Unmade in China

Ode to Joy.

And Charlotte and Alma.

Unmade in China

The Hidden Truth About
China's Economic Miracle

Jeremy R. Haft

polity

Copyright © Jeremy R. Haft 2015

The right of Jeremy R. Haft to be identified as Author of this Work has been asserted in accordance with the UK Copyright, Designs and Patents Act 1988.

First published in 2015 by Polity Press

Polity Press
65 Bridge Street
Cambridge CB2 1UR, UK

Polity Press
350 Main Street
Malden, MA 02148, USA

ISBN-13: 978-0-7456-8401-7

A catalogue record for this book is available from the British Library.

Library of Congress Cataloging-in-Publication Data

Haft, Jeremy, 1970–
    Unmade in China : the hidden truth about China's economic miracle / Jeremy Haft.
        pages cm
    Includes bibliographical references and index.
    ISBN 978-0-7456-8401-7 (hardcover : alk. paper) – ISBN 0-7456-8401-7 (hardcover : alk. paper) 1. China–Economic conditions–2000– 2. Industries–China. 3. China–Social conditions–2000– I. Title.
    HC427.95.H324 2015
    330.951–dc23
                            2015002742

Typeset in 11 on 14 pt Sabon
by Toppan Best-set Premedia Limited
Printed and bound in the UK by CPI Group (UK) Ltd, Croydon

For further information on Polity, visit our website: politybooks.com

Contents

Figures

Acknowledgments

There are so many people I wish to thank who have made this book possible. My family, first and foremost. To my wife Joy and my daughters Alma and Charlotte, whose patience and support have sustained me through it all, you have my undying love and thanks. Thanks also to my mother Joy Gillman, my sister Hilary and brother Adam, and Fred Drucker, Rhoda Sweeney, John Drodow, and in memory of Arthur Gillman and Sandy Drucker.

I also would like to thank the wonderful team at Polity, in particular Louise Knight and Pascal Porcheron, who have been at my side all the way.

Thanks, also, to my researchers. To Yue Sheng, your meticulous and thoughtful work has been invaluable to me. And thanks to Trip Taylor and Elizabeth Schieffelin, whose contributions are greatly appreciated.

I'd also like to thank Susan Golomb and Krista Ingebretson at the Susan Golomb Literary Agency for all your help and support to make this project a reality.

To my friends, who were a port in the storm: Jon Mozes, Glen Roberts, Gary, Cyndi, Max, and Sam Eisenberg, and Richard and Lenora Steinkamp. I thank you all.

I'd also like to acknowledge many people, mentors and friends, for all their insight, guidance, and support. Charles Freeman III, Marc Ross, Hani Findakly, Lisa Konwinski,

Molly Wilkinson, Mike Stokes, Bernard Schwartz, Jim Sasser, Derek Scissors, William Reinsch, Jeff Bader, Ken Lieberthal, Douglas Paal, Daniel Ikenson, Elizabeth Economy, Dan Rosen, Chris Nelson, William Zarit, Victor Cha, Pietra Rivoli, Elaine Romanelli, Arthur Dong, Charles Ludolph, Chris Papageorgiou, Lisa Shields, Ted Alden, Wade Sheppard, Brent Franzel, Chris Lapetina, Dave Hyams, Matt Geller, Dave Evans, Adam Fels, Hanadi Shamkhani, Tony Clayton, and my original mentor, Ted Tayler. Thank you all.

To my friends at Bikram Tenleytown – Elaine and Max Rosenberg, Debbie Nachmann, Adam Pearlstein, Barbara Ryan, and Ambiya Binta – you kept me sane through it all.

A special thank you, as always, to Wang Feng, for your enduring friendship and wisdom.

And to my Georgetown writing group, Dr Carole Sargent at the helm with Tim Jorgensen and Anne Ridder, your support sustained me. Thanks, finally, to my friends at Cornell, James Manning, Marty Broccoli, Michele Ledoux, Chris Watkins, Lee Telega, and Max Pfeffer.

Preface

The proof of China's might is in your waistband. And in the collar of your shirt; the chair you're sitting on. The mug on your desk. The phone in your pocket. The toy your child is chewing on.

Just look around you. Everything seems to be "Made in China" these days. So it must be "the China Century." And as China rises, America falls.

The logic goes something like this. It's a global economy, a flat world. If China can make anything we can, only cheaper and at the click of a mouse, then we surely haven't a prayer. We're on a race with China to the bottom – in wages and, ultimately, quality of life.

The flat world is tilting east, and all our good jobs are flowing to China.

The pundits agree. Just look at today's paper. There's a story on the front page about surging Chinese imports, flooding our markets with cheap goods and killing US jobs.

Then there's an op-ed on the back page. It says that China is already the world's second-largest economy. And that major financial institutions like the International Monetary Fund predict China will overtake the United States economically in just a few short years.

Politicians agree too. In the 2012 presidential election between Mitt Romney and Barack Obama, both candidates trimmed their sails to the headwinds of China's economic power. In a contest that the pundits still insist had nothing to do with foreign policy – Americans, they claim, were weary of wars in Iraq and Afghanistan and, with unemployment nearing 10 percent, were focused on kitchen-sink issues (like losing the kitchen sink) – the election was actually dominated by foreign policy. The campaigns spent nearly US$50 million on ads about China. And China was a frequent theme on the stump, especially in bellwether Rust Belt states like Ohio hit hard by the recession. The candidates and their surrogates flogged China again and again.

Romney's refrain: Obama is too soft on China's "cheating," its undervalued currency that keeps the prices of its exports artificially low.

Obama's refrain: Romney is an "outsourcing pioneer," sending jobs to China while he ran Bain Capital.

The implicit message in both campaign themes? If China can steal our jobs out from under us, through currency manipulation and outsourcing, America must be losing the competition for the next century.

Interestingly enough, before 2012, the typically pro-labor Democratic candidates were the China hardliners and the pro-trade Republicans the China softies. Now, talking tough on China was the bipartisan goose that laid the golden eggs. In both Democratic and Republican campaigns, the focus-group Svengalis told the messaging mavens to hit China early and often.

The polls show why. A recent Pew survey asked which is the world's leading economic superpower – *today*, not at some point in the future. More Americans than not said China.

Think about that. More Americans today believe that China, not America, is the world's leading economic superpower. You may be nodding your head in agreement.

So you probably won't be surprised to learn that nearly 60 percent of British said China, too. And across 21 countries, the majority of respondents voted China over America as the world's leading superpower.[1]

No surprise, right? China's might, and its dominance in the coming century, are just obvious. The ubiquitous labels on our products are proof enough of this irrefutable truth.

And if you square that truth with America's jobless recovery, our cratered-out industries, shrinking middle class, crumbling infrastructure, paralyzed government, uncompetitive wages, and thicket of regulations, then the corollary to China's rise is also an irrefutable truth. America is in decline.

But you don't need a poll to tell you which way the wind is blowing. At your next family get-together, try saying "My (*fill in the blank*) was 'Made in China.'"

How did they reply? I'm guessing you didn't all join hands and sing "We are the World..."?

Did you get an earful of invective? *Outsourcing, currency-cheating, idea-stealing, cyber-spying Commies!*

To be sure, China's rise is an emotional issue. Millions of Americans have lost jobs, homes, and pensions since the Great Recession of 2008. When the news media, politicians, and pundits almost universally blame China, it's hard not to get angry.

But something deeper is at play here, too. There's a thought-provoking psychological study that was conducted during the 2004 US presidential election between George W. Bush and John Kerry. Scientists wired electrodes to the skulls of Republicans and Democrats and showed them left- and right-leaning political statements, monitoring their brain functions. Each time a partisan statement was flashed on the screen, the areas of the subjects' brains that lit up were not the centers of reason, as you'd expect. They were the emotional centers.[2] Feelings, not logic, tend to drive our responses to political issues.

So it goes with China. One mention of "Made in China," and the feelings just come spilling out. The problem with basing beliefs on feelings, of course, is that feelings are sometimes immune to facts. Just ask the Chinese. Remember that Pew poll? The one that asked which is the world's leading superpower? The only country that overwhelmingly replied that China is *not* the world's leading economic superpower today...was China. They said America.

Could the Chinese know something about their fabled rise that we don't?

Yes. Because to stand on the ground in China and actually make things – make shirts and toys and apples and oil rigs – there is a reality that contradicts every widely held notion about China's so-called rise. Seen from the inside looking out, China is not a manufacturing juggernaut at all. It's a Lilliputian. China is not a lethal competitor. It's an economic helpmeet. China is not a killer of American jobs. It's a big job creator.

That's right. China actually *supports* millions of jobs in the United States.

But in order to see this, you've got to do more than watch the news or visit a couple of factories or talk to some Chinese businesspeople. You must walk the line where raw materials are formed into products. You must see for yourself how these products are made, step by step, from inputs to outputs. And ideally, you must try to wring safe products out of this system.

What you'd see would surprise you. You'd discover that nearly everything we're told about China's rise is wrong;

that, in fact, the very core of China's supposed might – how China *makes* things – is riddled with risk.

Now in any human endeavor there's always risk. It's a law of nature. Things fall apart. So the science of making things is to minimize risk. Of course, risk can't ever be completely eliminated. But you strive to achieve a successful outcome again and again, reliably, not randomly, as often as possible. An airplane that flies. A bridge that holds firm. A medicine that cures, not kills.

China is deceptive that way. It looks like a manufacturing powerhouse until you draw back the curtain. Then, you see risk everywhere.

Consider the "Made in China" safety scandals. In the past few years, we've seen baby formula spiked with melamine, an industrial chemical that caused renal failure in over 300,000 Chinese infants and killed six. We've seen melamine-laced pet food, too, that killed hundreds and injured thousands of dogs and cats in the United States. We've seen bad batches of the blood thinner, heparin, administered in American hospitals, killing 81 patients and sickening hundreds more. We've seen lead paint on Mattel toys. We've seen rotting Chinese drywall, installed in tens of thousands of US houses. We've seen exploding tires; faulty ignition switches; poison toothpaste and cough syrup; cracked welds on the San Francisco Bay Bridge; even "honey laundering," in which more than one third of the honey that Americans consume is now deemed counterfeit – smuggled from China and laced with unsafe additives.

Whether it's food, drugs, toys, tires, or bridges – pick any Chinese import – there have been big safety breaches. And this is not to mention the safety lapses in China – which are even more frequent, widespread, and deadly. Exploding watermelons, glow-in-the-dark pork, resold gutter oil, tainted seafood, scraps of animal skin in milk, arsenic in soy sauce, cadmium in rice, paraffin and ink in noodles, bleach in mushrooms, resin and starch to make fake eggs, poison gel caps and lethal antibiotics, collapsing roads and bridges.

There have been *thousands* of safety scandals in China just over the past few years. You can track them on a popular iPhone app called "The China Survival Guide" and on the website "Throw it out the window" (http://www.zccw.info).

Most of the "Made in China" safety scandals go unnoticed in the United States. But when a story is newsworthy enough, our media tend to seek a villain – a nefarious criminal ring, a factory with lax quality control, a corrupt bureaucrat. When the Mattel lead paint story broke, for example, the media spotlight shone on the owner of the Chinese paint factory. With the poisoned baby formula, it was employees of the Chinese dairy firm, its middlemen, and suppliers that were the culprits. The underlying assumption in these news stories is that China's frequent safety breaches are caused by a discrete set of bad actors.

The Chinese authorities agree. They repeatedly insist that each lapse in safety represents "one bad apple in the bunch," and that "more than 99 percent of Chinese exports are safe." So China's crackdowns typically hinge on criminal prosecutions. When ten people died from poisoned antibiotics, China executed its chief food and drug regulator.

But these diagnoses miss the deeper problem. The sheer volume and variety of safety lapses, which number in the thousands and span every Chinese industry, indicate that something deeper is going on than mere one-offs. The "Made in China" safety scandals cannot be blamed on a group of wrongdoers. They are endemic. China's entire system is to blame for these ongoing safety failures.

The risk that Chinese goods will be unsafe begins in the very ground, where crops are grown and livestock fed. Then it moves through China's firms and farms to the long supply chains that link them up to the regulators that govern them. With each node of production, risk is baked into the system.

Systemic risk in China has major implications for America. It's a major threat but also a major opportunity. The threat is easier to see than the opportunity. We hear about the threat often enough from many quarters. Chinese imports are unsafe. Despite a hundred years of evolving safety regulation in the United States after Upton Sinclair's *The Jungle* exposed nauseatingly unsanitary conditions in slaughterhouses, the jungle is back! And it's our biggest source for imported food, drugs, and consumer products. But, given the scope of systemic risk in China, how it permeates every level of manufacturing and agriculture, if anything, we're still underestimating how dangerous Chinese imports are, and we need to do a much better job defending ourselves.

Yet systemic risk in China also presents a major opportunity. As China struggles to make safe goods reliably, it must import them. Imagine you're a parent in China. You live in a brutally competitive, Darwinian economy with no social safety net to speak of. So if you've got some money in your pocket, you're going to spend it on products that you think will be safe for your family. Increasingly, that means Chinese are buying American.

Though we rarely hear about it, China imports hundreds of billions of dollars' worth of US manufactured goods, services, and agricultural products each year. In fact, China has shot up to become our third-largest export market behind Canada and Mexico.

And we're not talking about a handful of multinational corporations selling China airplanes and semiconductors. In nearly every congressional district across America, exports to China have been skyrocketing for the last decade. Between 2003 and 2012, in 401 out of 435 congressional districts (that's 92 percent), American exports to China doubled, often tripled, or, in some cases, grew tenfold and more.

So "Declining America" is selling products to "Rising China" hand over fist. With all that's famously wrong about our economy, we're still able to sell our wares to China from almost every congressional district. Exports support jobs. When China buys goods and services from US firms and farms, it employs Americans. But exports are only part of the jobs story. Chinese imports support American jobs, too. All those products need to be transported, warehoused, and retailed. And Chinese investments in American firms support jobs, as well.

But America is not alone. China also supports lots of jobs in Europe. The Chinese market is one of the fastest-growing export destinations for European goods and services. In fact, the EU is China's number-one source of imports today, beating Taiwan, Japan – and America, which ranks as China's fifth-largest source for imports. These exports to China support over three million European jobs.[3]

Wait a sec. China, a job creator? Many of you are shaking your head: No. That just can't be. Everything we see and hear about China tells us the opposite is true. But stay with me.

This book will take a new look at China's so-called rise and the implications for American and European competitiveness in the coming century. You'll walk the supply chain of how stuff is made – or really unmade – in China. You'll see firsthand how risk is a systemic defect in China's economy. And you'll see how this risk gives rise to threats and opportunities for the West.

Forget the pundits and politicians. Exploring China's secret supply chain is the only way to get a clear picture of China's competitiveness. For when it comes to accurate economic data, China is a black box. Its official metrics are

highly unreliable, partly because they're politically moti-
vated and partly because comprehensive research on any
given topic in China is either rare or non-existent. So the
aggregate data are untrustworthy, and the small case studies
are misleading.

That's why China's own government officials disregard
measurements of China's economic size, trade volume, and
exports as untrustworthy. Yet US academics, media, and
politicians swallow these false numbers whole and regurgi-
tate them as fact. A lack of good economic data has contributed to our China myopia. China looms much larger in the
world because we are looking at it through a false lens.

This cockeyed view of China's economy causes many
problems: bad governmental policies; squandered job opportunities; ignored risks to our health and safety; and, above
all, a false sense of self. We see a distorted image of America
through the refracting lens of China. We seem puny. Uncompetitive. On the decline. Yet to stand on the ground in China
and see how things are actually made, you'd realize that the
opposite is true. America is still vital. We're still competitive.
And China really needs what we make.

But systemic risk in China is difficult to discern. The
Chinese supply chain is opaque, complex, and well guarded.
Few ever glimpse more than distinct parts of it. Doing business in China is like being one of the blind men groping
around the elephant. It's really hard to get a sense of the
entire beast. You focus on your area. And try not to lose
your shirt. But with enough years and variety of experience,
a more complete picture begins to emerge.

My long and circuitous journey through China's long and
circuitous supply chain began in 1998. I had just completed
a successful tech start-up, and if I'd learned anything from
that experience, it was that companies rarely follow the
linear forecasts in business plans.

So, even though the stock market was rocketing up, and venture capitalists were shoveling money into any start-up with a dot-com in its business name, and the conventional wisdom was to "get big fast," I was determined to go slow. Before circumscribing a business plan, I needed to understand how things are really made in China.

The next year and a half were spent leading a group of engineers on a door-to-door investigation of China's supply chain – the long linkages of companies that make things. We traced the flow of goods and materials from beginning to end, starting way up the chain at raw materials and wending down through manufacturing and distribution.

Our team visited hundreds of factories. Nearly one thousand, in fact. We inspected physical plant and equipment. We interviewed managers. We bumped along countless dusty back roads and drank countless cups of scalding green tea, the flimsy plastic water-cooler cups melting to magma in our hands.

Back in 1998, that investigation was the most comprehensive field study of China's supply chain done to date. A colleague at Dun and Bradstreet, the commercial data powerhouse, coveted *our* data. Black gold, my business partner used to call it.

Years later, a venture capitalist looked over his glasses at me and asked, if I had to do it all over again, would I have lavished eighteen long months and precious seed capital on that industrial walkabout. To his smirk, I answered yes – because that investigation laid bare the secret workings of China's intricate supply chain. And it prepared the way for all the years that have come since – a crazy odyssey, in which we battled every sort of Scylla and Charybdis, bobbing along the churning wine-dark sea of China's economy.

Over the years, we've made (or tried to make) just about everything that could be made in China – from auto parts to oil rigs, door knobs to dental-bite blocks, valves and vents, louvers and lavatory deodorizers, drinking glasses and digital music players, chum buckets and stadium chairs, refinery tank farms and fencepost caps. From big steel infrastructure to little plastic parts, heavy industries to light, we've run the gamut of "Made in China."

These days, we're flowing the other way, selling American agricultural products and services to China. In a public/ private partnership with New York State and Cornell University, we're working to create American jobs through building markets in China for an East Coast state unused to exporting food to the Far East.

Like the man said. *Veni, vidi, vi-buyi, vi-selli, vi-shpilkes, vi-know-now.* I came, I saw, I imported, I exported, I got gastrointestinal reflux, but I got some understanding of the way things really work on the ground.

Having never studied Chinese in school, I came to China a newbie, ears and eyes wide open. Through all the years, I've tried to stay that way. To me, it's the only way to make sense of China's complexity. This book, therefore, is written in plain language about a complicated topic. Too often, academic texts about China's political economy are so obtuse as to be inaccessible to all but the most technical reader, while popular rhetoric about China from our pundits and politicians peddles gross generalities and distortions, playing on our fears. It's time to put a stop to that.

And so, like the ancient thespians, I ask that you suspend your disbelief for a moment and join me on a journey rarely glimpsed. To uncover China's secret supply chain, we will explore three themes. The first is the nature of systemic risk in China's manufacturing and agricultural sectors. Using firm-level data and recent case studies, the book will seek to illuminate how risk pervades each aspect of China's production platform – from the ground, to firms and farms, to the chains that link them up, to the regulatory structures that govern them. While many books and articles have analyzed individual aspects of China's business environment, none to date has provided a comprehensive view of risk in the system and its implications for the West.

That will lead to the book's next two themes: first, how Chinese imports are more dangerous than we imagine, and what we can do to defend ourselves, especially from unsafe food and drugs; second, how the phenomenon of risk presents an opportunity for the West to create jobs through providing the goods and services that China struggles to make safely.

Yet, before we can swoop down to the ground, we must first begin up in the air by looking at the typical ways we use to describe China's might – and how these misleading metrics give rise to widely believed falsehoods. From there, we'll move one level down, to look more closely at the impacts of Chinese risk on our economy – the threats to our health and safety, as well as all the jobs China supports. At that point, we'll sink to the ground to burrow our way along the length of China's supply chain. To see how food, drugs, toys, tires, cars, computers, buildings, and bridges are really made – from raw materials to fabrication to distribution.

Hopefully, at that point, you'll see the same startling truths about China's economy that I've been bowled over by. That far from a manufacturing powerhouse, China struggles to make a toy safely, much less a nuclear power plant. That China's rise is mostly a ruse, and its economic might a myth. And why that's really bad news and really good news for us.

1
Three Myths

China's rise is as self-evident as the rising of the sun.

Before Copernicus, that is.

Just imagine it. You look out the window of your sixteenth-century digs, and you see how the sun moves around the earth. You learn in school how this is so. You hear the same thing from leading scholars and politicians. Your eyes, your learning, your leaders: everything tells you the sun moves around the earth. But it doesn't.

Same goes with China. Everything tells you that China is about to eclipse America. The ubiquitous "Made in China" labels. The lessons in school about declining empires. The "rising China" rhetoric you hear from pundits and politicians. The news stories about outsourcing and China's wholesale theft of our jobs. But that doesn't make it true.

Because when it comes to China's rise, our eyes, ears, hearts, and minds mislead us. The labels are an illusion, the lessons in school inapplicable, and the rhetoric and punditry steeped in falsehoods. Make no mistake. China's imminent eclipse of the United States is about as true as the earth's centering the universe. And, like ol' Copernicus, we can debunk these untruths with reason. Notions of China's economic might are premised on three widely propagated myths.

Myth #1: China's Economy is about to Surpass US

So you're sitting on the couch watching the news, and they run a story about how China is the second-largest economy in the world, poised to surpass the United States.

What's the basis for this assertion? The mother of all macroeconomic metrics, the gross domestic product. GDP tries to measure the value of how much a nation produces in goods and services during a given time period. There are two ways to calculate GDP. One is through income, tallying up how much everyone in an economy earns. But the more common way is by measuring expenditure, how much every-one spent – that means consumer spending, plus business investment, government spending, and exports (what we sold other countries in goods and services) *minus* imports (what we bought from other countries in goods and services).

GDP is the measurement conventionally used to size an economy. Often you'll hear "GDP" and "the economy" used interchangeably, such as "the US economy grew 1 percent in the first quarter." What's meant here is that gross domestic product grew by 1 percent in the first quarter – or, that spending across the economy (minus imports) grew by 1 percent.

The claim that China is about to overtake the United States is typically based on GDP calculations. Here's an example from an opinion piece by Charles Kenny, a senior fellow at the Institute for Economic Development, which recently ran in the *Washington Post*. "America," Kenny warns, "will soon cease to be the world's largest economy. You can argue about why, when and how bad, but the end is indeed nigh."

(You always need to worry when you see "nigh" in a sentence.)

Kenny goes on:

According to the Penn World Tables – the best data to compare gross domestic product across countries – China's GDP was worth $10.4 trillion in 2011, compared with a US GDP of $13.3 trillion. But with China's economy growing 7 to 10 percent a year, compared with the recent US track record of less than 3 percent, China should take the lead by 2017 at the latest.[1]

Well, the Penn World Tables may be a good source to compare GDP across countries, but GDP is a lousy metric to compare economies. Let's say you wanted to measure your family's wealth. Would you start on January 1 and add up everything you spend through December 31? So let's say you shell out US$100,000 over the next 12 months on food, rent, school, and other expenses. Then the value of your household wealth is US$100,000?

Not at all. To gauge your family's wealth, you'd want to look at your assets and liabilities. What you own minus what you owe. That number would be a much more accurate picture of your finances, not how much you spend in a given year.

Well, it's the same with national economies. GDP tries to show one year's economic consumption through expenditures. But that number has little bearing on how wealthy a country is: how much it owns – what its households, businesses, and government have collectively saved – minus what it owes. By describing China's economy in terms of GDP, we actually understand very little about the nature of China's true economic strength.

As the economist Derek Scissors of American Enterprise Institute reminds us, if you build a skyscraper, tear it down, build it again, tear it down again, and build it yet again, you will keep adding to GDP, but this activity would add little economic value.

A silly analogy? Consider China's property market. Since the 2008 global recession, China's government has cranked opened the floodgates of what is arguably the largest fiscal stimulus the world has ever seen. That money has flowed through China's banks into business loans that have mostly financed construction – adding significantly to China's GDP. It's now estimated that investment makes up 70 percent of China's GDP – the largest imbalance between investment and consumption among major economies in the world. All that investment is creating a big problem of overcapacity, glutting China's property market with empty houses and malls, excess infrastructure and manufacturing capacity. A recent Chinese government report, looking into the phenomenon of "ghost cities," cites US$6.8 trillion in "ineffective investment" – deeming almost half of the total investment in China's economy from 2009 to 2013 as wasted.[2] Because each time another white elephant is erected, it may grow the overall GDP, but it acts more like a drag on China's economy than a boost. A building goes up, but it sits empty, causing the builder to default on the loan and the workers to be fired. GDP may be boosted, but few jobs are created.

So the popular notion that China's GDP must grow by a certain percentage a year – *in order to sustain job growth* – is off the mark. China's GDP growth, in and of itself, does not necessarily create jobs. In fact, it often destroys them. And if job creation is an important indicator of economic strength, then GDP is also an inappropriate metric because of the way imports are *subtracted* from the overall total. The math would have us believe that imports – buying goods from other countries – somehow diminish the overall value of an economy. Yet imports actually create jobs.

When goods arrive from other countries, what happens? They need to be transported, warehoused, retailed, and serviced, which supports jobs in trucking, rail, air, storage, marketing, construction, law, finance, and customer service. What's more, though you'd never know it from the "Made in China" label, many imported products from China actually contain inputs that are "Made in the USA": the cotton in your khakis; the cardboard in your Amazon.com box; the steel in your faucet; the chip in your iPhone; the photovoltaic polysilicon in your solar panel; the nacelle in your wind turbine. From the perspective of jobs, subtracting imports from the overall GDP number is misleading. It misses all the jobs it takes to bring those imported products to market, as well as all the jobs to make the components that go into those imported goods.

But, putting aside the notion that GDP is an inappropriate metric with which to size economies, China's GDP numbers, in particular, are pure fiction. Even China's top officials disregard them. There's a famous story about how Li Keqiang, China's current premier and an economist by training, characterized China's GDP statistics as "man-made" at a dinner with US Ambassador Clark Randt, when Li was head of the Communist Party in Liaoning province in 2007. Li said he considered just three metrics to judge the growth of his provincial economy: electricity consumption, rail cargo volume, and bank lending. "By looking at these three figures," a US diplomatic cable reported, "Li said he can measure with relative accuracy the speed of economic growth. All other figures, especially GDP statistics, are 'for reference only,' [Li] said smiling."[3]

It's charming that Li finds China's false GDP metrics so amusing. I wish our economists did, too. Year after year, China's provincial GDP numbers actually *exceed* the national GDP numbers by several hundred billion dollars. The parts add up to more than the whole. In 2009, the total GDP numbers from China's provinces topped the national GDP number by a whopping US$430 billion; in 2010, by US$570 billion; in 2011, by US$750 billion; in 2012, by US$930 billion.[4]

This disconnect between provincial and national statistics has been a long-term problem. In 1985, the provincial statistics agencies were separated from China's National Statistics Bureau (NSB), allowing each province to tally up its own GDP numbers. Since then, there's been a widening gap between provincial and national GDP.

Some economists blame the discrepancy in provincial and national numbers on different statistical methods employed by each bureau, as well as the problem of double counting. When a company is located in two provinces, it's difficult to determine where these firms' statistics should be booked – so both provinces count them in their numbers.[5]

But the root of the problem lies in how provincial officials are promoted in China's Communist Party. Though China's governmental system is federalist in nature, having divested a great deal of autonomy to the provincial governments, China's Communist Party remains the boss, the ultimate employer of governmental officials at all levels. Party careers live and die based primarily on GDP growth. The faster growing a province, the more chance an official will have for promotion. So there is a huge incentive to inflate numbers. The director of the National Statistics Bureau, Ma Jiantang, said as much when he remarked in April 2012 that distortions in China's official statistics are less about aberrations in accounting methodologies and more about fudged numbers.[6]

The NSB has toiled over the past decade to clean up its bookkeeping – by cutting out middlemen in the reporting of metrics that can distort the numbers and by segmenting the economy into more categories so that a greater degree of economic activity is captured. Until 2004, China's economy was measured in 16 industrial sectors. Since 2005, it's 94. Indeed, many China watchers say the numbers are improving, but there's no evidence to support that supposition. True, it's a good sign that national GDP is pegged lower than the total of the provinces. But consider that, since the 2008 recession, China has been hosing stimulus money into its economy like a fireman at an inferno. Yet, if you look at economic indicators that should track with GDP, you can see China's national statisticians are up to their old tricks. Electricity consumption, imports, and exports are all way down, pointing to a sharp contraction. Yet China's GDP keeps sailing smoothly along, growing much more quickly than any other major economy.

No wonder Chinese officials at the highest levels tend to ignore their own GDP statistics. But major financial institutions like the International Monetary Fund (IMF) routinely publish reports that take China's GDP numbers as gospel. It's not that IMF economists necessarily believe China's data. (Some IMF staffers, off the record, acknowledge China's GDP metrics are not to be trusted.) It's just that disputing these numbers – officially and publicly – would probably cause a dustup with China, a big client of the IMF.

So whenever you see a pundit touting China as the world's second-largest economy based on its GDP numbers, you need to be very skeptical. China's GDP numbers are fiction, and GDP is the wrong metric to judge the true size and dynamics of China's economy.

The same goes with China's famously red-hot economic growth. Like China's trumped-up GDP statistics, its growth metrics are also fictional. The numbers from the provinces year after year outstrip the growth rate of the whole country. For example, in April of 2013, when all of China's 31 provincial governments released GDP growth rates, none was lower than the national GDP growth rate – a statistical impossibility. The sum of the parts can't be growing faster than the whole. Yet most US economists just lap up these growth numbers as proof that China is about to overtake us.

Charles Kenny of the Institute for Economic Development writing in the *Washington Post* exemplifies the narrative we hear over and over again: "with China's economy growing 7 to 10 percent a year, compared with the recent US track record of less than 3 percent, China should take the lead by 2017 at the latest."

Now hear this! China will eclipse America a week from Tuesday at 2:47 in the afternoon. Their GDP numbers say so.

You see this kind of reporting all the time. America's decline is a frequent refrain in the news media – without a single caveat about the reliability of China's numbers or how all the microeconomic indicators show China is contracting fast. Here's another recent example from business writer Robert Samuelson, again in the *Washington Post*, who states that "the US economy is no longer the world's largest," and that China will overtake America's economy "sooner than many experts predicted."

Samuelson is referring to new World Bank figures touted in a blog post by economist Arvind Subramanian, the Dr Kevorkian of global trade, who administered a lethal injection to the US economy in his book *Eclipse* by asserting "China's rise and America's decline" using GDP numbers that nobody in China takes seriously and which aren't appropriate to size an economy anyway. Samuelson writes that the new World Bank figures indicate "that China's GDP in 2014 will hit $16.8 trillion compared with $16.1 trillion for the

United States. (All these figures are in 'constant' 2011 dollars.)"[7]

Oh, really?

Ask a senior Chinese government official if this comparison is valid. As soon as the World Bank findings were published, China's National Statistics Bureau stated that it did not agree with the methodology in the report and "expressed reservations" about the conclusion that China would soon overtake the United States economically.[8] Yet China's published GDP growth figures are validated by organizations like the IMF and the World Bank, then parroted by think-tankers like Charles Kenny and Arvind Subramanian, then touted by editorialists like Robert Samuelson, then spun by politicians up and down both sides of the aisle – and you wonder why these fictions take on the weight of truth.

As for Samuelson's " 'constant' 2011 dollars" qualification, this refers to another metric used to make the case that China is about to ram us in the global economy. It's a bit of economic legerdemain called purchasing power parity, or PPP. This construct attempts to make apples to apples comparisons between two economies – so that a unit of currency spent in, say, Manhattan would equal a unit of currency spent in Beijing.

By adjusting China's fictitious GDP with PPP, as per the World Bank's recent study, Samuelson can assert that China's economic size will reach US$16.8 trillion in 2014 compared with America's US$16.1 trillion. But PPP is a highly misleading metric. For one thing, prices tend to vary widely within a single country, as well as over time. And by trying to force parity between a highly developed, wealthy nation like the United States and a mostly rural, poor country like China paints a false picture of reality. In China, more than one million people still reside in caves, one billion people live in abject poverty, and a typical Beijing middle-class income is about US$12,000 per year.[9]

What's more, PPP numbers for China rarely take into account a really important metric in pricing. Inflation. As prices rise in a country, then a single unit of currency will be able to buy you less. But, in China, as you might imagine, inflation is a very sensitive number from a political standpoint. In a 2013 Pew survey, Chinese citizens were polled about the issues they take most seriously.[10] Rising prices topped the list as a very big problem, more than official corruption, wealth inequality, pollution, and even food safety. So authorities tend to downplay how much prices are really rising. China's true inflation rate is always much higher than what is officially reported.

Outside institutions, then, are forced to reckon Chinese inflation from afar. Consider when the World Bank adjusted its PPP numbers for China in 2005. Inflation, it was reckoned, had grown by 40 percent since the last time this metric was calculated, thereby causing the World Bank to downwardly adjust its PPP numbers for China by 40 percent. Poof! China's economy lost nearly half its size with an accounting adjustment.[11]

The new World Bank PPP numbers which Subramanian and Samuelson tout as proof that the US economy is toast for China's marmalade aren't any more accurate than the ones from 2005, though. An independent, comprehensive survey of Chinese housing prices since 2005 didn't occur, so the new PPP/GDP data for China can't be correct.

These statistics may seem unbearably trivial. Yet they are chapter and verse in the hymnals of journalists and politicians. We see China's economy as big and rich based on what we hear from opinion leaders. And opinion leaders see China as big and rich based on specious GDP/PPP figures. "A deeper look, though, shows that the People's Republic of

China is still far smaller and poorer than the US on the most important economic dimensions," writes Derek Scissors, "so its true global weight is correspondingly limited."[12]

Just how much smaller and poorer is simply not knowable by comparing GDPs – the amount China and America supposedly spend in a given year. You need to look at national wealth: how much a country's government, households, and firms have saved minus what they owe – or, what a company would call its balance sheet. Credit Suisse, in a 2013 survey, estimates US private wealth at US$72 trillion.[13] The US Federal Reserve puts American private wealth at closer to US$80 trillion. Compare this with compared with China's estimated private wealth of US$22 trillion. So American households are around *US$50 trillion* wealthier than Chinese households, and we're about to be surpassed economically by China? Really?

Even when you consider government savings and debt in the equation, America is way, way ahead in size and wealth. Factoring in China's governmental holdings, as well as its significant liabilities, you can estimate China's total national wealth as between US$30 trillion and US$35 trillion – a generous approximation and one that's probably too high. Now, considering America's public sector debt, as well as its holdings, US total national wealth can be put around US$65–70 trillion. So there's still about a US$35 trillion delta between the national wealth of China and America. *US$35 trillion.* This is why all this talk about China's imminent eclipsing of the United States is absurd.

And there are strong arguments to be made that it never will. You wouldn't know it looking at GDP numbers, but the fundamentals of China's economy keep its leaders up at night. "There are structural problems in China's economy, which cause unsteady, unbalanced, uncoordinated and unsustainable development," remarked Wen Jiabao, China's then premier, during a press conference from the National People's Congress in March 2007. It's a settled truth among China's top officials that investment spending as the mainstay of economic growth is unsustainable. China is struggling, therefore, to transition its growth from investment spending to consumer spending. Yet China's massive stimulus measures keep exacerbating the imbalances.

Most of China's stimulus money has financed infrastructure building. Yet China still lacks a mature bond market to support long-term infrastructure investment, so financing for these big construction projects takes the form of short- to medium-term bank loans. Since local governments by law must maintain balanced budgets, debts to banks have been kept off the books through agencies called local investment companies. Like the moribund Enron Corporation, which used complex off-balance sheet entities (named after Star Wars characters) to hide its liabilities, China's local governments keep their debt segregated from official budgets. China's published tally of local government debt as of 2013 was 17.9 trillion RMB – about US$2.95 trillion.[14]

But we can safely assume that number is much larger, if you imagine all the off-balance sheet debt the official numbers are not taking into account. Then consider corporate debt, which is significantly worse in China than in the United States. A look at the list of Fortune 500 companies in 2013 shows 95 Chinese firms among the group in industries, like steel making, chemicals, and power generation – "sectors," according to China's *Xinhua* news agency, that are "grappling with overcapacity."[15] In these industries, *Xinhua* reports, "[T]he average debt to equity ratio for non-financial Chinese companies on the list came in at 4.42, much higher than the 2.79 seen in US companies, a sign that Chinese companies are relying too heavily on borrowed money for business expansion."[16] We can only guess at the value of non-performing loans amidst this debt portfolio, but, given China's significant excess capacity, the number must be vast.

In order to put China's growth on a more sustainable path, a whole host of drastic reforms will need to occur. Because China lacks a viable social safety net, the Chinese middle class saves all the money it can to pay for health care and retirement costs. (The upper class spirits its money out of China as quickly as possible, preferring to park it in safe, dynamic economies like the United States.) But with China's negative interest rates, to put those savings in a bank, you'd actually lose money against the rate of inflation. So Chinese consumers with savings often invest in property, a second or third house or apartment, pumping more and more hot air into the real estate market and exacerbating the problem of excess capacity. Residential property makes up about 75 percent of all real estate development in China. This drives up demand for steel (40 percent of China's steel sells into real estate) and ripples out into the economy at large, as China's property market devours cement, glass, appliances, hardware, electrical fixtures, and so on. UBS estimates that, when considering the entire upstream supply chain, as much as 25 percent of China's final demand derives from real estate, a big, big bubble.[17]

So rebalancing China's economy from investment to consumption isn't something that can be done with a wave of the Autocrat Fairy Godmother's wand. It's a complex, risky, and long-term project, involving ground-up reforms in China's banking and insurance industries, health care, pensions, currency, and real estate. Reforms that are vehemently resisted by a powerful group of vested interests, which Professor David Shambaugh of George Washington University calls "the Iron Quadrangle" – state-owned firms, China's internal security apparatus, the People's Liberation Army, and conservatives within the Communist Party. These interests hold great power within China's ruling elite and work to block liberalizing reforms needed to address China's structural problems. "Beijing's political gridlock is similar to Washington's, and Xi Jinping's mandate for change is about as narrow as President Obama's," notes Shambaugh in a piece for the *Washington Post*, "Don't Expect Reform from China's New Leaders."[18]

In the meantime, America, though seemingly on the ropes, remains endowed with the attributes of an enduringly competitive economy. We have considerably more natural resources – water and arable land – and considerably less pollution. We have a much smaller labor force than China's, but it's much more productive. For every US worker, it takes China eight to achieve the same level of productivity. And we have a much wealthier, more balanced society – despite rising income inequality and concentration of wealth, our per capita average income is about US$48,000 a year. China's? US$3,000. Adjusted for PPP? It's US$6,000.

And even if we follow Arvind Subramanian's flawed GDP logic, America is still way ahead (see Figure 1.1). Let's compare US GDP per capita to China's. "According to the International Monetary Fund, per capita GDP in China last year reached $6,747, which was a level of economic output per capita that was first reached in the US back in 1882," notes Mark Perry of the American Enterprise Institute in April of 2014.[19] When you adjust for PPP, China's per capita GDP is on par with the United States in 1912. Perry continues, "And even if China's output per person grew at 7% for the next decade, it would still only be at a level the US reached in 1951."

The reason America retains its advantage, Perry asserts, is innovation. "Most global innovation surveys put the

1.1 US real GDP per capita, 1800–2014

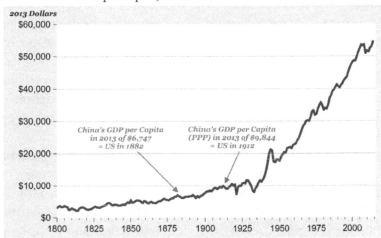

2013 Dollars

China's GDP per Capita
in 2013 of $6,747
= US in 1882

China's GDP per Capita
(PPP) in 2013 of $9,844
= US in 1912

Source: Global Financial Data

United States at or near the top." China often doesn't even rank in the top thirty. Innovation is an outcome of deeper structural strengths. Our system of government for centuries has permitted the free flows of capital, people, and ideas which gives rise to economic creativity. The extent to which China restricts the flow of capital, people, and ideas is the extent to which China holds itself back as an innovator. You can't lead the next century if your sole accomplishment is making a cheaper copy of a spark plug.

So, what's clear, across a number of economic indicators – most notably, national wealth – is that China is nowhere *near* equivalence with the United States. And given China's unfavorable demographics, chances are China may never catch up. We tend to imagine China with a limitless number of cheap laborers. Yet, demographically, China is starting to resemble Japan. Decades of the pernicious one-child policy are tipping the balance from youth to elderly.

It is estimated that in 20 years (one generation from now), about 20 percent of China's population will be 65 or older. As a matter of comparison, Japan, which has been grappling with economic stagnation since 1991, has a population in which about 20 percent is 65 or older. In other words, China's plentiful, youthful labor force will sharply constrict beginning in 2015 and will be a significant drag on China's economy. Soon, China will go from being a country younger than America to a country older than America.[20]

That the majority of Americans and British seem to believe China is already the world's sole economic superpower is startling when you consider the facts. China is actually a much smaller, poorer, and demographically older country than we imagine, racked with debt and struggling to right a severely imbalanced economy while trying to maintain control over the world's largest civilian population.

Myth #2: Everything is "Made in China"

OK, you say, but just look at all the product labels around you. Put the economic theories aside and use your eyes, man!

To which I respond with an old Marxist saying (Chico, not Karl): *Well, who ya gonna believe, me or your own eyes?*

Because the "Made in China" label is actually an illusion, like the sun appearing to move around the earth. Chinese-made goods comprise just a fraction of what we buy day to day. Based on data from the Census Bureau, the Bureau of Labor Statistics, and the Commerce Department, the US Federal Reserve asserts that 88.5 percent of goods and services we purchase daily are made in the United States. The Fed explains that this is because we devote about two-thirds of our consumption to services, which are usually locally produced. And as for products, just 11.5 percent of our personal consumption expenditures go to foreign-made goods, a quarter of which are made in China – which means that Chinese imports account for only 2.7 percent of US personal consumption expenditures. This may seem counter-intuitive, given that everything seems to be "Made in China," but Chinese goods dominate just a few categories, like house-wares, electronics, toys, and furniture.

Fine, you say, but the flood of cheap Chinese imports in these categories costs American jobs. If imports kill jobs, we should see unemployment levels rise as imports rise. Let's compare US imports to US employment levels from the early 1980s until now (see Figure 1.2).

Since 1981, imports have been rising steadily, while unemployment has been trending down, except for the period since the Great Recession of 2008, which slowed trade *and* caused significant job losses.[21] Looking at the last 30 years, there is no correlation between imports and job losses.

But what about Chinese imports specifically? Don't those cost American jobs? We certainly hear this claim a lot in the news. And it was a dominant theme in the presidential election between Barack Obama and Mitt Romney. Remember the second presidential debate between the two candidates? The "town hall" format, in which Obama had to score a palpable hit after his lackluster first-debate performance?

One hour and thirty-one minutes into the proceedings, ten minutes before the end of the night, the moderator, Candy Crowley of CNN, lobbed at the candidates a "Made in China" question made to order: "Mr President, we have a really short time for a quick discussion here. iPad, the Macs, the iPhones – they are all manufactured in China. One of the major reasons is labor is so much cheaper [t]here. How do you convince a great American company to bring that manufacturing back here?"

And so, with Crowley's question, the candidates launched into their China spiel. Romney talked currency

1.2   US unemployment rate and US imports, 1981–2011

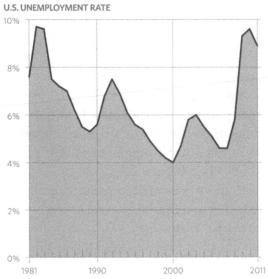

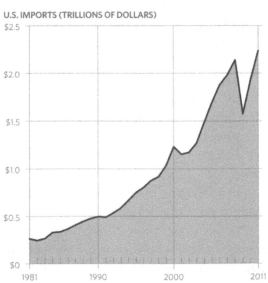

Source: US Department of Labor

manipulation. Obama talked job training. Yet neither addressed the premise of Crowley's question: that iPhones, iPads, and Macs are all "Made in China," which by inference costs America jobs.

But they aren't, and they don't. They're only *put together* in China, and importing these products actually supports American jobs.

Crowley's assumption touches on a common perception that China is the factory floor of the world. But that's misleading. China is more like the assembler for the world. China usually functions like a giant vacuum, hoovering parts from around the globe, which it then assembles and re-exports. This is especially true of consumer electronics, like the iPhone and iPad.

If you turn over an iPhone these days and read the label on the back, you see a hint of this dynamic at play. The phone doesn't say "Made in China." It says "Designed in California. Assembled in China." This is an important distinction. But it's one that's lost on US trade statisticians. America measures trade as if *Leave it to Beaver* were still on television.

US government data consider a product is "made" in the last country that shipped it to us. This method ignores how products are actually manufactured today – usually from components that are produced in many countries, then assembled in still another country, before being exported to us.

Let's consider Candy Crowley's example of the iPhone. It's designed, including its software, in America, and the components are manufactured in Japan, South Korea, Germany, and the United States before the phone is assembled in China (by a Taiwanese-owned factory).

Figure 1.3 shows the breakdown of the value added to a typical iPhone. You see Japan, Korea, Germany, and the

1.3   Apple iPhone major components and cost drivers

Manufacturer	Component	Cost
Toshiba (Japan)	Flash memory	US$24.00
	Display module	US$19.25
	Touchscreen	US$16.00
Samsung (Korea)	Application processor	US$14.46
	SDRAM-Mobile DDR	US$8.50
Infineon (Germany)	Baseband	US$13.00
	Camera module	US$9.55
	RF transceiver	US$2.80
	GPS receiver	US$2.25
	Power IC RF function	US$1.25
Broadcom (US)	Bluetooth/FM/WLAN	US$5.95
Numonyx (US)	Memory MCP	US$3.65
Murata (Japan)	FEM	US$1.35
Dialog Semiconductor (Germany)	Power IC application processor function	US$1.30
Cirrus Logic (US)	Audio codec	US$1.15
Rest of bill of materials		US$48.00
Total bill of materials		US$172.46
Manufacturing costs		US$6.50
Grand total		US$178.96

Source: Yuqing Xing & Neal Detert 2010, How The iPhone Widens The United State Trade Deficit With The People's Republic of China, ADBI Working Paper Series, http://www.adbi.org

United States on the list of component manufacturers. Do you see China? No. Because iPhones, on the whole, aren't manufactured in China; they're just assembled there. China, in fact, adds only a smidgen of value to each iPhone it assembles. So while an iPhone costs about US$179 to make, China contributes only US$6.50 worth of value in putting together the parts that are made elsewhere. But because China is the *last country to export* the iPhone to the United States, trade statistics consider it as 100 percent Chinese-made!

This methodology gets us into trouble. It makes China seem much mightier than it is. In 2009, the United States imported 11.3 million iPhones at a price of US$179 per unit, contributing just under US$2 billion to America's trade deficit with China. But if we accounted for the actual value that China adds to the making of an iPhone, that deficit would shrink to just US$73.45 million.[22]

Candy Crowley's example of the iPad is another good illustration of this dynamic at play. To make an iPad, China imports components from around the world, including the United States, and adds just US$10 in value through the assembly of a product that takes about US$275 to manufacture. Again, America considers each iPad it imports to be a 100 percent Chinese-made item, even though China adds just a fraction to the value of an iPad.

Every imported iPad, then, increases the United States–China trade deficit by a full US$275. So iPad imports contributed US$4 billion worth of trade deficits with China in 2011, according to *The Economist*. But if we measured the actual value China adds to the iPad, the deficit would only be about US$150 million.[23]

The data I'm using for the iPad and iPhone were not handed down to me from a bearded sage atop Mount Ararat; they're freely and easily accessible. Yet journalists like Crowley continue to peddle the same pernicious falsehoods about China – that everything is made in China, implying America can't compete.

We never seem to hear that the "Made in China" label is misleading, that it doesn't really mean the product is actually *made* in China. What we hear far too often instead is that China cheats. It keeps its currency low, making its exports unbeatable, driving a huge trade imbalance that costs millions of American jobs. Yet, according to the recent head of the WTO, Pascal Lamy, if we accounted for China's actual

value-added contribution to America's
deficit with China would probably be m
Japan has already warmed to this noti
a trade accounting system that discerns
mediate goods and their countries of
Trade Organization and the Organizat
Cooperation and Development are also
their systems. But many US pundits and
blissfully ignorant of the shortcomings in
Case in point: there's an oft-quoted stu
nomic Policy Institute (EPI), which asserts
imbalance with China has cost America a
jobs. This study is frequently cited by
media, and trade groups as a reason to
China by closing markets, jacking up imp
officially designating China a currency ma
Treasury Department.
During the heated midterm congressio
2010, for example, Democratic and Republi
Congress co-signed a letter to the House lea
it to apply more pressure on China to let its
ciate against the dollar. China bashing is
areas where both parties in deadlocked W
heartily agree. The letter cited the EPI study
China's currency manipulation is causing the
imbalance, which is killing millions of Ameri
Yet this widely touted EPI study is wrong
levels. Let's begin with the methodology. Dr
who produced the study, took US trade deficit
and ran them through a data model produced
of Labor Statistics (BLS). The first problem with
is that our trade deficit numbers with Chin
exaggerated, as just discussed, because 100 pe

value of Chinese imports are attributed to China – not to the countries that actually made the components. So Scott is using bad data as the input to the model.

The second problem with the methodology is that the BLS model Dr Scott employs was never intended to be used in this way. The BLS input–output model was actually meant to predict how many jobs would be created from activities like construction projects. "It wasn't meant to hypothesize about job displacement because of imports," said James Franklin, Chief of the Division of Industry Employment Projections at the Bureau of Labor Statistics.[26] Mr Franklin went on to characterize Dr Scott's methodology as "a common misuse of the data ... [which] doesn't square with standard trade theory." So the EPI study runs false trade-imbalance statistics through an inappropriate model.

But putting methodology aside, the EPI study makes some colossally incorrect assumptions about trade. It posits that a dollar spent on imports is a dollar not spent on US goods and services. So, in other words, for every dollar's worth of imported goods from China, the EPI study subtracts a dollar's worth of contributions to US labor wages: hence, job losses. But this assumption totally misses the reality of modern trade – that an imported product cannot be valued solely by the thing itself, but must also include all the steps involved in bringing the product to the consumer: the jobs in transportation, warehousing, retailing, marketing, construction, finance, and customer service.

According to the Federal Reserve Bank, scores of academics, and *The Economist* magazine, for every dollar spent on imported goods from China, about half the value actually flows to American firms. Returning to the example of the iPad, *The Economist* says, "The main rewards go to American shareholders and workers. Apple's profit amounts to about 30% of the sales price. Product design, software development and marketing are based in America. Add in the profits and wages of American suppliers, and distribution and retail costs, and America retains about half the total value of an iPad sold there."

Or, as the Federal Reserve Bank puts it:

> if a pair of sneakers made in China costs $70 in the United States...the bulk of the retail price pays for transportation of the sneakers in the United States, rent for the store where they are sold, profits for shareholders of the US retailer, and the cost of marketing the sneakers. These costs include salaries, wages, and benefits paid to the US workers and managers who staff these operations.[27]

The Fed estimates that, for every dollar spent on imports from China, about 55 cents pay for US services.

There are actually millions of jobs associated with the US services that support Chinese imports.[28] And counter to conventional wisdom, even the lower-value Chinese imports of apparel and toys support over half a million American jobs. Let's consider the apparel industry, a big category for Chinese imports. The economist Derek Scissors with colleagues Charlotte Espinoza and Ambassador Terry Miller calculate the estimated number of jobs supported by Chinese apparel imports in a paper called "Trade Freedom: How Imports Support US Jobs."[29] I like their methodology because they use actual business numbers for their calculations, not macroeconomic extrapolations.

To estimate US jobs supported by Chinese apparel imports, Dr Scissors et al. begin with the total value of sales by the US apparel industry in 2010: US$158.8 billion. Then they work their way to the value added by US workers in supporting these Chinese imports – the amount left over from total apparel sales after subtracting profits, cost of goods, import charges, and the value of Chinese content. What's left over is US$21.67 billion dollars, an estimate of the value of services that US jobs provide Chinese imports once they reach our shores. If you divide that number by the average worker compensation (wage plus benefits) in the apparel industry of US$61,051, you get 355,000 jobs. It's not an exact number, obviously, but a good guess.

Scissors then uses two other methodologies to get to a similar conclusion. One way is to take the total number of jobs in retail apparel sales in 2010, which was 1.6 million. Multiplying this number by an estimate of the market share of Chinese imports in this industry (0.36) gives another approximation of how many jobs in retail are supported by Chinese imports: 580,000 jobs. Scissors then looks at the latest available data from the IRS in 2009, when imports were lower, and that indicates 245,000 jobs were supported that year by Chinese imports.

So whichever methodology you choose, imported Chinese apparel supports hundreds of thousands of American jobs. Same with toys and sporting goods. Employing the same methodologies, Scissors demonstrates that Chinese toy and sporting goods imports support about 221,000 US jobs.

Now expand the aperture across all categories of imports from China. In 2013, the US Census put this number at about US$440 billion. If we use the Federal Reserve's estimation that about 50 cents of each dollar goes to US firms, that's about US$220 billion. Subtract estimated corporate profits of US$22 billion (10 percent) and divide US$198 billion by an average wage of US$60,000, and you get about 3,300,000 jobs. A very back-of-the-envelope calculation, but a clear indication that Chinese imports support *millions* of jobs in the United States.

There's another major flaw in the logic of the EPI study when it assumes that every dollar spent on Chinese goods is a dollar not spent on US-made goods. Many Chinese imports *contain* US inputs. So a dollar spent on Chinese imported goods usually *does* support US jobs because many American industries provide the content for the imported products.

You wouldn't know it because of the deceptive "Made in China" label, but Chinese hardware, like faucets and doorknobs, often contain US recycled steel. Chinese clothes often contain US cotton. Chinese furniture often contains US lumber. Chinese boxes often contain US pulp. Chinese solar panels often contain US PV polysilicon. Chinese consumer electronics often contain US technology. The list goes on.

Cardboard boxes are a great example. You may be surprised to learn that the box from your latest Amazon.com purchase, though stamped "Made in China," is probably American. Decades of widespread deforestation in China have depleted its resources for making quality pulp. So paper products made in China tend to be derived from inferior inputs, such as sorghum, grass, and bamboo.[30]

It's easy to assume that cardboard boxes are basically interchangeable. But the quality of the pulp determines how strong the box is. Ryder, the big logistics firm, learned that lesson the hard way, when a 30-foot-high wall of stacked boxes filled with television sets collapsed because of the inferior Chinese-made cardboard. Since it costs less to transport a sea container of scrap wastepaper from Seattle to Shanghai than from Shanghai to Beijing, firms prefer to use higher-quality American inputs when fabricating their boxes in China, rather than risk damaging the goods inside.[31]

Other products that seem to be entirely "Made in China" but that contain US inputs are metal goods, such as aluminum cans, engine casings, automotive parts, copper wiring, and stainless steel sinks. As with wastepaper, China is a major importer of American scrap metal. Still lacking a significant recycling industry, China is the world's leading importer of scrap copper, aluminum, and steel. In 2009, China imported 14 million tons of scrap, and in 2012, 22 million tons.[32]

The scrap comes from many different places – like old cars and their parts, discarded appliances, the remnants of dismantled buildings – which is shipped to China in sea containers. The scrap is then shredded, dusted, refined, and sold to steel mills that fabricate it into products for export back to the United States. Making metal products from scrap consumes up to 90 percent less energy than using new materials.[33] And since the integrity of recycled steel does not degrade much with the proper processing, the reincarnated products may live their new lives, get scrapped and sent to China again – then re-re-exported back to the States.

Clothing is another product that often contains US inputs. The United States is the world's largest cotton exporter. China, in turn, is the world's largest cotton importer. In 2011, China bought 30 percent of US cotton exports.[34] As with pulp, China struggles to produce high-quality cotton. Since its mills can procure premium imported American cotton for about the same price as local cotton, they import. University of Missouri professor Jung Ha-Brookshire contends that, in the apparel industry, American firms contribute to the "cotton production…fabric production, design, product development, branding, marketing [and] distribution" of these "Made in China" goods. On the other hand, Chinese firms contribute only the lower-value functions of "sewing, packing [and] shipping" the items. Many American clothing imports, then, are designed in the United States, made from US cotton and fabric, assembled in China and sold by American firms in American stores.[35]

The fact that it's cheaper to transport raw materials halfway around the world than from city to city is a trend that may not last. If the United States moves toward adopting policies that factor the economic impact of the carbon footprint of goods (such as a carbon tax or a cap-and-trade system), then the external costs to the environment of transporting goods by sea, air, rail, and road would be priced into the overall cost of goods sold. Still, other costs are already tipping the balance away from China. Labor costs in China have been rising sharply for years and, in 2015, China's average labor cost per unit is expected to outstrip that of the United States.[36]

This trend is already evident in the surge of manufacturing jobs being "re-shored" or "insourced" – in other words, brought back to the United States. Examples abound across industries. Consider the German engineering firm Siemens AG, which opened a new factory in Charlotte, North Carolina in 2011 to produce huge gas turbines for electric plants, creating 825 high-paying manufacturing jobs.

Commenting on why Siemens chose Charlotte, Eric Spiegel, CEO of Siemens's US subsidiary, said, "A lot of things that were offshored in the past were offshored because of low-cost labor, but that no longer is the most important factor. The reasons you bring a plant like this to the United States are higher-skilled labor, access to the world's best research and development, and good sound infrastructure."[37]

Michelin North America is another example. It opened a new plant in South Carolina to make 12½-foot tires for construction and mining vehicles, creating 500 local jobs. Michelin's US chairman said they chose South Carolina because of the state's strong technical schools and good infrastructure, with nearby seaports in Charleston and Savannah, Georgia.

General Electric is yet another example. Appliance Park, a sprawling manufacturing hub in Louisville, Kentucky, built in the 1950s, had been on the decline for decades, a few years ago employing a small fraction of its original labor force. But, in 2012, GE began opening new assembly lines at Appliance Park to make products that had previously been made in China and Mexico. GE's CEO, Jeffrey Immelt, wrote about this turnaround of Appliance Park in the *Harvard Business Review*, stating that offshoring is "quickly becoming mostly outdated as a business model for GE Appliances." GE is investing US$800 million in Appliance Park and staffing up its labor force. "I don't do that because I run a charity," said Immelt. "I do that because I think we can do it here and make more money."[38]

A number of factors are driving this trend. In addition to access to skilled labor and good infrastructure, the cost model of manufacturing in the United States is proving more advantageous than China. Domestically sourced natural gas allows manufacturers to power their plants much more cheaply than in China. Natural gas costs four times more in Asia than in America. And Chinese labor rates are five times higher than in 2000 and are predicted to keep rising by at least 18 percent a year.[39]

Bearing that in mind, let's reconsider Candy Crowley's question from the second presidential debate: "iPad, the Macs, the iPhones – they are all manufactured in China. One of the major reasons is labor is so much cheaper [t]here." No, Apple products are not "all manufactured in China." They're simply assembled there. And no, labor is not "so much cheaper there." On a unit-for-unit cost basis, American and Chinese labor costs are now on par, essentially eliminating the low-wage advantage China enjoyed. When you factor in all the complexity of doing business in China,

it's no wonder more and more firms are bringing their manufacturing back home.

Myth #3: China's Currency Manipulation Kills Jobs

Candy Crowley's question may have been wrongheaded, but
Mitt Romney's response was telling. He agreed with her
premise and attributed China's competitive advantage over
the United States to "cheating" on China's currency, the
renminbi or yuan.

China has a closed financial system. As such, China's currency is managed, and its long-standing policy has been to
peg its currency exchange rate to that of the US dollar. So
with the decline of the dollar's value, China's currency has
declined in value as well. Romney's argument, which you
hear a lot from Republicans and Democrats alike, is that this
artificially low value has allowed Chinese goods to achieve
an unfair pricing advantage – making them cheaper than
domestically produced American goods, and therefore killing
American jobs. Though it has become almost universally
accepted, however, this claim about currency and jobs is
simply untrue.

Compare China's currency value with US unemployment
over the past two decades. What we typically hear is that
when the yuan is cheaper, America bleeds jobs. But that just
isn't borne out if you look at the numbers (see Figure 1.4).

Going back to 1991, there is zero correlation between US
unemployment levels and China's currency value. Except for
the Great Recession of 2008 and a blip in 2003, unemployment has been mostly trending down, regardless of whether
the yuan is rising or falling in value. If there were any truth
to the argument that China's currency policy kills American
jobs, it would be reflected in the data. The sharp decline in
value of the yuan in 1993–4, for example, would trigger US

1.4 A weak yuan does not cause US unemployment

1991-2000: The yuan-to-dollar exchange rate falls and the yuan becomes undervalued. But U.S. unemployment declines.

1991-2000: The yuan-to-dollar exchange rate rises and the yuan becomes less undervalued. Yet U.S. unemployment rises.

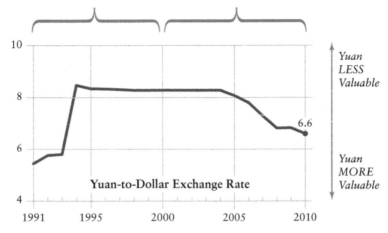

Yuan LESS Valuable

6.6

Yuan MORE Valuable

Yuan-to-Dollar Exchange Rate

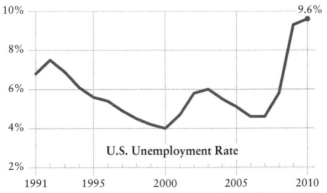

9.6%

U.S. Unemployment Rate

Source: Derek Scissors 2011, *The Facts About China's Currency, Chinese Subsidies, and American Jobs*, The Heritage Foundation, http://www.heritage .org/research

job losses. But if you look at US unemployment levels in 1993–4, they continue on their downward trend – in other words, America keeps adding jobs despite China's falling currency value.

Now, fast forward to today. China's central bank has allowed the value of its currency to rise against the dollar about 25 percent since 2005. Yet America's unemployment has surged during this time since the Great Recession of 2008. If the currency scolds were right, then the appreciation of the value of the yuan should have contributed to job creation in the United States. It hasn't.

Bottom line, with a US labor force of over 130 million people, China's real impact on the US economy is marginal. Certainly, it's not nearly as central as our politicians and news media would have us believe. By and large, American policies steer the American economy, not some faraway bean counters in Beijing. Which is why the currency argument is so politically expedient. It's a whopper of a red herring that distracts us from the real causes of our economic ups and downs – namely, US fiscal and monetary policies, and issues like immigration, health care, education, and housing.

Rather than confront these tough domestic challenges and potentially alienate voters and donors, blaming China for US unemployment scores political points while providing the cover to do nothing controversial. Ironically, though they wrap themselves in the American flag, if left to their own devices, the currency scolds in Congress would actually kill US jobs, not save them as they purport. Case in point: Senators Lindsey Graham, a Republican from South Carolina, and Chuck Schumer, a Democrat from New York, have repeatedly put forward a bill in Congress that would punish China for alleged currency manipulation. Each time the bill is revived, Graham and Schumer declare their legislation would protect American workers, and senators from both sides of the aisle clamor to sign on as co-sponsors. The last incarnation of the bill was called the "Brown, Sessions, Schumer, Graham, Stabenow, Burr, Collins, and Casey *Currency Exchange Rate Oversight Reform Act of 2013.*" The "Brown" among the co-sponsors is Senator Sherrod Brown, Democrat of Ohio. In a press release on his website that trumpets the revival of this legislation, guess what research is cited as the proof that China's currency policy kills American jobs? Dr Scott's fictional EPI study.

Yet, aside from the fact that specious research is used to justify this legislation, if the Graham-Schumer bill were ever made into law, it would do the opposite of its intended purpose. Here's how things would play out. China would be designated a currency manipulator, and a series of retaliatory steps would occur, including raising the tariffs on a broad swath of Chinese imports. By making it more expensive for China to sell us their goods, America's imports from China would decrease. But since many of the goods that America imports from China *contain* US components, then US exports to China across a number of categories would also decrease, ultimately killing jobs. A sharp decline in Chinese imports would also kill jobs in all the industries that bring those imports to market once they arrive in America.

The solar panel industry is a good example of how raising tariffs to protect jobs achieves the opposite result. The largest US solar panel manufacturer, SolarWorld Americas, initiated a case before the Commerce Department in 2011 that claimed US solar-panel makers were being harmed by Chinese subsidies, allowing China to dump cheap panels on the United States. The Commerce Department ruled in favor of Solar-World Americas, and, in 2012, in the midst of an election in which Romney frequently attacked Obama for being soft on China, the Obama administration jacked up tariffs on imported Chinese solar panels by a minimum of 31 percent.

Politically, this move may have played well to those wanting Obama to "get tough on China," but ultimately it was a policy misfire because solar panel fabrication is just one node in a long value chain. Analysis of the solar-panel industry has tended to focus exclusively on the fabrication of panels. Yet when you consider the whole chain, beyond just the panels, the United States, in fact, is a net exporter in the solar industry. That means, overall, America *sells* more solar energy products than it buys.

In 2010, the most recent year of an analysis of the solar industry that considers the entire value chain, US net exports of solar energy products to the world reached US$1.9 billion. And, contrary to the narrative that the United States is the hapless victim of Chinese dumping, America is actually a net exporter of solar products *to China* – totaling more than US$240 million in net exports in 2010. In other words, we sell more solar products to China than we buy.[40]

Our top solar export to China is the expensive, high-tech capital equipment used to make the solar panels. Our second top export is the PV polysilicon, the raw material that goes into the crystalline silicon photovoltaics, the active element in solar panels that converts sunlight into energy. China imports these items to fabricate and assemble the panels, relatively lower-value functions in the chain. China then exports the panels back to us. Once the panels arrive, there are several important services that support tens of thousands of jobs. The panels must be transported, the site must be prepared, permits must be filed for, and the system must be installed and maintained. So if you look at the whole chain, the majority of the financial value in an installed photovoltaic system flows to America. In 2010, installations of US solar energy systems were valued at US$6 billion – and 75 percent of that was captured by US firms.[41]

However, when tariffs are raised on just one part of the solar chain – the solar panels – then demand for imported Chinese panels decreases, which in turn decreases demand for US exports of capital equipment and PV polysilicon, plus the demand for all the services associated with selling, permitting, installing, and maintaining the systems. And so the policies meant to safeguard US jobs by punishing China actually achieve the opposite effect. Jobs are killed, not saved.

Tires provide another example. You raise tariffs on tires, as Obama did in 2009, and you may help one part of the value chain but you hurt others. According to a study from the Peterson Institute of International Economics, Obama's tire tariffs could have saved about 1,200 jobs in tire manufacturing – a fact Obama often touts when trying to prove his I'm-tough-on-China credentials. But the tariffs, in dampening Chinese imports, raised tire retail prices by US$1.1 billion in 2011. Higher prices slowed consumer demand, which cost about 3,700 retail jobs. So, politically, Obama may have looked like he was acting tough and protecting American workers, but the move was actually a *net job loss* for the tire industry.[42]

As illustrated by solar panels and tires, Obama's employment policies are often in conflict with one another. Consider the National Export Initiative, a centerpiece of Obama's job creation program. With a goal of doubling US exports in five years, the policy makes sense, as exports have been a leading edge in US economic growth since the recession of 2008, and boosting exports creates jobs. Yet, while Obama tries to create jobs by supporting exporters with his right hand, the left hand levies tariffs that punish exporters, kill jobs, and provoke retaliatory trade protectionism by the Chinese.

The blunt cudgel of tariffs is too clumsy a tool to protect jobs in value chains that span the United States and China. Usually, American value is added at the beginning and end of the chain: in the beginning with invention, design, engineering, branding, and the manufacture of components; and at the end with transportation, warehousing, wholesaling, retailing, and service. China usually occupies the middle phases, which sometimes may involve engineering and manufacturing, but mostly consist of assembly. In the case of the iPads and iPhones and scores of other Chinese imports, China functions as the assembler – with virtually no engineering or manufacturing.

Contrary to the popular notion of a zero-sum game, then, in which job creation in China means job destruction in the United States, Chinese and American industries are usually symbiotic – with the higher-value functions performed by American workers. In this process, the majority of value and profits in Chinese imports to the United States are captured by American firms.

But the fact that our retail shelves are lined with labels that say "Made in China" gives the impression that nothing is made in America anymore and lends credence to the myth of American economic decline at the hands of the Chinese. This fallacy is propagated by wrongheaded media coverage, such as the ABC series *Made in America*, and parroted by politicians of both parties. Especially during election seasons, the decline of US manufacturing is shouted from the rooftops. And this decline is seen as the canary in the coal mine for America. The death of US manufacturing presages the death of the US economy in the coming century. And China is to blame.

Except US manufacturing isn't in decline. Up to the economic collapse of 2008, "US manufacturing was setting new performance records almost year after year in nearly all relevant statistical categories: profits, revenues, investment returns, output, value added, exports, imports, and others," notes Daniel Ikenson of the Cato Institute in testimony before Congress in 2011.[43] And, since 2009, US manufacturing is growing again. From 2009 to 2012, according to manufacturing.gov which uses data from the Bureau of Labor Statistics, factories hired nearly 500,000 workers – 139,000 of them during the first four months of 2012 alone. Sheer manufacturing output from 2009 through the end of 2011 increased by 20 percent as well.

True, there was much gnashing of teeth and rending of clothes in 2011 when China was said to have overtaken the United States in manufacturing output. But, again, this needs to be put in some perspective. The comparative measurements of value are in dollars – and China's 25 percent appreciation in the value of the yuan since 2005 has made its production outputs more valuable. Also, we need to bear in mind the nature of most Chinese manufacturing – assembly and low- to mid-technology products. China, on the whole, does not compete with the United States in its manufacturing sweet spot: namely, high-tech, high-value manufacturing. So the fact that China churns out a lot of stuff that it assembles from components made in other countries should not presage the death of US manufacturing.

In truth, American factories have mostly exited lower value added, low-tech industries, like apparel, toys, housewares, and furniture. "US factories make lots of things," continues Dr Ikenson in his Congressional testimony, "in particular, high-value products that are less likely to be found in retail stores – like airplanes, advanced medical devices, sophisticated machinery, chemicals, pharmaceuticals, and biotechnology products."

Of course, we rarely hear from the cable news networks or the echo chamber of political rhetoric that US

1.5 US manufacturing employment 1950–2014

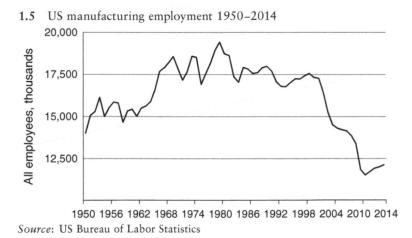

Source: US Bureau of Labor Statistics

manufacturing is on the rise. What we hear about, instead, is job losses in manufacturing. Yet, despite the fact that the manufacturing sector has been steadily adding jobs since 2009, it's true – factory employment is way down from 1979, when manufacturing employed 19.4 million Americans.

Since then, manufacturing employment in America has been trending down (see Figure 1.5). According to the US Bureau of Labor Statistics, that number in July 2014 was 12.16 million jobs. But, interestingly enough, Ikenson reminds us that manufacturing employment started declining after 1979, "fourteen years before the implementation of the North American Free Trade Agreements and 22 years before China joined the World Trade Organization. So the downward trend in manufacturing employment, along roughly the same trajectory for 30 years, began long before the common scapegoats for manufacturing job loss even existed."

If free trade agreements and trade with China are not the cause of declining employment in our manufacturing sector, what is? You'll notice in the early 2000s that manufacturing

1.6 US manufacturing employment 1998–2014

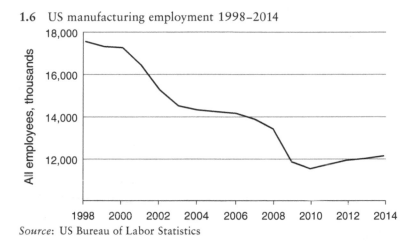

Source: US Bureau of Labor Statistics

employment fell off a cliff (see Figure 1.6). From 1995 to 2002, factories shed 2 million jobs, or 11 percent of manufacturing employment. To hear our news media and many politicians explain this phenomenon, the culprit was China and the scourge of outsourcing. Not so, claimed the Clinton administration, which sought instead to liberalize trade with China.

The pro- and anti-trade battle lines were drawn in 1999, as Congress clashed over whether to grant a special economic status to China: Permanent Normal Trading Relations. If approved, PNTR would end the usual yearly review of China's economic record and set the stage for accession to the World Trade Organization. David Axelrod, the man who would become President Obama's political strategist, produced negative ads meant to kill the bill for the powerful labor union, the AFL-CIO. Axelrod used the "Made in China" label to get his point across.

"Behind this label," the commercial darkly intones, "is a shameful story of political prisoners and forced labor camps, of wages as low as thirteen cents an hour, of a country that routinely violates trade rules, flooding our markets, draining American jobs." The legend "800,000 American jobs lost" flashes on the screen.

The assumption is that, if the United States is losing jobs, China is gaining them. But during the same period, from 1995 to 2002, China lost 16 million manufacturing jobs – or 15 percent of its manufacturing employment. In fact, there was a global dip in factory employment during that period of about 22 million jobs, of which China made up the lion's share. Yet, according to a study by Alliance Capital Management, global industrial output rose during that time by 30 percent.

This trend has continued since then. Even as American manufacturing employment has, by and large, been declining from its peak in 1979, the total value of US manufacturing has been trending upwards. With productivity gains – driven by advances in manufacturing technology – we are able to produce more with fewer workers.

In the United States, for example, "97,000 steelworkers produced 9.5% more steel in 2011 than 400,000 workers did in 1980," according to the Center for Innovative Media at George Washington University.[44] As Chinese firms acquire better technology, they are shedding workers, too. So the notion that when the United States loses jobs, it is just shipping them over to China is a fallacy. China is shedding more jobs in manufacturing than the States.

Certainly, some degree of outsourcing has gone on in the past couple of decades. We can see the proof from GE's Appliance Park, which is bringing the jobs back from places like China and Mexico. But the actual number of jobs outsourced has been grossly overstated in a vacuum of good data. According to the Congressional Research Service, "No comprehensive data exist on the number of production and services workers who have lost their jobs as a result of the movement of work outside US borders. The only regularly collected statistics on jobs lost to the out-of-country reloca-tions of work come from the BLS series on extended mass layoffs."[45]

The Bureau of Labor Statistics' mass-layoff data are based on surveys conducted from companies that have at least fifty claims for unemployment insurance filed during a five-week period. The *extended* mass-layoff data, referred to above, are a subset in which private-sector nonfarm employers state in a survey whether fifty or more workers were separated from their jobs for at least 31 days. A further subset, and one that is closest to representing the true number of jobs outsourced, is the quarterly list of "out-of-country reloca-tions." In other words, these data measure firms that had massive layoffs of 50 or more employees who had not yet been hired back within 31 days and whose jobs had been relocated overseas.

A pretty good estimation, but certainly not complete, as the data are based on unemployment insurance claims which don't usually reflect part-time or seasonal labor. Trying for a clearer picture, then, economists often employ additional data, such as the levels of US direct investment abroad and imported intermediate goods, to extrapolate broader out-sourcing numbers. But here we're getting into the realm of pure conjecture. That a business is investing in another country does not necessarily mean it is firing domestic employees and shipping those jobs overseas. Nor does the import of intermediate goods necessarily spell the loss of jobs here at home, as many jobs are required to transform those components into final products.

Trying to measure outsourcing is not only highly imper-fect, it's easily politicized because it stokes America's fears of economic inadequacy. In a 2012 survey of Michigan mil-lennials, 73 percent said outsourcing jobs to China was a top concern.[46] Yet, if we look at BLS's out-of-country relocations, which is a reasonable place to start since it gives us a good baseline of full-time laborers whose jobs have been sent overseas, outsourcing is a much, much smaller trend than typically portrayed in the news media. According to the BLS's out-of-country relocation data, just 2,687 American jobs were outsourced to other countries in 2012.

"With over 134 million jobs in the United States, that means about 1 in every 50,000 was shipped to another country last year," writes Tom Gantert of the Mackinac Center for Public Policy, a nonpartisan research institute in Michigan. Even if we expand that number significantly to fudge the part-time and seasonal labor that might be outsourced, the overall figure still represents just a small fraction of the US workforce. "Most jobs are gained and lost due to regular turnover; only a microscopic fraction is lost due to plants relocating abroad," says James Hohman, also of the Mackinac Center.[47]

A good snapshot of what Hohman means is provided by the year 2009. It was an especially bad year for American employment amidst a severe economic retraction. The United States lost 30.8 million jobs, while creating 25.3 million jobs. BLS out-of-country relocations for 2009 numbered 10,378, representing 0.03 percent of job losses.

That fact is that in America, millions of jobs are usually created and lost every year. It is convenient to blame the job losses on another country such as China. Demagoguing currency, outsourcing, and the trade imbalance let politicians tap into our anger and insecurity while misdirecting our attention from the true causes of our economic ups and downs.

To gauge America's true competitiveness, we need to disregard these widely held – and emotionally fraught – notions of China's might. China isn't about to surpass us economically. Everything isn't made in China. And China's currency policies have negligible impact on US employment.

Let's focus our attention, instead, on the real impacts of China's economy on the United States. Not the threat of currency, but unsafe imports. Not the notion of job destruction, but job creation. Before we swoop to the ground to explore the root causes of systemic risk in China's economy, it's worth taking a look at its symptoms in America.

2

Jobs and Jeopardy

What's the first image that comes to your mind when you think of China? Is it the "Made in China" label? Shuttered American factories? Chairman Mao in red wrestling spandex body-slamming Uncle Sam?

How about a river of pigs? You may remember it was in the news a little while back? Not all the reporting on China paints a false picture. We sometimes see glimpses of the true nature of China's economy.

Swine River is one of those times when the curtain gets pulled back and we can view China for what it really is – not the Wizard of Oz, but the little guy nervously working the levers.

Do you remember the story? The big river that runs through downtown Shanghai was choked with diseased pigs. Big sows and hogs. Tiny pink piglets. More than 16,000 bloated pig corpses were scooped from the water in February 2013 and the months ahead.

Imagine that. You're gazing at the Thames or the Hudson or the Seine, and a tide of dead piggies bobs by. And to make matters worse, many of the pigs were infected with porcine circovirus – a nasty bug that causes pneumonia, atrophy, and ulcerative skin lesions in the animals.

Thousands of rotting, diseased pig corpses were marinating in the drinking water supply. Not surprisingly, there was a run on bottled water in Shanghai.

How the pigs got in the Huangpu is still a mystery. The pig farmers upstream aren't fessing up, of course. *Why*, however, is more widely understood. A tough governmental crackdown on the common (but illegal) practice of fobbing diseased pigs off on slaughterhouses forced farmers to dump the dead and dying piggies into the drink.

Like so many other bizarre events in China – the traffic jam to Mongolia that lasted eleven days, the 10,000 cannons strafing the clouds with silver iodide during the Beijing Olympics to keep the rain away – the Swine River got some play for a few media cycles, then was mostly forgotten. Yet the river of pigs shows us how systemic risk on the ground gives rise to two outcomes for the West: jobs and jeopardy.

The Threat: Unsafe Imports

The jeopardy is more obvious than the jobs. Swine River flows right into your supermarket and drugstore. China is the top exporter of many food and drug products to both the United States and the European Union (EU). And because of the feeble screening mechanisms in place, which can inspect just a small percentage of these goods, Chinese imports present a clear and present danger to our safety.

Of course, the United States has had its own share of food safety lapses: the Peanut Corporation of America, which caused a massive outbreak of deadly salmonella poisoning at schools and nursing homes; pink slime, cow cartilage and connective tissue doused in ammonia added to ground beef sold in most of America's supermarkets; *E. coli* outbreaks in cantaloupe and spinach; salmonella in chicken processors; poison steroid shots made in compounding pharmacies. So has the EU: Dutch pig farms spiking their feed with illegal steroids, horse meat being sold in IKEA meatballs, regular eggs being passed off as organic.

But China's safety lapses are much, much more widespread, frequent, and severe. Not dozens or even hundreds, they've numbered in the *thousands* just in the past few years. And that's just in China. In the United States and the EU, far and away, Chinese imports dominate product recalls.

In 2010, Chinese imports comprised a whopping 58 percent of all product recalls in Europe. And, more recently, in 2013, 22 percent of all safety warnings in the EU were for Chinese-made goods. Just look at Figure 2.1 to see how China compares with the rest of the countries the EU imports from in number of safety warnings. Do you see a pattern?

Similarly, in the United States, of the 1,861 import alerts issued by the Food and Drug Administration between 2011 and 2014, China topped the list with 131 alerts, as compared to 45 for Taiwan, 41 for Japan, and 39 for South Korea.[1] The US Consumer Product Safety Commission also tracks product recalls for non-food and drug-related products. In the years 2000–2013, again, China was number one – and way ahead of the pack (see Figure 2.2).

If you look at the numbers year by year, China's safety threat is actually trending worse, not better. In 2000, 26 percent of US product recalls were from Chinese imports. By 2005, the percentage grew to 47 percent, then to 66 percent in 2007. In 2012, almost 52 percent of product recalls were from China – still double the amount of recalls in 2000.

But the amount of Chinese safety lapses in EU and US imports is dwarfed by what happens in China, most of which we don't hear about. Some of the more extreme safety lapses do reach our media, of course. For example, in 2008, we witnessed the scandal of melamine-poisoned baby formula, which sickened 300,000 Chinese babies and killed

2.1 2013 EU safety warnings by country of origin

Source: The European Commission 2013, RAPEX Facts and Figures 2013

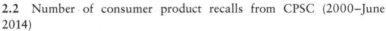

2.2 Number of consumer product recalls from CPSC (2000–June 2014)

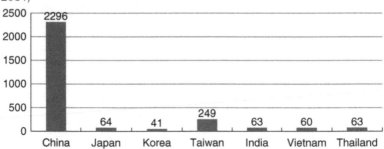

Source: United States Consumer Product Safety Commission, *Find Recalled Products by Country/Administrative Area of Manufacture*, viewed June 24, 2014, http://www.cpsc.gov

six – not the first incident of contaminated formula killing kids in China, by the way. But there have been thousands of grisly safety incidents that we haven't seen over the past few years: duck meat marinated in goat urine to make it taste like lamb (I would hate to be a food tester in *that* lab); gutter oil used for cooking in restaurants and in pharmaceuticals; meat laced with banned steroids; apples doused in arsenic; rotten peaches spiked with toxic bleaching agents and packaged in bags that used to contain animal feed. The list goes on and on.

What's terrifying about China's safety issues is that they're now ours, too. The Swine River flows into your local supermarket, restaurant, and hospital. Juice, fish, chicken, food additives, vitamins, medicines – many of the food and drugs we consume, if they weren't "made" in China, were processed there in some way, or contain Chinese-made ingredients, and therefore pose a considerable health risk.

Even as China's safety record worsens, our imports grow. US imports of Chinese-made food products have

2.3 Total US food imports from China (billions of lbs)

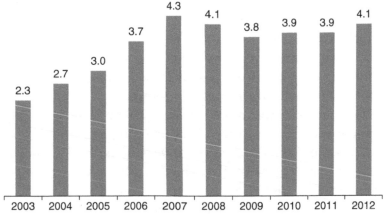

Source: Patty Lovera 2013, *Testimony Before The House Committee On Foreign Affairs Subcommittee On Europe, Eurasia, And Emerging Threats, Hearing On The Threat of China's Unsafe Consumables*, Food & Water Watch, http://www.foodandwaterwatch.org

tripled over the past decade, reaching over 4 billion pounds in 2012.[2]

The list of Chinese-made staples in our diet is long and scary. Two-thirds of the apple juice Americans drink is made from Chinese apple concentrate; 80 percent of the tilapia and half the cod; 40 percent of the processed mushrooms; about a quarter of the garlic. China also produces 80 percent of the world's ascorbic acid. So the vitamin C in your kid's chewables? Guess where *that* comes from?

And because of our country-of-origin labeling rules, most of the time, we *do* have to guess where our food is coming from. Take fish, for example. These days, about 86 percent of the seafood and fish we eat is imported, and one-quarter of that is from China.[3] Two top Chinese exports to the United States, tilapia and shrimp, are popular food items in

America. Shrimp is our number-one seafood choice, and tilapia is in the top four behind tuna, salmon, and pollock.[4] China's exports of shrimp and tilapia are aqua-farmed, which is not good, as China's terrifying aquaculture practices have recently come to light. One study describes how Chinese fish farms use untreated chicken manure and human waste to feed shrimp and tilapia.[5] Yum.

But perhaps even more eerily, with popular items like salmon and crab, the seafood is often caught in America but processed in China and exported *back* to us, with no indication of that activity on the labeling. Many fisheries in the northwestern United States prefer to send their catch to China for processing. "There are 36 pin bones in a salmon," says Charles Bundrant of Trident Seafood, "and the best way to remove them is by hand."[6] That kind of operation is China's sweet spot – low-skill, low-value labor, which offsets the price of transporting the catch 14,000 miles back and forth across the Pacific Ocean. Same with Dungeness crab, which often gets de-shelled and filleted in Chinese processors before being exported back.[7]

We have no idea how much fish and seafood is exported and re-imported, though. The US Department of Commerce's National Oceanic and Atmospheric Administration (NOAA), which oversees the seas, does not track re-imports. So your box of fish sticks may say something like "Caught in the Cold, Blue Alaskan Waters," but what it doesn't say is "Processed in an Unsafe Chinese Factory."

Chicken is next. Soon, chicken will be making the same round-trip tour that salmon and crab do. The US Department of Agriculture recently designated China's poultry processing as "equivalent" to that of the United States. As such, we've been told that American chicken processed in China is safe for consumption, even though US inspectors will not be allowed access to Chinese chicken-processing plants. And labels won't necessarily need to say where the chicken was processed. So the chicken in your can of noodle soup, or the breaded and fried buffalo wings at your local bar, or your McNugget may have been anonymously processed in China.[8]

Chicken isn't the only product where US inspectors are barred or discouraged, though. The pulverized ginger you get at your organic market is another example. There's a good chance it comes from China. And though it's been certified organic by a reputable certification service, that service had to take the word of a Chinese certification company because foreign firms are not allowed to inspect Chinese farms. Inspectors are also prevented or discouraged from visiting factories of active pharmaceutical ingredients that go into many of the medicines we take.

The Food and Drug Administration, with a small staff of twenty-seven to cover all of China, keeps pushing for more access. Even so, it's estimated that the FDA is able to inspect about 2 percent of Chinese imports today. That's really scary when you consider the source. We're buying food and drugs from "The Jungle" and not inspecting 98 percent of them. The FDA claims it screens all Chinese imports via electronic surveillance. Before food and drugs are exported from China to the United States, documents must be submitted in advance, and the FDA says it targets "high-risk" products.[9]

But cases like Baxter's tainted blood thinner, heparin, reveal that the FDA's database is not up to the job of effective electronic surveillance. The source of the bad batches, the Chinese active pharmaceutical ingredient manufacturer, wasn't even on the FDA's list and slipped right through the surveillance unnoticed. Other drug-related industries, such as vitamin supplements which import many of their ingredients from China, aren't even regulated by the FDA and are subject to zero US governmental inspection or oversight.

Despite reassurances from the FDA, our food and drug supply has been overrun by imports. Almost 90 percent of the seafood we eat is imported, as well as about two-thirds of the fruits and vegetables. And about 80 percent of the active ingredients of the drugs we take come from China and India.[10] The FDA is obviously totally overwhelmed, and we're sitting ducks.

Many articles and books have described the severity of the danger we face from Chinese imports. But they tend to blame corruption and malfeasance. Though underhandedness certainly plays a role in dangerous Chinese outputs, it's by no means the main cause. Dangerous goods emanate from a risky system. Even well-meaning manufacturers and government officials are typically thwarted by it. Later chapters will explore why.

The Opportunity: Jobs

That same risky system supports jobs in the United States and Europe. Lots of them. Let's take another look at Swine River. To see the threat is pretty easy. To see the opportunity, not so much.

Pigs started bobbing down the Huangpu in February of 2013. By mid-May, Shuanghui, China's largest meat processor, made a US$4.7 billion bid to buy Smithfield, America's largest pork producer. The succession of these two events, if not directly causal, is indirectly so. Grisly safety scandals in China's meat industry had already rocked the country many times before you could fish for diseased pigs in Shanghai.

In 2011, China's largest meat processors, Yurun and Shuanghui, were exposed in the Chinese media for adulterating their pork with clenbuterol, a poisonous additive in pig feed that is used for slimming hogs. Yurun's brave response? Nothing to see here, folks. We've destroyed the single contaminated pig! (As if we are to believe that just one pig was fed the clenbuterol.)

The safety scandals didn't go away, of course. Ongoing quality control allegations forced Yurun's founder to step down as chairman of the board in 2012. And, after negative media coverage about clenbuterol, Shuanghui had to recall thousands of tons of tainted pork,[11] and the company's shares went into freefall. Their trading was suspended after three straight days of 10 percent declines, costing the firm an estimated US$200 million in value.

For Shuanghui, then, the Smithfield acquisition was just as much about securing pork supply (China eats a lot of pork – about 20 million hogs per month) as by a desire to improve its food safety and quality control practices. Pork accounts for two-thirds of the meat eaten by Chinese consumers, says Dr Ben Embarek of the World Health Organization's Beijing office, but only half of it goes through slaughterhouses that are subject to inspection.[12]

Shuanghui's purchase of Smithfield will support about 46,000 US employees. And this purchase is part of a growing trend. Chinese investments in US companies keep reaching record highs – doubling to US$14 billion in 2013, buoyed by deals in food (read: Smithfield), real estate, and energy. Inbound Chinese investment is one of the ways China directly supports American jobs. American exports to China support jobs as well. And both are outcomes of China's risky system. As China struggles to make things safely, its consumers clamor for foreign goods. Increasingly, that means they buy from, and invest in, America.

Consider China's baby formula safety scandal. Imagine you're a parent in China. Chances are you have one kid, whom you'd prefer not to poison with tainted formula. So you do everything you can to buy foreign brands, which you trust more. The result? Baby formula shortages around the world. "Chinese are buying up infant milk powder everywhere they can get it, outside of China," reports Edward Wong for the *New York Times*. "And that has led to shortages in at least a half-dozen countries, from the Netherlands to New Zealand."[13] With limited supply and strong demand, baby formula prices in China have shot up – at least 30 percent since 2008, according to the *People's Daily*, as reported by Edward Wong. "Some 28-ounce cans cost more than $60."[14]

Sixty bucks for a can of baby formula? Yes, because Chinese consumers are scared of domestically produced formula. It's not surprising, given all the lethal safety lapses in the past few years. In a Pew Survey "Growing Concerns in China," published October 16, 2012, 41 percent of Chinese respondents said food safety was "a very serious problem" – up from just 12 percent in 2008. It's not just infant formula. Chinese consumers who can afford it opt to buy as much imported food as they can, and they're willing to pay a premium.

That's why, despite the significant added cost of exporting food halfway around the world, plus the high Chinese import tariffs that these items encounter when entering the country, America still enjoys a significant trade surplus with China in agriculture. According to the US Department of Agriculture (USDA), the United States exported US$30 billion worth of agricultural products to China in 2012 and imported just US$10 billion.[15] That's a fivefold increase from the value of our ag exports to China in 2003. China is now the top destination for US ag exports, and, since 2008, America exports more food to China than to Europe, representing 18 percent of total US agricultural exports to the world.[16] So while our politicians keep griping about trade imbalances to China in manufacturing – imbalances, by the way, that are highly inflated and misinterpreted – you rarely hear a peep from them about our big trade surplus to China in agriculture.[17]

Those exports support farm jobs across the country. Yet, when China is Topic A, exports are rarely touted. In fact, no one I talk to seems to believe that America actually exports anything to China at all. People are usually shocked to hear that we do. But we're not just exporting dribs and drabs, it's a tidal wave of exports.

In all sectors and in all states, in fact, in almost every congressional district, exports have been skyrocketing for the last decade. It bears repeating: between 2003 and 2012, in 401 out of 435 congressional districts (that's 92 percent), American exports to China doubled, often tripled, or, in some cases, grew tenfold and more.[18] So not only is America selling a lot of stuff to China, nearly every part of the country is.

Contrary to the popular opinion that uncompetitive America doesn't make anything anymore, the United States is actually an exporting goliath. In 2010, the United States became the world's top exporter, and the second-largest exporter of merchandise. In 2013, the United States exported a record US$2.3 trillion of goods and services to the world. (Comparatively, we imported US$2.7 trillion of goods and services – remembering that this figure does not attribute the actual value added per unit, so a portion of that value was derived from American-made components.)

Exports support jobs. Lots of them. By 2010, US exports directly supported 10.7 million jobs, according to the US Commerce Department. Our exports recovered from the recession faster than Germany's, the leading export nation of Europe, and exports made up more than 46 percent of the growth in America's economy from 2010 and 2011 alone – led by US manufacturing. Given that China is our

2.4 Total US exports to China (US$ billion)

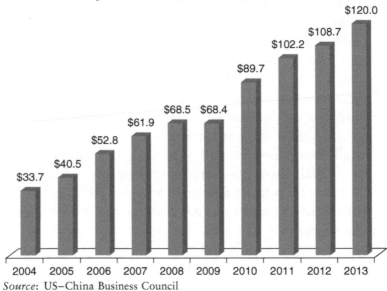

Source: US–China Business Council

third-largest export market, as well as our fastest-growing market for many products and services, US export growth in large part can be attributed to Chinese demand.

You might argue that the steep growth in exports to China derives from our starting from an extremely low base. You sell China an ear of corn. Then you sell it two. Suddenly you've doubled exports. True, 15 years ago, China was ranked in twelfth place in American export markets. But, since then, it has rocketed up to number three – just behind Canada and Mexico, our neighbors to the north and south.

The year 2013 set new export records to China (see Figure 2.4). We exported US$120 billion worth of goods to China, a 10 percent rise from 2012. In comparison, America exported US$300.3 billion to Canada, up 2.7 percent from 2012, and US$226.2 billion to Mexico, up 4.7 percent from

2012.[19] Our 2012 exports to Hong Kong (which are the latest numbers available) totaled US$44 billion. So China and Hong Kong together represent about US$168 billion in goods exports in 2013. If you add services exports, the number rises to over US$198 billion.

And, speaking of services exports, agriculture isn't the only trade surplus with China. US exports of private services to China – including travel, education, financial services, licensing, engineering, consulting, and R&D – reached US$30 billion in 2012 (the latest data available from the US Trade Representative), representing a US$17 billion trade surplus – up 455 percent since 2001.

So in actual value, not just in relative growth, China is buying a lot from America: in ag, services, and manufacturing. And, over the past decade, American exports to China grew at a rate of 255 percent versus 111 percent to the rest of the world (Figure 2.5).[20]

Now, given the fact that many Chinese imports contain American inputs, you may ask if the reverse is true. What portion of US-exported products is actually American made? The International Trade Commission (ITC), an independent US governmental agency that advises Congress and the executive branch on trade, estimates that about 87 percent of US exports is made in the United States.

So imagine an auto part made in Detroit, exported to Canada where it is combined with other components, then re-imported by the United States for final processing before it is exported to China. Of course, the percentage of American content in other sectors, like business services and agricultural products, is much higher – over 95 percent, according to the ITC.[21]

Most of what we sell to China, then, is American made, unlike a lot of what China sells us. Our top manufactured imports from China in 2013 were electrical machinery

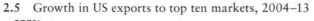

2.5   Growth in US exports to top ten markets, 2004–13

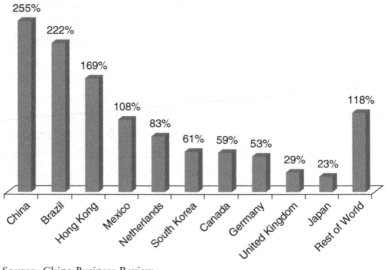

Source: China Business Review

(US$117.5 billion), non-electrical machinery (US$100.4 billion), furniture and bedding ($24.1 billion), toys and sporting equipment (US$21.7 billion), and footwear (US$17 billion).[22] Each of these categories has a very high concentration of non-Chinese value-add.

US top exports to China, on the other hand, were grain, seed, and fruit – think soybeans to feed all those hogs (US$13.8 billion), aircraft (US$12.6 billion), machinery (US$12.2 billion), electrical machinery (US$11.4 billion), and vehicles (US$10.3 billion). US top ag exports, specifically, were soybeans (US$13.4 billion), cotton (US$2.2 billion), hides and skins (US$1.7 billion), and distillers' grains (US$1.4 billion). Although dollar values on private service exports are not available through US government data sources, we do know that American top private-services export categories to China were education and travel, professional and technical services, and royalties and licensing fees.

2.6   US exports to China by state, 2004–13

State	Exports 2013	2004–13 Growth
1. California	$15.7 billion	136%
2. Washington	$11.4 billion	535%
3. Texas	$10.4 billion	118%
4. Illinois	$6.4 billion	380%
5. New York	$5.0 billion	171%
6. South Carolina	$4.9 billion	949%
7. Michigan	$4.6 billion	616%
8. Georgia	$3.9 billion	319%
9. Ohio	$3.9 billion	243%
10. Minnesota	$3.5 billion	426%
11. Pennsylvania	$2.9 billion	274%
12. Oregon	$2.9 billion	348%
13. Iowa	$2.9 billion	441%
14. North Carolina	$2.8 billion	261%
15. Indiana	$2.5 billion	358%

Source: China Business Review

What's truly astounding is how broad-based these exports are. They not only span every economic sector, they span most of the country. Forty-two states achieved triple-digit export growth to China since 2004. That means they doubled their exports. Seven states saw their exports grow fivefold. And, since 2009, 17 states doubled their exports yet again. The list of top 15 US state exporters to China between 2003 and 2012 is jaw-dropping. Figure 2.6 gives the growth numbers (reflected in percentages), along with 2013 export values.

In the top 15 exporting states, there are some real surprises. Michigan's exports to China grew sixfold (this being the state where 73 percent of surveyed millennials said they were worried about outsourcing to China). Ohio's exports more than tripled. Indiana's exports more than quadrupled. These states are usually associated with the decline of America's manufacturing power.

Yet, when hearing about these bullish export numbers, those in the know will often scoff that China has relegated the United States to a third-world country, buying crops and scrap from us. We certainly sell a lot of that to China. In fact, soybeans are still America's top export to China at US$13.4 billion in 2013. One out of every four rows of soybeans grown in Iowa gets exported to China.[23]

But waste and scrap exports are actually declining. Copper waste and scrap at US$2.8 billion in 2013 was a decline of 6 percent from 2012, aluminum waste and scrap at US$2.3 billion was a 5 percent decline from the year before, and paperboard waste and scrap at US$2 billion was a 9 percent decline. As China's manufacturing sector has slowed in the face of slackening demand from industrialized economies still recovering from the recession, China's demand for scrap, which is used as an input to production, also cools. Even with softening demand, though, it is estimated that nearly *all* US recycled paper and plastic is exported to China.

In the meantime, America sells a lot of higher-value goods to China, too, as well as services. The top two exporting states to China are California and Washington. California's top export to China is computer hardware. Companies in Silicon Valley, such as Qualcomm, make semiconductors that are sold to China for assembly into consumer electronic products like phones that are then shipped back to us as finished goods. Of Washington State's US$7.9 billion in exports to China, almost US$5 billion goes to the aerospace industry. Lockheed Martin, Honeywell, General Dynamics, and, of course, Boeing are based in Washington – and China is buying airplanes as it expands commercial aviation. Boeing exported 120 airplanes to China in 2013, a 50 percent increase from 2012. Texas, ranked number three for exports to China, is a leading manufacturer of chemicals. Dow, Dupont, and other companies export chemicals to China, such as the petrochemical resins and additives needed to make plastic. Many of those plastics are incorporated into housewares, toys, and sporting goods that get exported back to us.

Other higher-value exports include cars, where China is America's top-selling overseas destination.[24] In 2009, the United States exported 28,757 units of cars and light trucks to China. In 2010, it was 99,694. And in 2011, it was 136,222. That's hockey-stick growth.[25] Passenger vehicles were Michigan's third-top export to China in 2013. And that includes luxury cars. China is Cadillac's top export market – over half of Cadillac's exports go to China.

But wait. Didn't we just read that Detroit is on the ropes, that America's car companies can't compete internationally? That we'll soon be driving Chinese cars? Yes, Detroit – uncompetitive Detroit, with its infamously intransigent unions and expensive employee benefits and pensions – is making cars that the Chinese can afford and love to buy. Chinese consumers consider foreign automotive brands to be more prestigious and higher quality than domestic brands.

In 2007, there was much hoopla about a joint venture between Chrysler and China's Chery Automobile Company to produce cars in China that would be exported to the United States. Many predicted that America would begin importing the Chinese-made vehicles by 2009. A bit after the joint venture was announced in 2007 and the pundits started panting over the advent of Chinese imported cars, I remarked on the dais of a conference that if China were exporting cars to the United States by 2009, I'd eat my tie. Other speakers said I was crazy – that China's manufacturing acumen was undisputed, and that China would most certainly be exporting cars to the United States by then.

Well, the joint venture was disbanded in 2008. Insiders said it was because Chinese engineers could not overcome the technical challenges of meeting American and EU safety and emissions standards.[26] A 2007 crash test of the Chery Amulet sedan in Russia, China's top automotive export market, proved this point. The front end crumpled like an accordion on polka night. The Russian auto magazine that sponsored the test declared it was one of the worst safety performances they'd ever seen and demanded Chery pull out of Russia's auto market.[27]

As of this book writing, more than seven years after my prediction about China's auto exports, my tie remains uneaten. I predict it will stay that way for years to come. And, as China's auto makers struggle to make good cars, Chinese consumers clamor for imported ones. That's why automotive vehicle and parts exports are supporting thousands of jobs in Michigan, Ohio, and South Carolina.

But exports to China aren't just the purview of the likes of GM, Dow, and Boeing. Small and medium-sized firms are actually leading the charge – comprising 92 percent of US businesses exporting to China and 35 percent of the value of exports.[28]

The examples abound. There's W. S. Darley of Itasca, Illinois, which makes firefighting equipment and employs 215 people with annual sales of about US$110 million. Darley is a family business founded in 1908. Of the 50–100 fire trucks they build per year, most are exported to China, which has 171 cities with a population of at least one million people (compared with nine in the United States). China is eager to ramp up the municipal services these cities can provide and is on a buying binge for items like fire engines.[29]

Oransi of Austin, Texas is catering to another Chinese urban need. Breathing. Given the abysmal air quality in most Chinese cities, including Beijing, consumers are not only wearing masks outside, they're using air purifiers inside.

Oransi created a special line of air purifiers for the China market. They're high end, with a price tag of US$2,000–3,000 each. Oransi expects China sales in 2014 to double the company's 2013 revenues of US$5 million.[30]

While Oransi developed a totally new product for China, other companies with sagging sales in the United States are finding strong demand in China for their core business lines. Wallquest, based in Wayne, Pennsylvania, makes wallpaper – not a popular item in the US home market these days. So the family-owned firm turned to China. As proof that Chinese consumers pay a premium for American brands not just for safety but also for cachet (what advertisers call "consumer aspiration"), Wallquest's products sell from US$100–1,700 per roll. Approximately 30 percent of Wallquest's revenues come from China, which has allowed the company to staff up – going from 80 people in 2007 to 185 in 2013.[31]

Watermark of Brooklyn, New York, which makes faucets, is another example of a company that turned toward China after sales in the United States were circling the drain. As Watermark struggled to compete with cheaper imports from China, rather than shutter the factory, the family-owned business decided to sell to China. But rather than lower their prices, as you'd expect, they raised them. The strategy worked, positioning Watermark as a premium brand in a commodity market. Watermark has exported thousands of high-end plumbing fixtures to luxury hotels and condominiums in China.[32]

Ice cream is another success story. Though American brands Häagen-Dazs and Baskin Robbins control much more China market share, Bassett's Ice Cream, a fifth-generation family ice-cream maker based in Philadelphia, has become the largest US ice-cream exporter to China in less than five years. Its giant competitors, Häagen and Baskin, don't make their Chinese ice cream in the United States. Bassett does – and exports it in temperature-controlled shipping containers to the port of Xingang, where it's distributed to luxury hotels and ice-cream shops priced at US$7.74 for a large cone. Bassett's China exports went from zero to more than 20 percent of sales in less than five years.[33] Premium-priced cars, ice cream, air purifiers, and faucets sell better in China than the local, cheaper competition, disproving the widely held belief that our firms are on a race to the bottom with the Chinese on price. This is a function of China's risky system. Chinese consumers with disposable income will tend to spend more money on items they believe are safe. Since China has such a lousy reputation for quality *among Chinese*, imports are almost always preferred, no matter the category.

Then there's Georgia Chopstick, which is selling chopsticks to China. The Chinese go through 45 billion pairs of disposable chopsticks per year, and they're running out of forests. In Georgia, poplar trees are perfect for chopsticks – the trees are durable and grow back quickly. Georgia Chopstick makes 600 chopsticks per minute, 2 million per day, and is ramping up to 4 million per day. The plant runs six days a week and employs about a hundred people in Americus, Georgia, where unemployment runs around 14 percent, so the jobs are sorely needed.[34]

In another example of selling ice to the Eskimos, K'NEX of Hatfield, Pennsylvania is selling toys to China. This small business read the numbers – that 85 percent of toys sold in the United States are exported from China – and decided to buck the trend. They saw China's middle-class consumers with more disposable income preferring educational toys, so they started marketing their interlocking building toys to China in 2013 and forecast sales to ramp up to 10 percent of revenues by 2016.[35]

Many US service firms have also thrived in China – with persistence and grit. The Hoffman Agency of San Jose, California decided to enter the China market in 1999. Lou Hoffman, the firm's CEO, said,

> I thought I was in not just another country but another universe. It starts with the language, but goes much deeper. We couldn't do business on the phone or by fax. Placing our first classified ad took 14 hours. We had to do everything in person, and considering the traffic in Beijing, you could kill three hours so someone could see your face.

This business climate didn't scare Hoffman away, though. But instead of sending a member of his management team to Shanghai to build an office, Hoffman put off scaling his China capability for one year. He hired a Chinese national and stationed her in San Jose to learn the ropes, so she could ably bridge both cultures. Since then, Hoffman's China sales have grown, taking on high-profile clients such as China Unicom and Chinese venture capital firm, IPV.[36]

It should be noted that US exports to China are booming in every state and every industry, for small and large companies alike, despite China's famously undervalued currency. Though Chinese consumers can buy less with their money, they spend it hand over fist on US goods and services. Chinese consumers are voting with their wallets, and so are Chinese companies. China's corporate investment in US firms reached US$70 billion by June 30, 2014 – a record high. Though we hear a lot about China's investments in Africa, it's the United States that tops China's list, having received more investment than any other country. The reaction from America? Fear and loathing, from media, politicians, and the public at large. Keep China out!

But we've seen this movie before. In the 1980s, America was scared of surging Japanese investment. Yet Japan didn't take over America, and many Japanese companies in the United States employ lots of Americans. There's Nissan and Toyota and Sony. And there are those you wouldn't even know are Japanese, such as Consolidated Grain and Barge, a company that ferries grain up and down the Mississippi River. It employs thousands of Americans in several states, including Missouri, Ohio, Louisiana, and Indiana. The company is owned by ITOCHU, a Japanese conglomerate.

Just as Japanese investment in US firms employs Americans, so do Chinese investments. There have been several big-ticket acquisitions recently, including AMC Theaters in 2012 and Smithfield in 2013. And as a Japanese firm purchased Rockefeller Center in the 1980s, a Chinese insurance firm recently purchased the Waldorf Astoria Hotel. But there have also been scores of smaller deals, led by the financial, energy, real estate, and manufacturing sectors.

China's Holdings of Treasury Bills

In these moves, you can see how China is increasing its direct investment in American companies, as it begins to diversify its portfolio of US treasury bills, worth about US$1.2 trillion as of 2013. There's often a lot of anxiety over China's US debt holdings, that on any given Thursday, the Chinese could suddenly dump their T-Bills and wreak havoc on America's financial system. Since China is the second-largest holder of US government bonds after the US Treasury, politicians and media have seized on the idea that America's national security is somehow threatened by China's debt holdings.

Here's Mitt Romney in 2012, when accepting the Republican presidential nomination in Tampa: "Does the America we want borrow a trillion dollars from China? No."[37] And Sarah Palin in 2013, at the Iowa Faith and Freedom Coalition:

Didn't you all learn too in Econ 101 there ain't no such thing
as a free lunch? Our free stuff today is being paid for by
taking money from our children and borrowing from China.
When that note comes due – and this isn't racist, but it's
going to be like slavery when that note is due. We are going
to be beholden to a foreign master.[38]

And then, there's Barack Obama in 2008: "[T]he way [Presi-
dent] Bush has done it over the last eight years is to take out
a credit card from the Bank of China in the name of our
children.... That's irresponsible. It's unpatriotic."[39] And even
Jon Stewart's *The Daily Show*: when 2012 also-ran Republican Herman Cain was interviewed by John Oliver, Cain
was asked how he would respond to dire national security
threats, had he won the presidency. The scenario? China
wants to dump its holdings of treasury bills. Over to you,
Herman. Cain looks directly at the camera and says, "Why
you gotta play me like that, China?"[40]

So politicians and pundits from the right and left have
endorsed the idea that China has some kind of economic
stranglehold over the United States because of its bond holdings. Of course, many economists have argued that China's
appetite for US treasury bills has helped keep interest rates
low, aiding the recovery from the 2008 recession. But putting
that argument aside, there are many reasons why the dooms-
day scenario of China as our "foreign master" ain't gonna
happen, Governor Palin.

First, China's own laws prevent it from reinvesting dollars
in its own economy. China has amassed a big pile of dollars
from trading with America for three decades. We pay China
in dollars for all the products we import. But China's closed
economic system bars foreign currency from being invested
domestically. So China's dollar reserves can't be used to
build infrastructure and hospitals and universities. They've
got to be invested elsewhere.

And the fact of the matter is there's no other bond market in the world with the depth of that of the United States to absorb this amount of money. Europe doesn't have a continental bond market, and its national bond markets are too small to accommodate China's massive holdings. So, when it comes to safe, interest-bearing securities, there's nowhere else for the money to go.

Sure, you say, but countries don't always act in their own best economic interests. Just look at Russia's adventurist gambit to annex Crimea. It's economic self-immolation. So what *would* happen if China did try to dump its treasury holdings, even if it would hurt China's own interests?

The Pentagon did an assessment of just that scenario. In 2012, the US Department of Defense conducted its first analysis of China's holdings of US debt from a national security perspective. The report framed the issue this way: "Attempting to use US Treasury securities as a coercive tool would have limited effect and likely would do more harm to China than to the United States.... As the threat is not credible and the effect would be limited even if carried out, it does not offer China deterrence options [in a stand-off with the United States]."[41]

We get a glimpse of what the Pentagon is referring to when China lightened its load of treasury bills in the past. There's been no negative impact. In 2011, China's T-bill holdings dropped 12 percent – by US$163 billion. But rather than seeing a market plunge, "10-year Treasuries rallied... pushing the yield to 1.88 percent from 2.80 percent," according to Bloomberg News.[42]

Because as China sells, others buy. An interest-rate specialist at Credit Suisse explains this phenomenon: that if China dumped its holdings, others would step up. "[I]f treasuries were to sell off 50 basis points in the 10-year sector, you'd see a lot of demand from domestic and non-traditional foreign investors, including other central banks, which would step in to purchase at lower prices and somewhat higher yields."[43] Domestic investors would include the Federal Reserve Bank, which has the power to print money. The Pentagon's report affirmed that the Fed is "fully capable of purchasing US Treasuries dumped" by China and "reducing the economic impact."[44]

So the notion that China is somehow holding America over a barrel because of debt holdings is simply untrue. And as China diversifies out of bonds, a move it has been signaling for some years now, it increasingly invests in US equities. America is a highly attractive investment – with sound rule of law, an innovative, market-driven economy, and some of the best-run companies in the world. While China's continued appetite for US bonds helps keep interest rates low, its increasing appetite for US equities creates jobs.

Chinese Direct Investment in US Firms

The history of major Chinese investments in the US economy is short, basically starting in 2005 with Lenovo's purchase of IBM's ThinkPad business. Since then, there have been some rocky periods, like when state-owned oil giant CNOOC's bid to buy Unocal was blocked, as were Huawei's attempts to buy American telecommunications infrastructure companies. Although America is arguably the most open market in the world to outside investment, Congress and the Committee of Foreign Investment in the United States (CFIUS) watch for any deals that may threaten national security and have the power to block them – CFIUS by executive order and Congress by legislation. About US$40 billion worth of deals have been stopped since 2005, but more than US$70 billion have gone through. Since 2012, there have been 50 deals worth more than US$100 million with an average of about US$1 billion per month.

China's investments in US firms like Morgan Stanley, AMC Theaters, Smithfield, and many smaller deals that haven't had as much publicity – acquisitions of solar companies, battery companies, aviation companies, medical companies – all support US jobs and tie China more tightly into the international system of rules and norms. As fiduciaries in US firms, Chinese investors are regulated by our laws governing fraud, intellectual property, and contracts.

If you look at the actual deals, it becomes clear that China's corporate investments in the United States tend to complement and deepen industries where China struggles back home. Risk is usually a driving factor. So as China struggles to produce safe pork products, it buys Smithfield. As China struggles to move up the value chain in advanced manufacturing, it invests in US technology and advanced manufacturing firms – R&D facilities, energy firms, battery makers, and aviation companies.

Consider general aviation (GA), which comprises corporate and private jets. China has about 90 general aviation airports and about 1,000 planes compared to 5,200 airports and 228,000 planes in the United States.[45] China's increasing demand for private and corporate jets, combined with regulatory reform of its lower altitude GA airspace, is prompting Chinese GA firms to ramp up. Seeking to scale up and modernize, they are investing in US firms, a trend that supports US jobs. In 2012, Jilin Hanxing Group acquired a manufacturer of small aircraft, Glasair of Arlington, Washington. In 2011, China Aviation Industry acquired electric jet manufacturer Cirrus Industries Inc. of Duluth, Minnesota. Other recent Chinese acquisitions include Teledyne Technologies of Thousand Oaks, California and Epic Aircraft of Bend, Oregon.

As China struggles to build world-class, safe, advanced manufacturing products, like airplanes, its firms invest in the United States not only to service the US market but also to help modernize their operations at home. To date, there has been no evidence of asset stripping, in which the acquirer buys a company and sells off its assets. The research firm Rhodium Group analyzed 6,000 Chinese foreign direct-investment deals in the United States since 2000 and determined that a majority of the Chinese parent companies have either kept or added staff. Today, China remains a relatively small US employer, compared to Japan and Germany, but if China continues at its current pace of investment, its firms will employ 200,000–400,000 Americans by 2020.[46]

Politicians across the country have been aggressively courting this investment because of the jobs it supports. Several governors of both large and small states led trade delegations to China in 2013 and 2014, including Vermont, Washington, California, Iowa, Virginia, South Dakota, and Wisconsin. And mayors like Michael Bell of Toledo have been to China frequently to court job-creating investments. Mayor Bell, who has traveled to China four times over the past four years, has also hosted thirty delegations of Chinese investors. Bell's efforts have been rewarded. According to the *New York Times*, "In Blue Collar Toledo, Ohio, A Windfall of Chinese Investments," Chinese companies have invested in two local hotels, a restaurant complex, and a 69-acre waterfront property. "Huaqiao University," the article continues, "one of the largest higher-education institutions in China, recently signed an agreement to open a branch in Toledo." And, "there have also been preliminary talks between local officials and a Chinese company about an arrangement in which industrial tools would be produced in China, shipped for assembly in Toledo and labeled 'Made in the USA,' which would allow them to be sold at a premium" in China.⁴⁷

It's especially ironic, however, that in states like Ohio with booming exports to China and strong inbound investment – and therefore many jobs supported directly from Chinese demand – we often hear the loudest anti-China rhetoric. Ohio's exports to China have more than tripled over the past decade, and Chinese investment is flowing into cities that desperately need to create jobs, like Toledo. Yet Ohio's senator, Sherrod Brown, if he had his way would eliminate all these jobs supported by Chinese trade and investment.

Brown co-sponsored the latest version of the Graham-Schumer bill to punish China for currency manipulation, which passed the Senate in October of 2012. And when running for re-election, his campaign ads were rife with China bashing, distorting the truth about the job-creating benefits that China brings Ohio.

A typical Brown ad, with the title "Protecting Ohio Jobs," ran in 2012. It said: "Sherrod's spent his entire career standing up against policies that benefit China at the expense of American workers, and that's why he led passage in the Senate of a bill that stands up for Ohio manufacturing by cracking down on China's illegal currency manipulation."⁴⁸

Brown's rhetoric plays on our fears of China in the guise of protecting American jobs, but his policies, if enacted, would actually kill jobs, not protect them. By jacking up tariffs on Chinese imports, Brown would eliminate jobs in Ohio in three different ways. He'd kill jobs associated with China imports; he'd kill jobs associated with China exports; and he'd kill jobs associated with Chinese investment. Brown's ad does get something right: "Sherrod believes that if competing on a level playing field, no one does it better than the American worker." America's workers can and do compete with China – *today*, on a supposedly unlevel playing field. The Chinese are already buying Ohio's products and investing in Ohio's companies. Characterizing the working voters of Ohio as somehow disadvantaged in the competition with China does them a disservice.

But Brown was certainly not the only one who peddled untruths to Ohioans in the 2012 election. Romney and Obama carpet-bombed Ohio with China-bashing ads. Cleveland alone saw 4,722 negative China ads.[49] One of the Romney spots claims, "Under Obama we've lost over half a million manufacturing jobs, and for the first time China is beating us...It's time to stand up to the cheaters and make sure we protect jobs for the American people."[50] Obama's counterpunch, which hit the airwaves one day after Romney's, states, "Romney never stood up to China. All he's done is send them our jobs."

The two campaigns collectively shelled out US$45.7 million on TV ads that attacked China to score points about jobs and competitiveness.[51] And in the concurrent Senate election, Brown also invested US$3.7 million in ads demonizing China. China bashing must win votes because, in the 2010 midterm election cycle, Nancy Pelosi, the Speaker of the House at the time, urged Democratic candidates to hit China in their messaging, too. Internal polling showed voters strongly favored eliminating tax breaks for companies doing business with China.[52] So the 2010 election was dominated by anti-China rhetoric, too.

Even savvy political journalists, if inadvertently, helped perpetrate the myth that China is harming Ohio. During the 2012 election, in a piece for *The Atlantic*, "Why the Battle of Ohio is All about China," Molly Ball writes, "Ohio is dotted with shuttered factories, testament to a bygone era in the American economy; meanwhile, new factories seem to spring up hourly across the Chinese landscape. They're not unrelated developments, as labor is cheaper in China and more expensive in the US, but it's also the case that voters need a scapegoat for their economic ills."

By painting a picture of shuttered US factories alongside new Chinese ones, Ball asserts causality where none exists. Often, China is losing more jobs than America. And the factories that are springing up in China are usually white elephants of excess capacity, sitting idle – not the recipients of outsourced labor and transferred equipment that we imagine.

But Ohio isn't alone. South Carolina is another good example of the disconnect between China-driven job growth and anti-China political rhetoric. South Carolina's exports from 2004 to 2014 grew 949 percent, with transportation equipment, chemicals, machinery, and passenger vehicles topping the list. BMW, for example, makes cars in South Carolina, many of which are exported to China. In addition to booming exports to China, South Carolina also boasts US$656 million-worth of Chinese investment.[53] Those exports and inbound investment support lots of middle-class jobs.

Yet South Carolina's senior senator, Lindsey Graham, has led the decade-long crusade with Senator Chuck Schumer of New York to enact legislation that would brand China a currency manipulator, thereby jacking up tariffs on Chinese imports – a move that would kill jobs in South Carolina, not protect them.

Similarly, Michigan, whose exports to China have grown sevenfold over the last decade, heard mostly China bashing from its last governor, Democrat Jennifer Granholm. The self-styled "go anywhere, do anything for jobs" governor never went to the fastest-growing, largest market for cars. She failed to publicly acknowledge her state's exports to China and the implications of this trend on Michigan's competitiveness, and failed to visit China *once* during her two terms. Noteworthy, given Michigan's ailing automotive industry and China's booming car market.

Instead, Governor Granholm privately welcomed Chinese trade and investment delegations, while bashing China in public. In her 2006 election for governor, millions of dollars were spent by Granholm's campaign and the Michigan Democratic Party on ads bashing China as a job killer. And the China vitriol continued through her term. In August of 2009, toward the end of her administration, Granholm wrote in a fundraising letter, "Michigan stands at a crossroads: what kind of state do we want to be in the twenty-first century? Do we want to be a place where the unemployed suffer while we watch our jobs shipped off on a slow boat to China?" All the while, during the course of Granholm's two terms as governor, exports to China skyrocketed, and China invested in 32 local companies in deals worth over US$250 million. It should be noted that Republican Scott Snyder, Granholm's successor, has already made four trade missions to China as of this writing, with more planned, and Chinese investment levels in Michigan have risen to over US$1 billion – mostly in the automotive sector.

You'd think that politicians would jump at the opportunity to riff on American competitiveness: how Chinese consumers clamor for American products; how Chinese investors clamor to invest in US companies; how America *can* compete in the coming century.

Yet what we hear over and over again, from both sides of the aisle, is how China is a rapacious job stealer and America a hapless victim. Ultimately, this does a disservice to the American people and feeds into the false meta-narrative of "rising China and declining America." Among the success stories of small and medium-sized firms' exports to China are business leaders that bucked the trend and sold toys, faucets, chopsticks, and other unlikely products – often raising their prices, not lowering them. How many other business owners, if they were aware of the opportunities in China for the imaginative and bold, would choose not to shutter the shop but turn to China and create jobs at home?

Sadly, the din of China bashing from our politicians and news media contributes to an overall feeling of defeatism. This theme was typified in the 2012 election season. Curiously, we heard very little about the true causes of the cataclysmic economic crash and why millions of Americans lost their jobs and homes. Unregulated derivatives markets, mortgage-backed securities, subprime lending, banks run amok – neither presidential candidate dared delve into these issues. What we heard instead, over and over again, was how China is the culprit – how China is stealing our jobs, how China is stealing our economic primacy in the world.

Do you remember Mitt Romney's slogan?

Believe in America.

From the campaign that brought us such inspirational lines as "I like to fire people" and "Borrow money if you have to from your parents" – a campaign that seemed wholly disconnected from the anguish and anxiety of the American people amidst a wrenching recession – Romney actually managed to say something true.

America, in ways large and small, *has* ceased to believe in its own vitality, in the manifest destiny that each generation will do better than the one before. We've lost our faith in the American Dream.

Yet proof of enduring American competitiveness is all around us, in just about every congressional district. From China comes jobs and investment. But also jeopardy. To connect the dots and understand why these two opposing symptoms arise from the same cause, we need to walk China's secret supply chain and see firsthand the risk that suffuses it.

3

The Bad Earth

And so we begin our journey on the ground. Literally.

Polluted land, water, and air contaminate the crops that are inputs into China's food production. So the risk that eating Chinese fruit, veggies, and meat will poison you starts with the bad earth.

Recently, I spent a torpid Saturday wandering through a China expo on the national mall with my kids. There were kite makers, folksingers, dancers, and calligraphers. And scores of volunteers to staff the many booths. I overheard one, a Chinese student, lecturing an elderly American on the wonders of China's food. How it could all be considered organic because it's picked from trees and reaped from the ground. Sure. If your definition of organic means the food is rich in heavy metals, like cadmium and arsenic, pumped full of veterinary antibiotics, and doused in 11 different pesticides.

Poisoned Water, Land, and Air

Picture the map of China in your mind. It's a huge country, dotted with cities. You'd think that this mostly rural nation – where many of the workers are still farmers – would be the perfect setting for an agricultural powerhouse. It's difficult to fathom how a country so vast could be unable to produce enough food for itself – and not just enough food, but safe food.

China, however, lacks both food security and safety. It lacks land that can support crops and water that can fertilize them. It's a well-known fact that China consumes about 20 percent of the world's food but possesses only about 8 percent of arable farmland. Yet people are usually surprised to learn how little arable land China actually has. It's not a matter of sheer land mass, but land that can produce crops. Estimates vary, but basically, the amount of arable land in China would fit somewhere between the size of Texas (268,820 square miles) and Alaska (587,878 square miles).

And the arable land that China does have is in peril. For one thing, the deserts are encroaching quickly. It is estimated that one-quarter of all of China is now desert. And the desert is expanding at a rate of 1,900 square miles per year.[1] Drought, deforestation, and monocropping have all conspired to speed desertification, which China's State Forestry Administration reports has turned more than 400 million Chinese into environmental refugees.[2] Think of it. The entire population of the United States is rendered homeless because their towns are suddenly Saharan.

But, in addition to desert, urbanization is also destroying farmland. China's Ministry of Land and Resources estimates that each year, more than 3,320 square miles of arable soil was lost to growing cities between 1998 and 2006. Since these are official estimates, we can safely bet that they're on the low side. And China's push to urbanize, a central tenet of its economic policy, continues to this day.

That means that, each year, the cities lop off at least another 1 percent of arable land from the total. Consider this trend in terms of the coming century,[3] the supposed "China century." With more than one-quarter of its land already desert, if China continues at its current rate of urbanization and desertification, there won't be much arable land left at all in a few generations.

As with so many of China's challenges, there's a damned-if-you-do, damned-if-you-don't conundrum here. China's leaders see moving its rural population into cities as a key to continued economic growth. They plan to urbanize more than 400 million people by 2030. China's economic planners see the cities as the key to rebalancing China's economy. City-dwellers spend a lot more than country folk. So rapid urbanization is considered necessary to move from investment to consumption as the driver of economic growth. But it will wreak havoc on the land, water, and air.

Many western visitors to China are surprised by how many "big cities" there are. In fact, as China's urbanization experiment pushes inland, a typical second- or third-tier city is often the size of Manhattan. McKinsey predicts that by 2025, more than 60 percent of China's entire population will live in cities – up from just under half in 2010. And, by 2020, China's urban population is expected to expand by 350 million people. That's the entire population of the United States moving into cities before the end of the decade.

The cities don't just eat up arable land, though. They suck the water resources dry. China isn't naturally endowed with a lot of water anyway. It's estimated that, compared to the world's average per capita of freshwater availability, China falls far below the mark, with only one-third the average. And the water China does have is being wasted and polluted. Elizabeth Economy at the Council on Foreign Relations, an expert on China's environment, reports that "skyrocketing demand, overuse, inefficiencies, pollution, and unequal distribution have produced a situation in which two-thirds of China's approximately 660 cities have less water than they need and 110 of them suffer severe shortages."[4]

A big part of the problem is waste. In the movie *Karate Kid 2*, Jackie Chan, as the superintendent of a Beijing apartment building, chides the newly arrived Americans on wasting water. He points to a shut-off valve that keeps showers short. Use the switch, he says, and save the planet. The implication here is that China is a paragon of water conservation. Not so much. China's agricultural sector uses 66 percent of China's water and wastes more than half of it. And Chinese cities waste 20 percent of the water they consume through leaky pipes.[5]

With dwindling water supplies, China is scavenging for more and more water underground, and giant tunnels are forming – causing another alarming problem. Honeycombed below, China's wealthiest cities are sinking fast. Shanghai and Tianjin have sunk more than six feet over the past 15 years.

Water is scarce in China, and the water that's available? Usually polluted. The Xinhua News Agency reported that 90 percent of China's cities have polluted aquifers. Alarmingly, this groundwater provides 70 percent of China's drinking water.[6] Drink the tap water in a Chinese city, and you risk poisoning yourself. Over three-quarters of all the river water found in China's cities is deemed unfit for consumption or for fishing.[7]

Pollution in China comes from many sources. Most factories, for example, dump untreated waste in rivers and surrounding land. The polluted water is then used for crops and fish farms. China's officials have finally acknowledged the existence of dozens of "cancer villages" – municipalities near factories and polluted water, in which cancer rates are abnormally high.[8]

Polluted water not only sickens Chinese citizens, it contaminates the crops. "As much as 10 percent of China's farmland is believed to be polluted," reports Elizabeth

Economy.[9] China's Ministry of Land and Resources backs up that assertion, estimating that 10 percent of China's arable land is "poisonous" from heavy metals and pollution. And the results of a 2006 study by the Ministry of Environmental Protection and the Ministry of Land and Resources that was long kept secret have recently been released: 8 million acres of farmland, about 2 percent of China's arable land, is actually too polluted to cultivate at all.[10] As these are official statistics, it's a safe bet the actual figure is much higher.

Other official Chinese statistics are scary, too. The Chinese Academy of Agricultural Engineering states that heavy metals have poisoned 20 percent of China's farmland. That's 20 million hectares or about 77,240 square miles – around the size of South Dakota. And that's what the officials admit. One can only imagine the real figures. At a conference of the Guangdong Provincial Association for Science and Technology, Professor Luo Xiwen estimated that 12 million tons of grain *every year* is poisoned with heavy metals.

A recent report by the *China Economic Weekly*, a state organ, confirmed Professor Luo's observation that more than 12 million tons of grain have been contaminated by heavy metals. It is also estimated that over 10 percent of Chinese rice is tainted by the heavy metal cadmium, a carcinogen, from samples taken in 2007. Cadmium is described by the US Occupational Safety and Health Administration (OSHA) as "an extremely toxic metal."

Several studies have discovered high levels of heavy metals not only in rice and vegetables but also in meat and seafood.[11] That's because livestock and fish are often fed polluted inputs. But there are no comprehensive data on heavy metals found in China's food supply. Part of the problem is that different sorts of crops, and where they're grown, have variations in the way they soak up heavy metals from the soil.

In some areas, China has lower background levels of cadmium in the soil than Japan, but, since over half of China's arable land is low on microelements like potassium and phosphorous, the absorption of heavy metals can be much higher than what is deemed safe.[12]

Water is a big source of contamination, and so is the air. Spend some time in Beijing and you'd see what I mean. You get runny, red eyes. You wheeze. You suffer frequent colds. National Public Radio ran a piece recently about how Beijing is now considered a hardship post by ex-pats, and big corporations, who once had to beat back eager transplants to Beijing with a stick, have to beg to get their employees to move there.

During the 2008 Beijing Olympics, China did not want to show the world how grim and polluted the capital city is and undertook science-fiction-like measures to choreograph blue skies. Almost US$17 billion was spent reining in traffic and closing polluting factories. Fifty thousand people were hired to shoot silver iodide into the clouds to prevent the rain.

But Beijing is not an anomaly. Chinese cities are typically highly polluted. In fact, sixteen of the world's twenty most polluted cities are in China.[13] One key reason is China's coal-dominated energy economy. Though China may lack water and arable land, it's got plenty of coal, which remains the primary source for China's energy production. Though China is trying famously to green its economy, coal, the dirtiest of carbon fuels, still makes up 70 percent of China's energy mix.

The intensity of China's commitment to coal is staggering. From 2005 to 2009, China brought online the equivalent of the entire US coal-power plant fleet with 510 additional 600 megawatt plants. From 2010 to 2013, China brought online half again the entire US coal-power plant fleet. And over the next ten years, it is estimated China will bring online yet again the entire coal-burning capacity of the United States.[14]

Each year, China uses 4 billion tons of coal to generate power: the United States – 1 billion; the EU – 0.6 billion. Yes, China is investing in renewable energies, but all the talk about China winning the green energy war is absurd. China may have double the capacity for wind energy than the United States, but less than half of this capacity is even connected to China's energy grid.

Coal is ruining China's air quality and so is China's urban planning, which has embraced the automobile as the dominant mode of transportation. It's as if the planet has learned nothing since the days of Robert Moses, the master builder who put the car front and center in New York's urban design – at the expense of public transportation. This model of urban planning has been exported to China, where the authorities keep erecting more and more ring roads, highways, parking lots, and high-density, single-use residential buildings inaccessible to public transportation.

China is already the largest car market in the world, and 40 percent of China's oil is consumed by the transportation sector. That figure is expected to go up to 65 percent by 2035. China, which was once energy self-sufficient, is now a big net importer of oil.

Traffic has become so bad in the cities that you've got to factor in extra *hours* just to make it to a meeting on time. Famously, in 2010 there was a traffic jam outside Beijing that ran 60 miles and lasted 11 days. The cause was highway construction that waylaid a fleet of trucks hauling coal from Inner Mongolia to Beijing.

Soil contamination levels are not the only pollution data that Chinese authorities try to keep secret. The levels of particulate density in Beijing's air were also altered for years, making the pollution levels in the air seem less severe, until the US Embassy in Beijing started posting this data on its website.

It's all part of a vicious cycle. Pollution from cars, factories, and coal-fired power plants causes severe acid rain, which contaminates one-third of China's arable land.[15] With arable land scarce and water even scarcer, it's safe to say that China is well beyond the point of crisis in terms of its natural resources – putting its food supply in dire jeopardy.

Risk and Reward

So the agricultural and aquacultural products that China produces from its polluted land, water, and air are at risk of being contaminated by heavy metals. This is good news and bad news for us. The bad news is that our food supply is exposed to a clear and present danger from unsafe Chinese food imports. Based on data from the USDA and Food and Water Watch, many of our food products have a high degree of probability that they're made in China and are, therefore, risky. There's a three in four chance that the tilapia you consume will be from a Chinese aqua-farm; a two in three chance that the apples in your kid's apple juice will be from China; a fifty-fifty chance with cod; a 20 percent chance with garlic and frozen spinach. The list goes on with decreasing but still risky odds. Once we start importing processed chicken from China, that will also pose an additional and significant risk to our food supply.

Scarily, any health threats from heavy metals in the food we import from China would be slow to appear and often difficult to detect. Heavy metal exposure takes a long time to manifest itself. Chinese officials estimate that one-third of all Chinese children suffer from elevated lead levels. Cadmium, lead, arsenic, mercury, and chromium can all cause serious damage to humans who ingest them. Given how much food we import from China, those safety risks are now ours.

The good news, however, is that China's struggles to produce safe (and enough) food mean China must import these items. Several major surveys from 2005 to 2010 all conclude that food safety is one of the issues that worries Chinese the most, and more than half of all Chinese do not have confidence in the country's food safety system. This consumer trend impacts trade flows. China has recently become the world's number-one importer of agricultural products.[16] Consequently, the United States runs a significant trade *surplus* with China in agriculture.

Today, China is the largest overseas market for US agricultural products, amounting to 20 percent of all our ag exports.[17] In 2013, the value of American agricultural exports to China broke a new record: US$26.7 billion. Agricultural exports from the EU have been booming, too. They tripled in the years spanning 2010 to 2013, rising from about 1 billion euros to over 3 billion euros.[18]

Yet, given all the bureaucracy involved with selling food products to China, it's amazing any food gets exported at all. You'd think that China's myriad food safety lapses would encourage the authorities to open the floodgates to safer imported products. But the opposite occurs. China is extremely protective of local agricultural interests and makes it hard to export food into the country – especially in areas where China's track record is the worst, such as dairy, pork, and seafood.

Responding to Export Challenges

Chinese food import regulations are complex and change often. It can literally take years to get your product into the market. If you're a dairy, meat, or seafood supplier, for example, your establishment must be inspected and approved by the appropriate US government agency. Then, many sets of documents must accompany the products on their journey, even for non-controversial items like cherries. You need a certificate of origin that verifies that: the products come from where they say they are coming from (this can be issued by a local chamber of commerce); a health certificate, providing third-party verification that the goods are safe for human consumption from the appropriate government agency; a certificate attesting that the wood pallets the products are exported on have been fumigated; a packing list; a commercial invoice; and sometimes other documents.

Chinese customs have the authority to inspect, detain, or reject any products coming across the border – and often do. Horror stories abound among food exporters who've had their goods seized by Chinese customs for no apparent reason other than bureaucratic fiat. These types of hurdles are euphemistically called "non-tariff barriers," and China has a thicket of them, not just for food, but for all product categories. That American exports to China keep surging year after year is a testament to China's real demand – and the saintly patience of US exporters.

The US government helps a great deal. There are battalions of civil servants at the Commerce Department and the US Department of Agriculture who assist exporters with the bureaucratic complexities of selling into Chinese markets. Many states also have their own offices in China that provide assistance. And on the level of policy, US government officials from various departments, such as the Commerce Department and the US Trade Representative, battle on behalf of US exporters to eliminate or mitigate the non-tariff barriers.

But, for food exporters, the wait is often worth it. Many of the agricultural products we sell to China are priced at a high premium. When you factor in the cost of transportation, plus import duties, the US price can often double. But often you can still make a higher margin than selling locally. Baby formula is a great example. But so is US-made honey and maple syrup, which are often sold in China for more than US$15 for a small bottle. Chinese consumers with disposable income, when offered a choice, prefer to buy these imported items. They perceive American foods products as being safer and therefore are willing to fork out the extra cash.

These premium prices support jobs along the export chain – in transportation, in wholesaling, and in farming. And, yes, while big agribusiness commands vast sales in the exports of goods to China (such as Monsanto and Cargill), a great many smaller farmers, breeders, and fisheries are also exporting to China and supporting local jobs.

A notable example is fisheries of Asian carp, a species first imported to America in the 1970s to help clean up wastewater ponds. This fish'll eat anything. An unintended consequence: the fish have multiplied and migrated, crowding out indigenous species. River and lake towns throughout the American South and Midwest, where these "pesc-y" invaders roam, have tried various unsuccessful ways to stop the spread of the carp. More and more outlandish solutions have been proposed, including electric barriers and poisoning the waters.

But entrepreneurs had a better idea. If you can't beat 'em, *eat 'em*! The fish are bony and generally not eaten in the United States, but the Chinese love them. Carp in China these days are often farm raised and are looked on suspiciously by the Chinese from a health perspective. So why not export US Asian carp back to China?

Several US fisheries have been established to catch and sell the invasive carp. As usual, getting them into the Chinese markets has been challenging. Consumers there prefer to buy live fish, and exporters have had to overcome this attitude by branding their frozen, dead fish as safer and higher quality than local aqua-farmed carp. Transportation costs are also high, as the fish must be shipped across the ocean in freezers and kept cold in China. Despite these high barriers to market entry, though, many US fisheries are exporting Asian carp to China in high volume, notably Two Rivers Fisheries, Schafer Fisheries, Heartland Fish Products, and Big River Fish.[19]

Many of these companies got their start from grants. Local and state governments award funding to firms that are exporting and creating jobs. Grants can also be secured through industry trade groups, like the Food Export Association's Market Access Program, which reimburses travel and marketing expenses for US exporters. And in addition to the Food Export Association, there are many not-for-profit industry groups that can assist small exporters through advocacy, education, and grants. Their local representatives work closely with exporters of all sizes, helping them navigate the complexities of Chinese regulations, sales, and distribution. There's also the Export-Import Bank, an independent US government agency, which not only provides buyer financing for large deals, such as in the aviation industry, but also provides a number of financing options for small firms trying to export.

Beyond grant funding, local and state governments also try to boost exports, some with greater success than others. California, for example, has an office in China and a governor who aggressively courts Chinese investment and purchases – in technology and agriculture, especially. Other states have tried to follow suit. Today, the United States sells mostly commodity agricultural products to China: soybeans and grain – to feed China's livestock, especially; and cotton to make textiles.

Yet China's food safety scandals give rise to significant demand for American dairy, produce, and protein – products whose export levels are still quite low compared to what we sell China in soybeans. America could be exporting so much more agricultural products to China, while creating jobs on America's farms.

In some cases, though, well-intentioned policies get in the way of successful exports. As the headquarters of agribusiness giant Monsanto, Missouri is an ag powerhouse. The state grows corn and soybeans and is also a major livestock breeder of cows, hogs, and turkeys. Indeed, America's largest live-hog exporter to China is based in Jefferson City, Missouri. From 2004 to 2013, Missouri exports to China rose 204 percent versus an 86 percent rise to the rest of the world.[20] Yet Missouri is ranked fifteenth in the United States in terms of total exports and could be exporting so much more, especially to China. It's true, Missouri's exports to China are increasing sharply, but export intensity remains low. Missouri sells primarily machinery and commodity agricultural products to China. But there are many products that aren't being exported to China that could be, such as life-science products and perishable foods.

Recognizing this potential, in 2008 a group of Missouri business leaders and politicians started cooking up something they called "the Big Idea" – an ambitious plan not just to boost exports to China in order to create jobs but to revitalize a troubled airport. Ever since TWA went belly-up and American Airlines sharply reduced its footprint at Lambert Field in St Louis, the airport was in a financial tailspin. As passenger travel volume plummeted, it took on more and more debt to stay aloft. Meanwhile, planes flying from China to nearby Chicago O'Hare Airport, teeming with cargo for distribution in the United States, often headed back to China empty. If St Louis could fill planes with cargo, that would be a huge win for Lambert Airport, for the airlines, and for Missouri agricultural jobs.

The idea captivated a number of Missouri and St Louis officials, business executives, the local Chamber of Commerce, and the World Trade Center. A so-called China Hub Commission was formed, and a high-priced consultant was hired to craft the strategy. Lambert Airport, however, lacked the basic infrastructure to handle a serious cargo operation. Remarkably, the airport had no cold warehousing facilities. This is critical for any product that needs to be kept chilled before shipment – such as perishable food items that are either fresh or frozen. Gate Gourmet, the airline catering company, had a warehouse near the airport with refrigeration, but storing frozen hog carcasses alongside food for airline travelers wouldn't exactly fly. Aside from lacking cold storage, St Louis-Lambert Airport had no livestock-handling pens, so transporting any sort of live animal (a major export from the region that travels by plane) would be impossible.

The airport, already buried under a mountain of debt, would need to invest even more money in building this infrastructure if it was to compete with O'Hare in Chicago and grow its cargo operations into anything resembling the China Hub that was envisioned. Enter the Missouri legislature, where a bill was proposed in 2011 to fund the China Hub to the tune of US\$480 million – nearly half a billion dollars in a state hit hard by the recession. US\$420 million of the proposed budget would go to tax credits for the building of infrastructure, and US\$60 million would go to trade credits to entice freight forwarders to route their cargo away from nearby O'Hare – a true hub with all the requisite infrastructure and business services.

Freight forwarders were at the center of "the Big Idea" strategy. The travel agents of goods, they route freight by means of the cheapest, most reliable routes. US$60 million in trade credits spread over eight years – providing discounts on transporting perishable and non-perishable items via Lambert – begs the question of why a freight forwarder would route goods away from O'Hare to an airport with minimal-to-no cargo infrastructure just for a slight discount on the cargo prices.

While the bill was still being debated in the Missouri legislature and before a single freight forwarder volunteered to re-route cargo from a major hub such as O'Hare to an airport with no facilities to handle perishable cargo, Missouri delegations traveled to China to convince an airline to begin flights into Lambert.

Much fanfare and huzzahs went forth as China Eastern Airlines agreed to start flying into Lambert to transport goods back and forth from Missouri to China. Then the bill in the legislature failed to pass, just as Chinese cargo planes began landing at Lambert. The first plane arrived. And suddenly the China Hub Commission realized: not a single freight forwarder had stepped up, and the inbound plane from China needed to be filled with Missouri cargo. There was much scurrying around until a local business executive from Emerson Worldwide agreed to stock the hold with components bound for factories in Asia. The second plane arrived and even less cargo was loaded. China Eastern executives realized what was going on and suspended the route.

The China Hubbers, though well intentioned and correct in seeing the big potential to create jobs through China exports, failed to see some basic facts – that freight forwarders are in business to make money, not run a charity, and that even saving 30 cents per kilo would not be enough of an enticement to route cargo away from a major hub like

O'Hare to an airport that lacks the most basic infrastructure to handle perishable freight. And that the key to filling planes with cargo is through *demand*, not supply. Through securing purchase orders from Chinese importers for Missouri agricultural products. With orders in hand, you can route your freight through whichever airport you choose. And you don't need nearly half a billion dollars in public financing to do it. In fact, you really don't need any public financing at all to pursue such a plan. Scores of Chinese importers would clamor to invest in the appropriate infrastructure near the Lambert Airport, once they started sourcing product from the region. Often, Chinese imports and investment go hand in hand.

But the China Hubbers failed to see that the way to fill planes, trains, trucks, and boats is not through bribing freight forwarders to act against their own business interests. It's through *orders*. Winning orders for Missouri goods. Orders put money in the pocket of producers, wholesalers, warehousers, and transporters. And with enough orders, planes could be chartered out of Lambert that could eventually bootstrap a real cargo operation. You don't even need a dedicated route from a major China airline. But winning orders requires boots on the ground in China. The only boots on the ground Missouri deploys in China are the Gucci loafers of a former senator who makes hefty fees from leading trade delegations to China that have had a questionable impact on anyone's bottom line except the senator's consulting practice.

Sigmund Freud said the definition of insanity is to do the same crazy thing again and again hoping for a different outcome. By this definition, the China Hub planners are nuts. After having spent hundreds of thousands of dollars paying the consultant who helped dream up this cockamamie freight forwarder scheme to begin with, they were either too embarrassed or too stubborn to change course. And so, ten years since the inception of "the Big Idea," Lambert is still declining, the China Hubbers are still trying to implement their bad idea, and Missouri's agricultural exports remain what they've always been – bulk commodity crops from big agribusiness, but not the perishable items from smaller ranchers and farmers that China's food safety scandals have created strong demand for.

Chinese Investment

The United States is not just a strong export platform for China, it's also a highly desirable place for China to invest in agriculture. When considering China's lack of arable land and clean water, it's important to bear in mind that a country's natural resources are a key component of its overall competitiveness. If you can't feed your own people, you are at the mercy of other countries. Americans tend to take for granted the natural resources their country is endowed with: plentiful arable land and water, and air that's considerably less polluted than China's. It has a population of less than one-quarter of China's as well.

Understandably, China is already making big investments in natural resources in Africa and, more recently, Eastern Europe. First, China tried to buy a big chunk of Ukraine, but annexing themselves to China met with some complaints by the Ukrainians. They've already got Vladimir Putin to contend with. So instead, China cut a deal to lease one-twentieth of Ukraine's farmland for 50 years at US$2.6 billion per year.[21]

Many experts believe that China's investment in Smithfield was in no small part because of the land associated with the deal – over 100,000 acres in Missouri, North Carolina, and Texas. In fact, if you Google "China investment in US

farmland," the web is abuzz with rumors about China gob-
bling up US agricultural acreage. In another version of
the-Chinese-are-taking-over-America story, the fear is that
China is quietly purchasing farmland out from under
America. Yet this claim is unfounded. Firstly, in many
Midwest agriculture states, such as Iowa, foreign ownership
of farmland is prohibited by law. And when you actually
look at the deals that have been done – and a couple of entities track this activity purchase by purchase (most notably
Dan Rosen at Rhodium and Derek Scissors at American
Enterprise Institute) – you can see for yourself that China
owns almost no US farmland at all. So the much-touted
Chinese invasion of the American heartland isn't actually
happening. And, by the way, the United States is still,
far and away, the world's largest investor in overseas
farmland.

So far, then, China's skyrocketing demand has not caused
starvation of exporting countries or severe environmental
degradation. But countries selling agriculture to China will
need to come to terms with the externalities of China's
demand sooner rather than later. While skyrocketing
Chinese demand for food is good for jobs, its sustainability
over the long term is still an open question, and export
nations will need to plan accordingly. "By 2030," reports
Heather Timmons in *Quartz*, "China will import almost
one-third of all food available in the world...up from 4%
in 2007."[22]

Bottom line, China's severe need for food, water – and
yes, clean air: a small jar of air from southern France was
recently auctioned in China for over US$800![23] – puts China
in a very bad competitive position and gives big leverage to
exporting countries with abundant farmland and water.

In order to stave off environmental catastrophe, China is
already investing funds to clean up its water, air, and land.

The investor, Jim Rogers, said, "Someone's going to make a staggering amount of money cleaning up China; the government has spent a lot of money and is allocating more. In 20 years, China will be one of the dominant pollution cleaner-uppers."[24]

That massive cleanup effort has already begun. It is estimated that China's market for environmental technology and services ranges from US$500 billion to US$1 trillion. As of 2010, US firms already commanded 40 percent of the revenues of the global trade in this industry, and are well positioned to capture significant market share in China.[25] To pave the way, Washington and Beijing have allocated funds to support green tech innovation, including the United States–China Clean Energy Research Center, which focuses on research, development, and deployment of clean-energy technologies. To get the job done, China needs a long list of products and services, including carbon-capture technology, municipal and industrial water treatment, hazardous waste remediation, air and water pollution monitoring, and waste-to-energy solutions. The combination of advanced technology and technical services puts these offerings squarely in America's sweet spot.

From China's bad earth, sowed with risk, American jobs are reaped.

4

Risky Business

Risk begins in the very ground, with polluted inputs. Then it moves in outwardly concentric circles of danger through firms and farms to the chains that link them up to the regulators that govern them. Rather than mitigate risk, Chinese firms and farms magnify it.

Let's begin with farms. Though we imagine China's agricultural sector as a powerhouse, it's actually a throwback to the Middle Ages – arguably, the most inefficient and primitive farming system in the modern world. In a recent report from the Chinese Academy of Science, agriculture was deemed the economy's "weakest link."[1] It also states that China is more than a hundred years behind the United States in agriculture and that China's agricultural productivity is equal to 1 percent of Japan's. For China to reach productivity levels comparable to most developed nations, the report states, China would have to shrink its number of farmers by about 90 percent. Given that there are around 300 million people employed on Chinese farms, according to China's National Statistics Bureau, Beijing will need to move nearly the equivalent of the entire US population out of the agriculture sector for it to become competitive.

China's policies have actually created this problem. Though the country has been moving toward a more market-driven system over the past 30 years, one of the bedrocks of capitalism – individual property ownership – has yet to take hold. No one really owns property in China; the state owns it all. Farms are owned collectively and over- seen by local party honchos. So farmers essentially lease land from their village. That has stymied growth in the agricul- tural sector, as Chinese farmers are unable to leverage the value of their farms to mechanize and improve efficiencies. China is wrestling with this issue and is experimenting with reforms that allow farmers to borrow against their farms and even merge little farms into bigger farms.

But arguably these are baby steps that do not go far enough. At present, the vast majority of China's farms are divided into tiny family plots of around 1.5 acres each. And they're relics of the past. The Chinese Society for Agricul- tural Machinery estimates that as much as one-half of all China's farms are still tilled by hand and beasts of burden, not machines.

The Threat from Farms

China's food safety issues can be traced to this sprawling, primitive agricultural sector, which is proving a nightmare to regulate. How can you police about two hundred million family subsistence farms, where desperate farmers take any measure to stave off starvation? Polluted air, water, and earth put tremendous strain on these farmers. Water scarcity and inferior organic content in the soil yield weaker crops, which in turn leads farmers to do whatever they can to make sure their crops survive and make it to market.

That often means rampant abuse of pesticides and antibi- otics. China is the world's largest producer and consumer of pesticides, and the world's largest producer and consumer of veterinary antibiotics. To combat pests and diseases, family farmers will drench their crops in chemicals, with no regard to the dosage or mix they are using. And they'll pump their herds full of antibiotics to try to prevent illness.

Various media reports in China have uncovered this widespread problem. In June of 2012, for instance, farmers from Shandong province, a major apple-growing area in China, were found wrapping young apples in pesticide-soaked paper. As usual, local officials insisted there was no foul play. "The apples passed the Ministry of Agriculture's quality checks in 2010 and 2011," said a Yantai city government official to the Xinhua News Agency. "We exported 217,000 tons of apples last year, and not a single quality dispute was reported." But independent tests confirmed that the paper used to wrap the apples was soaked in pesticide and arsenic-laden fungicide.[2]

Where do you suppose those 217,000 tons of exported apples wound up? Probably in your kid's apple juice. Two-thirds of the apple juice that Americans drink comes from China.

Yantai officials promised to step up quality control testing. But by the time produce leaves the farm gate, it's too late. Consider the case of vegetables from Anhui province, which the *Xinhua Viewpoint* followed from farm to table. The day before being taken to market, string beans were bathed in eleven different chemicals – seven insecticides, three fungicides, and one miticide – and eggplants in four different chemicals, The poisoned veggies left the farm gate uninspected where they moved to the local wholesale market, uninspected, to the city wholesale market, uninspected, and finally to retail, where they remained uninspected. "We don't have testing equipment – we're lucky if the county authorities come to test the food once or twice a year," explained one wholesale market official.

A lack of testing equipment is only part of the problem, though. In order to combat unsafe levels of pesticides, testing must be conducted *on every batch*, said An Yufa, head of the Centre for Agricultural Products Circulation and Marketing at China Agricultural University. When batches are coming from many thousands of different farmers, even if you have the proper testing equipment, effective oversight becomes almost impossible from a logistical standpoint. The current method of spot-checking the products, Yufa says, is akin to "drops in the ocean" – and the only way to truly monitor safety is at the farm itself, testing each batch.[3]

But given the structure of China's sprawling agricultural sector, that just can't happen. You're a family farmer who can barely put food on your own table. You're not going to buy expensive testing equipment and spend your time screening every batch of food before you cart it off to the market.

What's perhaps even more terrifying is Chinese farmers' reliance on veterinary drugs to breed meat, fish, and chicken. It is very common in China that antibiotics are used to *prevent* disease – not just to treat individual animals that are sick. And that when an animal does get sick, the whole herd or flock is administered antibiotics. The threat from this widespread and aggressive use of antibiotics is becoming more understood. Chinese ranches and aqua-farms are breeding grounds for antibiotic-resistant bacteria.

Though there are no comprehensive studies on the prevalence of antibiotic-resistant bacteria in Chinese meat, fish, and poultry, there are a number of smaller studies which have found antibiotic-resistant bacteria in fish sampled and tested from markets in Guandong, in pigs and poultry, and in seafood and milk in various parts of China. Antibiotic-resistant strains of bacteria have also been discovered in the manure that is used as fertilizer for crops.

The risk that Chinese produce and meat products will be contaminated by heavy metals, unsafe levels of pesticides, or even antibiotic-resistant bacteria is significant. And since the United States and Europe import so much food from China – often as anonymous ingredients with no country-of-origin labeling – we face a dire and immediate threat to our health and safety.

The Threat from Firms

But risky Chinese farms don't pose the only threat. So do risky Chinese firms. Back in the 1970s and 1980s, when America was gripped with another fit of "Chicken Littleism," the Great Japanese Menace was going to steal American jobs, sap American competitiveness, and take over the world. During those days, Japanese companies were actually doing some very innovative things, including figuring out ways to reduce risk in manufacturing. They designed quality control systems that would be the basis for what would become known as Six Sigma – procedures that were later adopted by the likes of General Electric and Pfizer.

In a salute to Japanese corporate know-how, American companies often tried to imitate Japanese business practice – in management style, quality control methods, and even rituals like standing in meetings, to keep them short. I don't know of a single company that tries to imitate Chinese business practice.

Given the famous "China Price," you have to wonder why. American companies often loudly complain that China is able to dump its products into our markets, sometimes pricing even lower than our cost of goods. Because of the "China Price," we believe that China is a formidable competitor, able to make whatever we can, only more cheaply. We imagine Chinese companies as highly skilled manufacturing machines, whose cutthroat business practices are made all the more lethal by undervalued labor and currency.

But labor costs in China are rising fast, the value of China's currency is rising too, and inefficiencies in China's manufacturing supply chain often lead to production costs that are *more* expensive than in the United States. A lesser-known policy is actually an enabler of the so-called "China Price." For more than 20 years, China has granted its exporters rebates on their value-added taxes (VAT) across thousands of products. Typically, the VAT is 17 percent of the difference between the manufactured price and the sales price – what's also known as the gross profit. That's a big chunk of profit and often means the difference between red or black ink in highly competitive industries. Chinese economic planners use VAT rebates as levers to promote exports of favored industries, refunding anywhere from the entire amount to something less. In 2005, for example, China increased its export rebates on high-value biomedical goods (an industry the authorities wanted to help) and reduced them for lower-value products like clothes.

The government has also used rebates to prop up its entire export sector during financial downturns. After the Southeast Asian Financial Crisis, China jacked up its export rebates nine times, as well as increasing the number of eligible products. After the 2008 recession, China raised its rebates again to insulate its exporters against sagging demand from the West.

The United States levies no VAT import tax, as some countries do, and its tariffs are low or zero in most import categories. So China's rebate system acts like a massive subsidy to the export sector. It is estimated that China distributes about US$100 billion worth of rebates per year. That's one trillion dollars in export subsidies a decade.[4] The rebate allows exporters to price really low, and still make good money on the back end. The "China Price," then, is not proof of China's might. It's proof of China's fundamental uncompetitiveness.

As you'd imagine, this practice is a source of widespread corruption. Companies typically over-invoice their VAT as a way of collecting higher rebates, according to Professor Cui Zhiyuan of Tsinghua University.[5] Another trick Chinese manufacturers will employ is a scheme to collect rebates even if the goods are not being exported. Often products are sent on a "one-day tour" or "round trip" through a bonded zone at the port, in which the manufacturer can collect an export rebate, then spirit the goods back into China.

The booming port city of Shenzhen has three bonded export zones, in which goods can be processed for export. Shenzhen's exports were reported to have grown 69 percent in the first quarter of 2013, a sharp increase over its three-year average. Yet, suspiciously, the value of the reported exports had grown much faster than actual port throughput, suggesting that this illegal activity is much more rampant than the authorities would have us believe. As Shenzhen made up 48 percent of China's export growth during the first quarter, you have to be very skeptical of reports that claim how China's rebounding exports are a sign of its economic recovery.[6]

The illusory "China Price" and China's fake export numbers disguise what are, by and large, highly uncompetitive companies. Corruption, weak corporate governance, untrained workers, disloyal management – the hallmarks of Chinese companies are certainly nothing to emulate – and nothing to fear competitively. In China, whether it's a large state-owned enterprise, a privately owned mid-sized firm, or a family farm, chances are it's a risky business.

Good companies run on a few basic principles. Above all, you need good governance. That doesn't just mean good managers. It means good corporate DNA, good structure, systems, and personnel.

When fretting about our competitiveness, we often forget that American and Western European companies benefit from the evolution and acculturation of 400 years of corporation law. A typical American company, therefore, will have several layers of governance. The stockholders elect a board of directors. The board appoints officers. The officers hire managers and staff.

Good companies build processes around these standard governance structures. Lines of reporting are established from corporate officers to managers to staff. With lines of reporting comes accountability. A staffer reports to a manager, who reports to an officer, who reports to the board, who reports to stockholders. With accountability come clear definitions of roles and responsibilities. Each employee knows what a good job is, and is rewarded for doing a good job and penalized for not doing a good job. Transparency in operations allows for these processes to function well.

All of this is considered basic good corporate governance in America. Now I'm not saying American companies are somehow holier than their counterparts around the world. Of course, US firms can be corrupt, pernicious, and destructive. As the details of the financial crisis of 2008 emerge, it is astounding what US investment firms did to make a buck – and all under the watchful eye of regulators, boards of directors, corporate officers, and managers.

But, at the very least, the conventions by which American companies operate are solid. And undergirding US business practice is a rule of law that functions comparatively well. For example, contract enforcement in America and the protection of intellectual property are fundamental guarantees of general fair play.

In China, there is no bedrock rule of law. Sure, there are plenty of laws on the books – many of them good laws – but their enforcement is extremely spotty, and often depends on whom you know and how much you are willing to pay. China is still a country ruled by administrative fiat, where paying off a judge to get a favorable ruling is normal.

Business as usual in China would be considered out-and-out fraud in the United States. It is a well-known custom in China, for example, that negotiations don't seriously begin until *after* a contract is signed. This would never fly in the West. Once a contract is signed, it's enforceable in a court of law – in China, not really. It is also typical business practice in China to keep multiple sets of books. There are numbers for your investors, numbers for the taxman, numbers for your local government, and still other numbers for your partners. This kind of practice in the United States or EU would land you in jail. In China, it's just another day at the office.

American corporate governance is codified in law. Board members are considered fiduciaries of stockholder capital. They are bound by law to safeguard this capital and can be prosecuted for malfeasance if they don't. In China, governance is typically an ad hoc affair. Corporations tend to be very murky. Ownership structures are often labyrinthine. Lines of reporting are often fuzzy, with no clear systems of accountability in place. Roles and responsibilities of employees are often vague. The murkier the firm, the riskier its outputs because quality control can't happen in the dark.

But a murky firm is often difficult to discover. Usually, it will have all the trappings of a well-run company. Its operations manual will read just like an American one. And it will probably have the proper international quality accreditation, such as ISO 9000 or 9001.

The International Organization for Standardization (ISO) sets standards that govern management and quality control in companies around the world. To win ISO accreditation, a firm must submit to an in-depth auditing process. Of the nearly one thousand suppliers my team inspected before launching our first trading business in China, just about all of them had received ISO accreditation. And over the years since, among the additional hundreds of firms we've either worked with or screened, it's been rare to find a Chinese export manufacturer that had not won some kind of ISO or other international quality certification, just as you would expect to find with their western counterparts. In fact, according to the ISO 2013 survey, 337,033 ISO 9001 certificates have been granted in China, compared to 34,869 in the United States.[7]

But, in China, ISO status is awarded to factories by for-profit registrars, and that often means looking the other way when audits reveal non-compliant practice rather than forfeit a fee. It also means that a factory can win accreditation by abiding by ISO standards on paper but not in practice.

I remember an ISO factory near the port city of Ningbo that we once hired to make stainless-steel air-conditioner vents for a large home builder in Alabama. The goods traveled to the United States wrapped in plastic, encased in stacked boxes, inside a sealed sea container. When the client unpacked the vents, they were wet. Everybody was dumbfounded. How could this have happened? We later discovered the ISO-accredited factory had put the vents in a part of its warehouse that had no roof – and the night before packing the vents for export, it had rained.

You'd think that keeping final products under an actual roof would be one of the eight management principles espoused by the ISO system. Having an international quality certification or an operations manual that says the right things doesn't necessarily mean a company can make things well.

There are millions of Chinese firms, ranging from mom-and-pop shops to large state-owned corporations, and you'd expect to find this kind of casual business practice in the small enterprises, but it's surprising to see it as standard operating procedure among China's largest companies as well. Deng Xiaoping, who took over leadership of China after Mao, understood this problem. He recognized how China's state-owned sector was a herd of dinosaurs, relics of the command-driven economy, which would not be able to withstand international competition if Deng liberalized trade. Many of Deng's economic reforms were targeted at trying to improve the competitiveness of these firms.

Yet, over the decades since, China has also pursued policies that have shielded these firms from competition, ultimately undoing Deng's goal. Most notably, Beijing has lavished a largesse of financial goodies on its uncompetitive state-owned sector. These include easy access to loans. Typically, nonstate-owned companies have a hard time borrowing money. State-owned firms, however, have access to loans and can borrow at well below China's stated rates. And when state-owned companies are having difficulty paying the loan back, the government will often wipe the slate clean or convert the loans from debt to equity. In the United States, it takes the power of a bankruptcy court to absolve debt, not the smudge of a bureaucrat's eraser.

In addition to below-interest loans, debt forgiveness, and debt to equity swaps (where non-performing loans are conveniently converted to equity), state-owned companies often receive their land for free or at highly reduced pricing. Energy is also often deeply discounted, as are raw material inputs. Since state-owned companies are legacies of China's old command economy, in which the factors of production were controlled, managers are acclimated to this way of doing business. If you ask the manager of a large state-owned firm how the year went, you will usually hear, *We had a great year. We produced 10 million tons of output.* But that's beside the point for competitive modern companies. The key metric is sales. How much product did you move? How many reorders? How much profit? Were your customers happy? It's quite rare in China, especially among state-owned firms, to hear this kind of analysis. They act as government-backed budget spenders, not market competitors.

Washington policy makers, think tanks, and trade groups wring their hands over the notion that these firms are somehow more competitive than their US counterparts. But, given the myriad incentives and subsidies that China fobs onto its state-owned firms, while erecting barriers like tariffs and ownership laws that make it hard to impossible for foreign firms to compete in certain markets, the opposite is true. These dinosaurs of the command economy are shocking examples of bad business practice and, therefore, risk. And the extent that these companies are shielded from true competition is the extent to which they remain stunted, uncompetitive, and ultimately non-innovative.

Shipbuilding

A vivid example happened recently, when Shell Oil was seeking to purchase an offshore drilling rig from China's newest, most advanced shipyard, Shanghai Waigaoqiao Shipyard (SWS), the jewel of the mammoth, state-owned China State Shipbuilding Company. Many drilling rigs these days are produced in South Korea or Japan. China has been vying to grab market share from these countries and has invested heavily in capacity building.

Before purchasing a rig from SWS, Shell performed an audit on the shipyard, as is customary before awarding a major contract to a new supplier. Even though SWS was considered the most modern shipbuilding facility in China, however, it flunked Shell's audit across every evaluation category. A company that makes offshore drilling rigs is basically a giant purchaser and assembler. It buys parts and puts them together (see Figure 4.1). So a good shipyard must have systems in place to monitor its suppliers, insuring the parts are compliant with quality standards of the end user, in this case, Shell. It must have good engineering to insure that the parts fit together safely. And it must have good workplace practices to prevent its assemblers from being injured on the job. SWS flunked in all of these areas.

First, SWS was found to have no coherent systems for purchasing components or managing the quality of suppliers. That's a big problem when most of what you do is buy content from subcontractors and put it together. Shell found that SWS had yet to implement subcontractor performance management systems or quality control procedures on the components the subs produce. Furthermore, SWS lacked procedures consistent with international standards in the selection and ongoing management of its subcontractors – an infraction deemed "a significant project risk to Shell" in the audit.

Aside from weak subcontractor oversight, the shipyard was found to have weak engineering capability. Before a complex job of fabricating a rig, a lot of design engineering and planning must happen (see Figure 4.2). SWS was discovered to have no front-end engineering and design capability (FEED), nor did it have the ability to oversee a vendor

4.1   Construction of a rig in dry dock

Source: iStock

perform this function. Shell noted that SWS also lacked the engineering capability to manage design changes mid-project – a big problem, as changes in design happen frequently on large engineering projects.

SWS also flunked Shell's audit of health, safety, and environmental (HSE) standards, citing "several high-risk activities." The audit went on to state that "locations are noted as not having the appropriate industry-defined HSE controls in place." If you consulted SWS's operations manual, though,

4.2   A tough job without in-house engineering

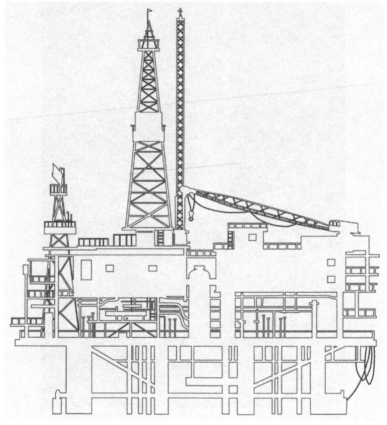

Source: shutterstock

you'd see many of the standards required in international practice. Like scores of China's laws and regulations, it's not so much a matter of what's in the book as what's enforced. As Shell's audit discovered, the shipyard had "not fully implemented several of the control procedures that are defined in their QSHE manual" (that's quality, health, safety, and environment). Further, the shipyard had no procedures in place to handle hazardous materials or defects that inevitably arise in the creation of such a complicated piece of equipment.

And, perhaps most importantly, Shell found that SWS lacked basic lines of reporting and clearly defined job responsibilities, generally undermining accountability and magnifying risk. Ultimately, SWS flunked Shell's audit because bad business practice instills risk into products. If you don't have the means to monitor the quality of the parts you purchase, then there's a risk that substandard parts will make their way into your final product. If you don't have the means to conduct the extensive planning and designing before a complex piece of equipment like an offshore drilling rig is built, there's a risk that the ad hoc engineering will be flawed. If you don't have a way to handle defects – to identify non-compliant parts and take corrective measures – there's a risk that your final product will be defective. If you don't have a means of defining clear lines of reporting, there's a risk that someone will screw up and no one will know. Having flunked every aspect of Shell's audit, lacking the most basic elements of a modern, well-run company, China's most advanced shipyard revealed itself to be a fly-by-night operation.

Shell decided to give the shipyard the opportunity to correct the citations in the audit. It granted SWS "conditional accreditation," meaning that "SWS must demonstrate the willingness in developing an improvement plan and implement remedial actions to address the audit action items...identified by the Shell evaluation team during the audit." Considering the severity of the infractions, this was generous. SWS didn't have to fix the problems. They just had to develop a *plan* to fix the problems and show they were taking basic steps to improve. The carrot was nearly US$1 billion in Shell orders and acceptance onto the Shell procurement platform, which would have allowed SWS to bid on additional billions of dollars' worth of future business. And it would have bestowed on SWS the cachet of being a supplier to one of the most prestigious international customers in the world.

To make the deal even sweeter, a grant was offered to SWS by China's National Development and Reform Commission, a powerful macroeconomic agency under the State Council, to fund any operational costs SWS might bear in implementing Shell's action items. So, to enable the order to go forward, SWS was presented with conditional accreditation and free money. Tellingly, SWS refused. Their domestic market was deemed big enough to ignore the inconvenience of improving their systems, even if that meant forgoing the large order and potential billions of dollars of future business from Shell.

This posture is typical of China's state-owned companies. Lazy, bloated, and uncompetitive, they tend to prefer the path of least resistance. China's government makes a lot of voluble pronouncements about how it's climbing up the manufacturing value chain, investing in advanced manufacturing, yet SWS is a common example of what this really means on the ground. A lot of noise and chest-thumping from government officials, but zero follow-through at the firm level.

Refineries

SWS is certainly not an anomaly. That's why many of the world's largest engineering, procurement, and construction firms (EPCs) – the companies that run large-scale infrastructure projects – ban Chinese-made steel on their jobs. There was the case of a recent project in Saudi Arabia, in which oil giants Conoco Phillips and Saudi Aramco sought to build a tank farm for a petroleum refinery. A tank farm, as far as infrastructure goes, is a fairly straightforward job (see Figure 4.3). The tanks are basically giant steel vats.

4.3 Tank farms for petroleum refinery

Source: iStock

Halliburton was selected as the EPC on the job. Companies from all over the world were invited to bid for the construction contract – from India, Europe, the United States, and China – with just one important caveat. Chinese steel was disallowed from the project.

This is a typical provision in large infrastructure projects these days. Chinese steel is infamous for its relatively low quality. Part of the problem is inferior inputs. In steel production, iron ore is mined from the ground and then processed to make different grades of steel for different industrial purposes. Higher-quality steel needs higher iron content. The percentage of iron in the ore must be 70 percent or more to be considered high quality by industry standards. However, China's iron content in its mined ore tends to be quite low – 50 percent or lower. That's the reason why China imports over half of the iron ore it uses to make steel.

The world got a glimpse of Chinese-made steel in action during the 2008 earthquake in Sichuan. Compared to buildings and bridges in California, many of which were built decades ago but have been able to withstand earthquakes of much stronger magnitude, the Chinese-made buildings collapsed like houses of cards.

Low-quality iron ore was part of the problem, as well as the notorious practice of steel thinning. In 2011, there were a number of Chinese media reports exposing this profitable and growing industry in China, in which regulation-thickness reinforcing bars are stretched to a thinner specification and sold for cheaper prices. As China urbanizes, it is rushing to build "affordable housing" for the migrating rural population at breakneck speed. Low-cost building puts pressure on developers' margins. Thinned steel is one way to claw back some profit while appearing to abide by architectural specifications. As reported in *The Australian*, "an inspection of a new affordable housing project on the island of Hainan found that four of the mega-projects had been using dangerously thinned-down reinforcement bars."[8] Residents of China's cities are familiar with the effects of slipshod building techniques, having to evade "glass bombs" as windows from modern skyscrapers come loose and plummet to the sidewalk.

But low-quality Chinese steel is not a new problem. In 2007, American and Canadian institutes of steel construction warned member companies to be especially cautious with Chinese supposedly "high-strength" steel inputs. The inspectors got suspicious when they discovered that documents meant to certify the strength of different types of steel tubes were photocopied *en masse* from a single original.

When tons of Chinese steel was then tested, "the welds failed horribly," said Dan Malone, construction manager for Garneau Manufacturing.[9] Malone added that, had the steel been processed into a finished product, "it would have killed somebody." Charles Bradford, president of Bradford Research, a metals consultant, said, "Most of China's 800-plus steelmakers are small fabricators who have no idea what quality is about, so there is a risk that some guy with a welding torch buys some hot-rolled coil steel and just welds it together."[10]

Similar risks can be found in large, state-owned firms, too. Companies like SWS may have the most modern equipment and hardware. Yet if their corporate governance is flawed – really, the company's software – then state-of-the-art hardware isn't sufficient to eliminate the risk of defective outputs. Looking from the outside in at a giant state-owned enterprise, it's easy to get suckered. California's transportation department was.

Bridge Building

Consider the San Francisco Bay Bridge, where the eastern and western spans needed a major renovation – an extremely complex job. The new eastern span was designed as a suspension bridge, with a single tower and one long steel cable. A real challenge to the builder.

In anticipation of this project, the California Department of Transportation, or Caltrans, which regulates bridge, highway, and railroad construction, refused stimulus money from the federal government because the funds would likely come with "Buy America" provisions for infrastructure. And California wanted to keep its options open.

Caltrans contracted reputable EPCs Fluor and American Bridge, whose bid for the job specified that they would be going overseas for the materials – specifically, China. At a projected cost of US$6.4 billion, California officials guessed that they would save about US$400 million on the job.[11] Of course, they weren't factoring in cost overruns from quality lapses. The project went way over budget and was ten years late.

Fluor and American Bridge hired a large Chinese state-owned enterprise, Zhenhua Port Machinery Company (ZPMC), to do the job. Astoundingly, given how complex the project was, the bridge-building contract was not awarded to an actual bridge builder. ZPMC is a world leader in making cranes to unload containers from ships. It supplies 80 percent of the port cranes used around the world.[12] It does not build bridges.

Caltrans justified the hire by citing ZPMC's giant 1.2-square-mile fabrication facility created specifically for the project, the firm's low projected costs, and its Chinese government backing. So a bridge-building newbie was hired to undertake a highly complex project with taxpayer money – the reconstruction of one of the most trafficked bridges in the world, vulnerable to earthquakes.

ZPMC's scope of work was to make 900 panels to be assembled into football field-long deck plates. Predictably, as the bridge spans were being fabricated, independent inspectors were finding that the bridge welds were defective. There were cracked welds in the girders meant to hold up the roadway. When California officials said those problems were fixed, more cracks were discovered in the welds that are supposed to join the deck plates to the girders.

The problems began as soon as ZPMC started production in 2007. The inspection firm tasked with quality control on the job, MacTec Engineering and Consulting, threw up a red flag when they found that up to 65 percent of the panels had defective welds.[13] MacTec inspectors on site in China stated that ZPMC had "failed to provide most of the quality control documentation required under its contract with American

Bridge and Caltrans, and had failed to produce a single test weld that conformed to the contract specifications."[14]

Shortly thereafter, MacTec inspectors on the ground complained of "random weld quality" on more than a hundred panels and urged the production process to stop until ZPMC improved its welding. In 2008, MacTec reported that cracked welds on a deck panel had been replaced, but that the welds were not tested by ZPMC as per the project requirements. When examining another panel that had been repaired, there were cracks in more than a dozen welds.

Rather than insist that the problems be fixed, Caltrans fired the inspectors. A new inspection firm was hired and a new set of looser inspection criteria was adopted. Caltrans insists this change in inspectors had nothing to do with MacTec's requirement that the welds on the San Francisco Bay Bridge be free from cracks. Caltrans director Will Kempton reassuringly said, "yes, we did modify the acceptance criteria...we developed what we think are acceptable standards."

Well, that's a relief.

Of course, ZPMC's shoddy production process should have come as no surprise to anyone looking at the company's history. Angling to get into the bridge-building business for years, this port crane producer made giant bolts for California's Carquinez Bridge in 2001 that were the wrong size. As stated in a report for the California State Senate Transportation and Housing Committee, "The San Francisco–Oakland Bay Bridge: Basic Reforms for the Future," Caltrans, which oversaw the botched Carquinez project, hired ZPMC anyway for the Bay Bridge – a much more complex project. It seems ZPMC still hadn't learned how to make bolts ten years later, as one-third of the giant bolts it produced for the Bay Bridge snapped as they were tightened into huge braces called shear keys.

When investigative reporters Phillip Matier and Andrew Ross from *San Francisco Gate* got a hold of the ZPMC Bay Bridge story, they started to press the California officials who thought it was a good idea to hire a Chinese firm with no expertise to build a complex, heavily trafficked bridge that is susceptible to major earthquakes. The official in charge from Caltrans defended the decision and said that ZPMC is so big, "they couldn't be a fly-by-night corporation," and added, "they couldn't command that kind of market share if they were putting out a shoddy product."[15]

But that totally misses the point. Firstly, ZPMC's market share is not in bridges. It's in port cranes. And they can command so much of the market because their products are heavily subsidized by the Chinese government. Walk the pier at the Port of Baltimore, for example, and you'll see a row of ZPMC cranes. The port saved millions of dollars purchasing them over other cranes.

Putting that aside, however, Chinese state-owned enterprises are by their nature large – and yes, they're often run like fly-by-night operations, which Caltrans would have known had they done their homework. If not Caltrans, then surely Fluor or American Bridge should have known ZPMC would be a risky choice. Other EPCs like Halliburton won't go near Chinese steel on large infrastructure projects.

Nuclear Power Plants

But risky business practice in large state-owned entities isn't limited to the steel industries. Another terrifying instance can be found in China's nuclear reactors. In an effort to diversify its energy portfolio away from coal, China is charging headlong toward nuclear. It already has 21 reactors online, another 27 under construction, and more in planning.[16]

"With the drive to construct many more power plants in a short period of time, there's a serious risk of reckless expansion and corner-cutting," warns Dr Bo Kong, Professor at the University of Oklahoma and Senior Fellow at the Johns Hopkins University School of Advanced International Studies. China, adds Dr Kong, "lacks safety culture."

Many problems in the construction of nuclear power plants have already been spotted in inspection, according to a report filed by Liu Weirui, Deputy Director of the Shanghai Nuclear Power Office. It's the same old refrain. As we saw in Shell's audit of SWS, there was found to be poor management and accountability at the construction firms. And in the operation of the power plants, there was a lack of technology proficiency, leading to incorrect working practices and a lack of understanding of how certain devices work.[17]

Anyone who's tried to make products in China will be nodding. Because this is a common problem, not just in the building of bridges or offshore drilling rigs or nuclear power plants, but also in toys, tires, toothpaste, or what have you. The basic culture of safety is lacking in a typical Chinese enterprise. Another alarming example of this phenomenon is in the handling of radioactive materials. Dr Kong writes of how four nuclear inspectors in May of 2013 *lost* radioactive material under their care and did not file a police report until the next day. Apparently, when they realized the materials were gone, they kept working.[18] Sadly, this is not an independent case. According to Chinese statistics, the location of two thousand batches of radioactive materials is unknown!

A lack of safety culture can be attributed not just to weak corporate governance but also to unqualified workers. As such, China's nuclear industry faces a shortage of trained personnel. According to official estimates in 2010, China had about 14,000 engineers and administrators and approximately 7,000 researchers. Each reactor requires 700–1,000 workers. With the current nuclear building boom, China would need 5,000–6,000 professionals each year over the next decade to staff the reactors. Yet the yearly supply of newly minted nuclear engineers, administrators, and researchers is currently only around 2,000. Contrary to popular belief that China graduates one million highly advanced engineers each year, China is actually struggling to keep apace with its nuclear personnel needs. China has six universities that educate nuclear specialists, but fewer than a third of the graduates stay in the nuclear industry after graduating.

The hardware of the companies is not the issue. Often China imports state-of-the-art equipment, as you might find at SWS or ZPMC. It's the software of the companies that makes them so risky. Unclear lines of reporting, a lack of functional accountability, vaguely defined roles and responsibilities, and badly conceived emergency planning all conspire to make China's nuclear reactors extreme risks to the health and safety of the Chinese and their neighbors. That a Three Mile Island- or Chernobyl-type incident hasn't happened yet is extremely lucky.

If you're just looking at the hardware, Chinese firms can fool you. Caltrans, for example, got taken in by how big ZPMC's facilities are. Like a Potemkin village, you think you're seeing something really impressive, when you're not. Even the most seasoned of spectators can be fooled. James Fallows, who has lived in China for years and reports from the factory floor for many publications, created a DVD series in 2009 for *The Atlantic* called *On the Frontlines: Doing Business in China*. It is divided into segments that explore different aspects of Chinese commerce and features a prominent section on quality control.

Surprisingly, Fallows and his co-host Emily Chang devoted their remarks in this section to downplaying China's quality control issues. There was no discussion about how risk is a systemic problem in China's manufacturing and agricultural sectors. In fact, the lethal safety scandals that had occurred by 2009, such as melamine-tainted baby formula and contaminated heparin, were completely ignored. Mattel's Dora the Explorer recall was chalked up to bad design in the United States. And the general issue of quality control was attributed to different cultural standards, as Fallows pointed out how Chinese still use open-air wet markets to sell fish and produce. As if safety were simply a matter of cultural preference.

Then, with the cameras trained on the outside of the factory that was tasked with painting the recalled Dora accessories, Chang pointed out how the building looked rather shabby. She then dispensed the following advice to her viewers: you can judge the quality of a Chinese factory simply by looking at the outside of it. Anyone who has done significant business in China knows this statement is untrue. It's perplexing that Fallows, who is no stranger to Chinese factories, would associate himself with such an assertion. A gleaming, giant facility, like SWS, might be a shambles organizationally. Or it might be corrupt, undermining effective quality control. Examples of this abound in the food industry.

Yurun, one of China's largest meat processors, has been cited numerous times by Chinese authorities for gruesome food safety violations. If you followed Chang and Fallows's advice, by looking at the outside of these processors, you'd see impressive, modern-looking buildings. Step inside, though, and you'd see something else: food mixed with fecal matter; food on the floor; food laced with chemicals.

Yurun's founder and (until he had to step down) chief executive, Zhu Yicai, is a former government bureaucrat, and his skill in growing the company from a single canning factory into a meat-packing giant has been attributed to his ability to wheel and deal with local government officials. In 2011, investors were said to be pouring over Yurun's financials, singling out suspicious line items, such as how 26 percent of pre-tax profits were accounted for as "government subsidies."

Pharmaceuticals

Not just state-owned enterprises, but also large multinationals can get tainted by China's culture of corruption. Pharmaceutical giant GlaxoSmithKline has been struggling to combat corrupt practices at its Shanghai research and development center. GSK was already in the crosshairs of Chinese authorities, who claim the firm had bribed doctors and government officials to boost drug sales, masking illegal payments through travel agencies. Then, an internal GSK audit from November 2011 revealed that research and development procedures were also probably corrupt. With a drug in development for multiple sclerosis and Lou Gehrig's disease, results of animal trials had been withheld until after human testing had begun. "That's kind of a Rock-of-Gibraltar-sized ethics violation," said Arthur L. Caplan, head of the medical ethics department at NYU Medical Center and the former chairman of a bioethics advisory committee at GSK.[19] The internal audit also discovered that employees were not properly documenting drug trials, obscuring whether patients had taken the proper dosage or whether there was any action taken when patients did not follow the testing protocols.

And the way payments were being disbursed by the Shanghai center to hospitals and clinics that ran drug trials was also flagged by the audit. Flat fees were being paid despite the number of patients enrolled in a trial, which could be construed as a form of bribery. The GSK audit states that "reputational, financial, and/or regulatory action risk where payments made to investigators regardless of actual work completed are perceived as bribery or corruption."

According to a report by McKinsey and Company, 13 of the top 20 global pharmaceutical companies have established R&D practices in China, many of which are under investigation by Chinese authorities for corrupt practices. "It's cheaper to do research there," said Eric G. Campbell, a professor of healthcare policy at Harvard Medical School, in an article about GSK that ran in the *New York Times*. "I have absolutely no doubt that with cheaper research comes greater risk"[20] – risk that corners will be cut and quality standards will be lowered.

Ultimately, when corporate governance isn't anchored in enforceable rule of law, the risk of unsafe outputs intensifies. Unsafe food, drugs, infrastructure, and consumer products leap immediately to mind. Yet, since a minority of Americans actually work in farms or factories, it's hard for many of them to gauge the competitiveness of China, where farms and factories are the mainstay of the economy. The "flat world" paradigm would have us assume there's a basic equivalence to an American company and a Chinese company. Because of the flattening effects of information technology, products are available from around the world at the click of a mouse, so US and Chinese firms must now be competing head to head. If you buy into the "flat world" perspective, it's easy to imagine, then, that China is populated by American-style corporations staffed by cheap Chinese labor – an unbeatable combination.

But assuming parity between China and the United States is misleading. The very DNA of American corporations – their governance, their personnel, their culture – is arguably centuries ahead of the typical Chinese corporation. You can't just leapfrog over 400 years of evolving corporation law and the acculturation of these conventions.

That's one reason why behavior that we'd consider to be out-and-out fraud is seen as business as usual in China. Keeping separate books for investors or auditors? Shenanigans like that would get you thrown in jail in America. Not so in China – it's just how business is done. Poisoning your fruit and veggies? Again, you'd be liable in the United States for any harm you cause others. In China, you just shrug and avoid eating anything you haven't grown yourself.

Bottom line, Chinese business practices are not a competitive advantage but a stiff headwind that keeps Chinese firms from evolving. If you can't make basic manufacturing products safely and reliably, it's really hard to advance to high-tech manufacturing. And as China struggles to evolve, it must import the products it needs to grow its economy – to house, feed, and power its population.

Risky Chinese Firms Support US Jobs

Let's consider the nuclear industry again. China's struggle to overcome risk in building and maintaining reactors has resulted in an export bonanza for the United States. America, not China, is designing the next generation of nuclear reactors being deployed there. Westinghouse and General Electric are inventing designs, in which cooling can occur in the event of a total electric failure, such as the one that happened at Fukushima in Japan. The United States is also manufacturing and exporting critical components for the "nuclear island." China's need for advanced nuclear design and next-generation equipment is creating many jobs in America. Just four Chinese reactors under construction have created 5,000 US jobs at Westinghouse and other suppliers.[21]

Despite the fact that America has mainly ceased building nuclear reactors at home, and therefore some of the largest parts of the reactors in China are being supplied by other countries, such as Japan Steel Works, in many cases, US nuclear technology cannot be replicated anywhere else in the world. An example is reactor coolant pumps, which are an innovative aspect of the next-generation Westinghouse design. Nuclear reactors produce power by using the heat from fission to boil water, which creates steam, which moves turbines, which generates electricity. The coolant pumps are a critical part of this process, moving water from the reactor vessel to heat exchangers and back to the vessel. In Westinghouse's design, the coolant pumps keep the radioactive materials separate from uncontaminated water.

However, pumps are components in reactors that tend to break or need maintenance. America's Curtiss-Wright Flow Control Company is building pumps for China's reactors that are unique in the world – sealed pumps that can run maintenance-free for 60 years. According to a piece in the *New York Times*, "Nuclear Industry Thrives in the US, but for Export," "Each is 23 feet tall, weighs almost 100 tons and pumps about 13,000 gallons of water a second. They sell for more than $10 million each, and there is nowhere else to buy them."[22]

Tyco International is also creating US jobs, testing valves for Chinese nuclear reactors. It recently opened a US$25 million lab in Mansfield, Massachusetts. Tyco manufactures the high-precision valves as well, each of which sells for US$10–30 million. The cost to maintain and service the valves earns Tyco another several million dollars a year. Manufacturing, testing, and servicing the valves supports US jobs.

Not just an importer of parts, designs, and services, China is providing a platform for the commercialization of next-generation American nuclear technology, too – especially small, modular reactors that can be deployed more nimbly than large reactors. One company in this space is Terra-Power, backed by Bill Gates, which is developing the traveling wave reactor that consumes a low-grade form of uranium. This would allow countries to use nuclear power without the enrichment phase, a necessary step toward weaponization. Another American firm, Babcock and Wilcox, is pioneering the manufacture of modular reactors. Similar to modular homes, the modular reactors are built entirely in a factory. That way, the construction quality control issues that Dr Bo Kong warns about are minimized, as the reactors are pre-fabricated in a remote facility and transported to the site.

You may be thinking that the Chinese will import these high-technology parts and designs and simply copy them, stealing American jobs in the end. However, reverse engineering is not as simple as you may think. A complex piece of technology is not easily copied, much less replicated over and over again safely.

Intellectual Property Theft and High-Speed Rail

China's high-speed rail is a perfect example. Looking at it from the outside, using the Fallows-Chang paradigm of what-you-see-is-what-you-get, the network is an awe-inspiring testament to China's infrastructure building prowess. In his 2011 State of the Union speech, President Obama warned that "our infrastructure used to be the best, but our lead has slipped."[23]

4.4 China's bullet train network

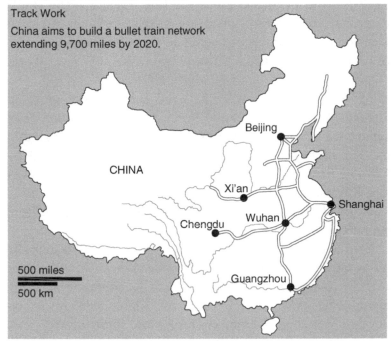

Track Work

China aims to build a bullet train network extending 9,700 miles by 2020.

CHINA

Beijing

Xi'an

Shanghai

Chengdu Wuhan

500 miles

500 km

Guangzhou

Source: World Bank

Has it really? Let's take a closer look. As China was rushing to blunt the impact of the global recession, it pumped billions of dollars' worth of renminbi into its economy as a stimulus, much of it for infrastructure building. The budget for high-speed rail ballooned to about US$100 billion per year. By 2008, the first high-speed rail line was already operational between Shenyang and Qinhuangdao in north-eastern China, construction having begun in 2004 (Figure 4.4). With the onset of global recession, Chinese planners wanted to build even faster, to double the amount of track as an antidote to an economic downturn. In 2008, ground was broken on the flagship Beijing–Shanghai line. Three years later, the line was open for business. Then, a year later, in 2012, the Beijing–Guangzhou line opened – the single longest stretch of high-speed rail in the world. In less than a decade, 6,800 miles of track had been built – more miles of high-speed railroad than the rest of the world combined.

Meanwhile, it is widely believed that technology from Siemens AG of Germany and Kawasaki Heavy Industries of Japan, the companies that partnered with China to build its first high-speed rail systems, was copied and used by Chinese firms to expand the network. The case of Siemens and Kawasaki is often cited as an example of China's state-sanctioned policy to replicate and deploy stolen intellectual property.

Yet the opposite is true. China's high-speed rail is actually an example of how systemic risk undermines China's ability to reverse-engineer and roll out advanced manufacturing technologies. On July 23, 2011, two high-speed trains collided in Wenzhou, China, killing 40 and injuring 192. This was the third fatal high-speed rail crash in the world. In 1998, 101 people were killed in Germany when a crack in a wheel derailed the train. And, in 2013, 78 people were killed in Spain when the conductor took a turn too quickly.

The difference between China's accident and the ones in Spain and Germany is telling. Spain's high-speed rail accident was caused by human error. Germany's was because of a single point of failure. But the accident in China happened because of systemic problems in design, construction, and operations of the railway.[24]

Before the Wenzhou crash even occurred, there were already scandals of rampant corruption in the construction of the high-speed network. The hard-charging railway minister, nicknamed Great Leap Liu Zhijun, had led his ministry in a headlong rush to build big – as fast as possible. Yet he presided over a vast honeycomb of corruption, characterized by Liao Ran of Transparency International as "the biggest single financial scandal not just in China, but perhaps the world."[25]

Even middlemen were getting rich on the subcontractor kickbacks. A project that might cost four billion yuan would net the middlemen 200 million. So illegal subcontracting began to flourish, in which a contract would be divided up and sold again and again, netting kickbacks each time, until the job would finally be hired out to the cheapest, most unskilled workers. Evan Osnos, in his eye-opening piece "Boss Rail" for the *New Yorker*, reported that "In November, 2011, a former cook with no engineering experience was found to be building a high-speed railway bridge using a crew of unskilled migrant laborers who substituted crushed stones for cement in the foundation."

Great Leap Liu was removed from office in February 2011 and charged with corruption. The new managers of the railway ministry then decreased top speeds from 218 to 186 miles per hour, characterizing problems with safety on the network as "severe."[26] Inspectors launched a series of safety checks up and down the line, but these measures failed to prevent the disaster that would occur in July.

After the crash in Wenzhou, in December 2012, having initially tried to cover up the incident, Chinese authorities released a report detailing an investigation into what happened. It revealed "serious design flaws" and a "neglect of safety management." Part of the problem was the speed with which complicated technologies had to be built and deployed. Investigators discovered how the signal in the Wenzhou crash that had shorted out was designed and fabricated in just six months by the state-owned China Railway Signal and Communication Corporation. A giant company with around 1,300 engineers, the crash investigators characterized its working culture as "chaotic," one which performed only "lax" inspection on the signals and "failed to discover grave flaws and major hidden dangers."[27] China Railway Signal and Communications Corporation is an ISO 9001 certified company, by the way.

Though rushed and risky, the signal was approved in 2008 for use on the high-speed network and deployed across the system. Then came the launch of the Beijing–Shanghai line, which was pushed one full year ahead of schedule to occur alongside the ninetieth anniversary of the Chinese Communist Party. When trains along the route faced delays, staffers were warned to hurry up or their bonuses would be cut. On the night of the crash, trains began backing up. Skilled operators would have stopped the trains to recover proper signal operations, but instead they scurried ahead to try to make repairs and keep the trains running. The investigating committee's deputy chief stated, "The maintenance people weren't familiar enough with their jobs, and they didn't want to stop the train. They didn't dare."[28]

Then, nearly a year after the crash, in March of 2012, a section of high-speed rail, about a thousand feet long, collapsed. The authorities first blamed a heavy rainstorm but later revealed that about five and a half miles of track would need to be replaced. The foundation was sinking. As reported in the *South China Morning Post*, the high-speed rail tracks should have been ballasted by concrete slabs reinforced with gravel and fly ash, a by-product of coal-power plants. "But all the coal-fired power plants in China and the rest of the world could not possibly produce enough high-quality fly ash for the thousands of [miles] of high-speed lines that have been laid annually on the mainland."[29] We can only imagine what kinds of low-quality inputs were substituted.

Building, deploying, and running complex systems requires much more than just an ability to copy a spec. To implement the development of advanced manufacturing, you need reliable quality control, which can happen only in companies that are transparent, with clear lines of reporting and managerial accountability. You need trained personnel. And you need effective oversight. "China's most famous public-works project was an ecosystem almost perfectly hospitable to corruption – opaque, unsupervised, and overflowing with cash," writes Osnos of the *New Yorker*.[30] With corrupt companies, untrained workers, rushed timetables, lax quality control, and regulators who looked the other way, China's high-speed rail is not proof of China's infrastructure prowess, as is usually thought, but rather a shining example of systemic risk in China's manufacturing base – and how this risk impedes attempts to reverse-engineer advanced technologies.

The People's Liberation Army and Cyber-Spying

At its peak, the railway ministry under Great Leap Liu was like a mini-empire, with its own courts and police. The only other bureaucracy in China with such power and independence is the military. Like the railway ministry, China's People's Liberation Army (PLA) gets huge pots of money from the government. The Center for Strategic and International Studies estimates that China spent between US$90 billion and US$142 billion in 2011 on its military – sums similar to what the railway ministry spent in the roll-out of its high-speed network.[31]

Policy wonks in Washington, DC, fret over China's military budget and its saber-rattling buildup of military hardware. Compounding this fear is China's widespread, state-sanctioned push to steal terabytes of military and industrial designs through cyber-spying. However, when considering China's military, it's useful to remember the lessons from China's high-speed rail boondoggle. You can't develop and implement high technology amidst a culture of secrecy and corruption.

As John Garnaut reported in *Foreign Policy*, one of China's top generals, Liu Yuan, the head of the PLA's General Logistics Department and the princeling son of a past Chinese president, has turned heads with a sharp, public rebuke of the military. Liu described an institution rife with corruption, where the buying and selling of offices is commonplace and where the behavior of officers is more befitting of a mafia family than a world power. "Certain individuals," Liu said, "exchange public money, public goods, public office and public affairs for personal gain, flouting the law and Party codes of conduct...They physically attack loyal and upstanding officials, kidnap and blackmail party leaders, and drag in their superiors to act as human shields. They deploy all of the tricks of the mafia trade within the army itself."[32] Outside observers of the PLA also note its fragmented and opaque command structure, the darkness in which corruption thrives.

Sound familiar? While the wholesale theft of military secrets is a serious issue, we should not make the mistake of assuming China can readily replicate and deploy these technologies just because hackers steal some specs. Risk permeates the PLA, just as it does the railway ministry, hampering any efforts to replicate advanced technologies.

Light Bulbs

The army, high-speed rail, shipbuilding, nuclear power, steel making, agriculture – risky business is standard operating procedure for China's firms and farms. A Chinese TV host put it best when he wondered aloud, "Can we drink a glass of milk that is safe? Can we stay in an apartment that will not fall apart? Can we travel roads in our cities that will not collapse?"[33]

One of the longest bridges in northern China crumpled in a heap of concrete and steel in August 2012. It had opened just nine months earlier. It was the sixth big bridge to collapse since July 2011, according to the Xinhua news agency. Critics in China blame "tofu engineering" – bad design, cheap materials, and corruption.

But you don't need to look at large infrastructure projects and weapons systems to see evidence of China's idiosyncratically risky businesses. The humble light bulb illuminates why GE chose China for production, then reconsidered. Since 2000, GE pursued a strategy in which light bulbs would be made in China alongside a research and development facility to speed innovations. GE is constantly working to improve the technology of its light bulbs, Thomas Edison's crowning invention which birthed the GE giant.

But GE noticed that its China operations were struggling to innovate. When R&D and production were based in the United States, big leaps in innovation would occur frequently. Instead of moving from A to B, there'd be a jump from A to E, then F to J, and so on. The advances in design were seamlessly implemented in production. In China, however, the R&D capability crept from A to B to C to D. And manufacturing struggled to implement these iterations while maintaining quality control. Ultimately, GE decided to move its R&D and production of the light bulb back to the United States.

The same attributes of Chinese business practice that give rise to risk – weak corporate governance, untrained personnel – also stifle innovation and the ability to evolve. So seemingly simple products like light bulbs become difficult to make in China, not just big infrastructure projects.

Yet this reality evades many Chinese academics. In *The Atlantic* magazine's DVD series *On the Frontlines: Doing Business in China*, a young Harvard professor recommends you give China sourcing a try by visiting one of the many trade shows there. You might as well, he says with a smile. But there was no qualification about the danger Chinese firms and farms tend to present to all but the most skilled and dedicated US importers. Giving China sourcing a try without the proper precautions has scuttled scores of US firms large and small. For to wring safe products out of the supply chain, you almost always need to invest countless hours in training your Chinese counterparts and installing your own stringent safeguards on site to insure quality.

Of course, not every single company you come across in China is a honeycomb of chaos and corruption. But after having worked with hundreds of Chinese factories large and small over the years in a wide variety of industries, as well as having worked closely with many others of similar background, the view from the ground is that the vast majority of China's firms grapple with similar issues. Even if management means well, a company that lacks line accountability need not be corrupt to be risky.

Now here's a scary thought. If you consider that the DNA of China's typical firms and farms is defective, imagine what happens when that DNA is replicated across China's gangling supply chains.

5

Chain of Fools

We measure China's might by what it makes. We look at any given product and suppose that it can be made cheaper in China. Because so few of us have ever walked a Chinese supply chain, we can only guess at how China makes things. So we employ false paradigms, like the "flat world," to imagine China manufacturing.

Consider how a laptop is usually purchased these days. We go to a website, customize the product's features, enter our payment information, and hit "send." What happens next? We envision a giant factory somewhere in the Chinese hinterland with workers scurrying around putting our laptop together – like Santa's elves on meager wages.

But that's not how things get made. Many companies must work together to bring a product to market. Like a line of kids playing hot potato, items get passed from one firm to the next as they're transformed from raw materials to final products. A simple plastic toy, for example, is actually quite complex, a manufacturing process that involves several collaborating companies.

The raw materials begin as petrochemicals, which are formed into plastic pellets, along with additives to give the plastic desired qualities, such as strength or flexibility. The pellets will need to be formed into the various parts of the product, so a mold must be designed and cut from steel. The precision of the mold depends on the specifications of the product. How much variance is permitted from the specification is called the "tolerance." So surgical instruments need a much tighter set of mold tolerances than, say, a bottle cap. But a bottle cap isn't that easy to make either. Take a look at those tiny threads that interlock the inside of the cap with the spout of the bottle. If just one of those threads is out of alignment, then the cap won't twist properly.

There are different kinds of molding processes, like blow molding, in which molten plastic is exhaled into hollow shapes like bottles; or injection molding, in which the molten plastic is pushed into an impression to form a solid object. Once the mold is designed and produced, the fabrication of parts begins. Then the parts must be assembled and painted; then packaged, which requires its own set of manufacturing processes, such as forming boxes from cardboard inputs, labeling, and shrink-wrapping, and tying those annoying metal twisty things around each part of the toy. Now the final product is ready to go on its journey to the customer.

The line of players looks something like that shown in Figure 5.1. In business parlance, this arrangement is called a "supply chain" or, if you want to sound hip, a "supply web." In America and Europe, these chains are highly evolved forms of commerce. In the early days of the industrial revolution, the chains were long, gangly, and chaotic, glutted with many firms large and small, some serving a purpose, others not. Each operation was handled by a

5.1　A supply chain

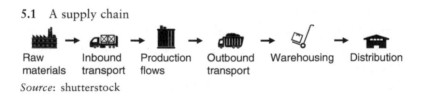

Raw　　　Inbound　　Production　　Outbound　　Warehousing　　Distribution
materials　transport　flows　　　transport

Source: shutterstock

discrete, specialized player. But, over time, the system became streamlined or "rationalized." Some firms were driven out of business, while others were absorbed and integrated into larger firms.

Today's platform for making things – whether it's goods or agriculture – tends to be pretty integrated and efficient. Domestic supply chains usually run on a minimum number of firms. So to make that toy in the United States, the discrete functions of manufacturing – the mold design and fabrication, the product creation, painting, and assembly, the packaging and labeling – will usually all occur under one roof.

The glaring exception to this rule is a supply chain that has been globalized. The allure of cheap input costs has driven many companies over the past three decades to diversify their upstream suppliers, turning to facilities overseas for intermediate inputs and assembly. Toys, consumer electronics, cars, medicines, even airplanes usually have long, complex, cross-border supply chains, which are often opaque. And when that chain extends into China, the risk magnifies significantly because, in China, it will typically take two to three times as many firms than in the United States to make and bring a product to market – whether that's an apple or an oil rig. Instead of moving through five or six firms, a product will often move through twelve, eighteen, or even more.

Fragmentation

If you imagine how risky an individual Chinese firm can be, imagine that risk compounded with each player that handles the goods. China's long, opaque supply chains exacerbate the risk that products will be damaged, contaminated, or spoiled along the way.

In business parlance, Chinese supply chains are described as "fragmented," meaning several firms are required to do a job that should take just one. And they're not just fragmented in one part of the chain. Severe fragmentation afflicts every node of food and product manufacturing. So instead of one factory to make a product, you may have four or five – a primary manufacturer and several subcontractors. Instead of inbound and outbound transportation each handled by one firm, there are often several firms involved in each step as goods pass through hauler after hauler. And middlemen of varying sizes and functions glut the chain at each node.

There are many causes for this fragmentation that are idiosyncratic to China's political economy. In an attempt to create a system that could house, feed, and, above all, provide maximum employment for a vast, far-flung, and growing population, Chairman Mao set up each province as self-sufficient. So a province would have its own steel mills, breweries, clothing manufacturers, auto plants, and chemical factories. Production outputs were planned by the central government and carried out by the provinces.

When Deng Xiaoping took the helm from Mao, he tried to steer China away from the horrific period that had just been endured, in which an omnipotent central government used its power to inflict wide-scale "reforms" that killed millions of people. Deng sought to wrest power from the central government and vest it in the provinces, enabling them to enact and enforce their own laws and to collect and spend their own funds.

In addition to experimenting with politics (federalism), Deng also experimented with China's economy (privatization). He supported the widespread adoption of Township and Village Enterprises (TVEs), in which individuals could form their own companies in partnership with local municipalities. In Deng's own words, the oncoming wave of TVEs was like an army emerging from the forest. Thousands of TVEs were formed, new entrants into the economy that rushed into industries with low capital requirements, such as apparel and toys. In many ways, these small businesses blazed the trail for China's emerging market economy.

Yet, despite divesting certain powers to the provinces and supporting (to some degree) the adoption of private forms of corporate ownership, the central government did hold on to one important power, as chief employer of government officials through the Chinese Communist Party. Advancement within the party structure was based on economic performance. If a province hit its growth targets, the officials were promoted. Nothing much has changed since then. Since the days of Deng, local officials' priorities, then, are almost exclusively economic growth, maximum employment, and tax inflows; a distant fourth is social welfare, and only if that supports stability.[1]

Though this bargain with the central government has allowed certain provinces to rocket up in wealth and prestige, federalism has augmented risk in China's manufacturing and agricultural sectors. Remember that China is not, as is often presumed, a capitalist economy with an autocratic regime. It's a hybrid economy, part communist, part capitalist. In China, they call it Chinese socialism, or capitalism with Chinese characteristics.

What has resulted from this belt-and-suspenders economy is a situation where descendants of Mao's original state-owned firms exist alongside hundreds of thousands of small and mid-sized nonstate-owned firms. Many of the dominant local companies are either owned by or closely aligned with local government officials and their families. These companies are often the engines of provincial economic growth. Their output helps the province's economic numbers. They deliver tax revenues. They employ workers. The better they do, the greater the chances for local political advancement – and, often, the more padding to the personal bank accounts of high-placed officials.

So these firms are usually shielded from competition. It's very common for provinces to employ tariff and non-tariff barriers to protect their home companies. A good example is the taxi fleet in Shanghai. If you've been to Shanghai, you'll have rattled around in the Volkswagen Santana. The Shanghai government owns part of the Volkswagen joint venture that makes these cars. So, to prevent rival Citroëns made in Hubei province from encroaching on Santana's taxi monopoly, the Shanghai government demands very high "license fees" on any non-Santana car. Hubei's government, in turn, dictates that all its governmental agencies buy Citroëns.[2]

These barriers hinder evolution and keep fragmentation entrenched. It arguably took America a century to rationalize its supply chains, sped by the dynamics of American capitalism. Private property rights and free flows of capital provided the ability to roll up smaller, specialized firms into larger, integrated firms. In China, it will probably take much longer, if it happens at all, because rationalizing China's supply chains would mean reforming its entire system of governance – not only making local bosses act against their own economic interest but also requiring the radical reform of China's closed financial system. In order to incentivize companies to acquire and merge with complementary companies, China's financial sector would need to be liberalized in a way that disfavors the state-owned firms. A market-based banking system and a vibrant private equity industry, underpinned by strong rule of law and contract enforcement, would need to be in place before supply chains could be rationalized. These are big reforms that go against the essence of China's closed communist system.

So China evolves in sputtering half measures. Part capitalist, part communist, Mao's state-owned relics mingled with nonstate-owned firms have created a mess. A fragmented, disorganized, complex, opaque supply chain. Any company – Chinese or otherwise – trying to do business on the mainland grapples with this complexity. China's supply chains are so fragmented, it's very hard to have visibility into the makings of a product and therefore hard to control quality.

Toys

Some of America's most respected companies have run aground on these fragmented shoals. Consider Mattel, the world's largest toy company. If publicity talking points are a window on the corporate soul, then Mattel's messaging reveals a sleeping giant, just weeks before its massive "Made in China" recalls hit. In a feature profile in July of 2007, "Toymaking in China, Mattel's Way," the *New York Times* portrayed Mattel as the gold standard in China manufacturing, an impression that was reinforced by Mattel's own staff and outside academics. Mattel had invested in China "before it was cool," says M. Eric Johnson, a management professor at the Tuck School of Business at Dartmouth, "and they learned to do business there in a good way. They understood the importance of protecting their brand."[3]

Yet it seems that pride goeth before the recall. While Mattel was preening in the pages of the *New York Times*, lead-laced toys were quietly rolling off the production line. A few weeks later, reports of lead contamination caused Mattel to recall nearly one million toys – the seventeenth recall in ten years – and its brand (and stock price) were in free fall. If you believed Mattel's press, it shouldn't have happened. In the *New York Times* article, the key to Mattel's mastery of China, according to outside advisors such as

Professor Johnson, was that it had invested in its own Chinese factories, twelve at the time of the recalls. Mattel presumed that asserting command-and-control over its own suppliers would eliminate risk.

Yet Mattel's problems in China highlight how difficult it is even for experienced international companies to manage the risks that come with China's fragmented supply chain – even when they own their own in-country factories. Subcontractors hoisted Mattel on its own petard. Many of Mattel's product lines were farmed out to 30–40 outside vendors. Those vendors, in turn, would job out the work to subcontractors that hired still other sub-subcontractors and even sub-sub-subcontractors. So although Mattel owned local factories, and even audited its outside contractors, it had not audited any of the subcontractors. A critical mistake – and one that would introduce significant risk to the process because, in China, the farther down the subcontractor rabbit hole you go, the riskier and riskier the companies you tend to encounter.

Mattel's two massive lead paint recalls in 2007 involved outside vendors that Mattel had worked with for many years – Lee Der Industrial, for 15 years, and Early Light Industrial, for 20 years. Yet, in both cases, the trusted vendors had subcontracted to firms that Mattel had not inspected. Even with those subcontractors in play, though, the lead problems should have been avoided, if you look at Mattel's manufacturing rulebook. Vendors must buy paint from approved suppliers. However, Lee Der Industrial, Mattel's vendor on the first recall, purchased paint from two nonapproved suppliers, Dongxin and Zhongxin, which, in turn, purchased lead-laden yellow paint pigment from a company that has since disappeared, Mingdai, which Mattel thinks was a trading company. Mighty Mattel, laid low by a sub-subcontractor. Similarly, Early Light Industrial, responsible for producing toys in the second recall, subcontracted the painting to Hong Li Da. It is thought that Hong Li Da chose to use alternative paint when a tub provided by Early Light ran out.

"Toymaking in China, Mattel's Way" in the *New York Times* eerily presages the cause of the massive recall about to come. The article mentions Elisha Chan, Mattel's director of product integrity and corporate responsibility, who "is charged with guarding against dangerous defects like lead-based paint."[4] Chan comments how Mattel's suppliers are "closely monitored" to guard against "fake or tainted supplies." Not so much. Toys doused in lead-laced paint snuck through Mattel's lines of defense, as well as those of the outside vendors that also had lead-detecting equipment.

Luxury Cars

Mattel's struggle is far from unique. Every industry sector in China is a fragmented thicket, and manufacturing is typically a murky, multi-tiered affair. A similar case is luxury carmaker Aston Martin, which recalled most of the cars it built since late 2007 – that's 17,590 cars – because a substandard plastic was used in the accelerator pedal arm.[5] As with Mattel's paint, Aston Martin's manufacturing manual specified what polymer must be purchased by vendors – a plastic produced by DuPont. Yet the counterfeit plastic that was used instead of the DuPont product meant the accelerator pedal could break off while driving. That would put a rather serious crimp on James Bond's getaway plans.

Like Mattel's lead-based paint, Aston Martin's counterfeit plastic hid amidst a long and shadowy supply chain. The accelerator pedal supplier was Precision Varionic International (PVI), a firm based in Swindon, England. PVI hired a subcontractor in Hong Kong, Fast Forward Tooling, to make

the accelerator pedal arm. Fast Forward hired a sub-
subcontractor in China, Shenzhen Kexiang Mould Tool,
which purchased the plastic from Synthetic Plastic Raw
Material of Dongguan, China.[6] Aston Martin is one of
the most prestigious automotive brands in the world. Shenzhen Kexiang is a tiny company, with five used injection
molding machines, registered capital of US$163,000, and 45
employees.[7] Like Mattel, Aston Martin was undone by a
pipsqueak.

Plastics News magazine, a prominent trade publication,
undertook its own investigation into what had happened. It
reads like an industrial version of *Rashomon*. Conflicting
versions of events make it difficult to figure out not just who
was at fault, but what actually happened. In an interview in
his factory, the general manager of Shenzhen Kexiang stated
flatly that his company had no record of ever even *working*
with Fast Forward Tooling. Of course, there was that one
time when some of Fast Forward's staff visited Kexiang and
asked them to produce some samples, using molds and materials that Fast Forward provided. Hmmmm. Already the
story sounds fishy: no record of having worked with Fast
Forward, except they did, but under unusual circumstances.
Why would Fast Forward need Kexiang to produce samples
with Fast Forward's molds and materials? To see whether
Kexiang's staff knew how to operate an injection molding
machine? Curiouser and curiouser. The general manager
added that he could not say for certain whether Kexiang had
produced the accelerator arm, as his company does many
jobs for contractors that frequently do not divulge the
end buyer.[8]

We see a similar muddle in Mattel's own investigation
into its lead paint recalls. Mattel struggled to come to grips
with what actually happened. Where the offending paint

was sourced from, how, and why. China's fragmented chain is like a shattered hall of mirrors. When unsafe products emerge, it's difficult to see exactly where they came from.

Mattel and Aston Martin are unfortunately not isolated cases. It's a common misperception that these types of large, global firms are policing their upstream supply chains, shamed into action after embarrassing revelations going back to 1996, when Kathy Lee Gifford's clothing line was exposed as made in a Honduran sweatshop. Yet each of the major China safety lapses over the past decade involved major multinational firms that lacked supply chain oversight – Mattel's lead-laced toys, Baxter International's tainted blood thinner, Fonterra's poisoned baby formula, Raytheon's counterfeit night vision parts for navy helicopters, Nestlé's Alpo doggie death treats, Firestone's flimsy tires, and on and on.

The year 2007 was an especially bad one for China recalls. Toys, toothpaste, tires, tools, bibs, batteries, dog food, dry wall – defective Chinese products were discovered in the United States again and again. Yet the worst was yet to come. In 2008, there were the deaths of almost 150 Americans from tainted blood thinner and the poisoning of hundreds of thousands of Chinese babies from formula laced with an industrial chemical.

During the torrent of 2007 recalls, the Chinese government tried to calm things down. Its Minister of Commerce, Bo Xilai, stated that more than 99 percent of Chinese exports are safe.[9] Yes, that would be the same Bo Xilai who was later convicted of bribery, embezzlement, and abuse of power as the head of a massive patronage network, while serving as the Communist Party chief in Chongqing.

The tainted official claiming China's exports are untainted.

Of course, corruption is often a factor in unsafe Chinese products. In an op-ed for the *New York Times,* "China's Corrupt Food Chain," Yanzhong Huang, a senior fellow at the Council on Foreign Relations, posits that the ongoing problem of China's food safety demonstrates "the collapse of the country's business ethics."[10]

That notion reinforces what we usually hear. With each new "Made in China" safety scandal, the western media and Chinese authorities seek out evildoers to blame. But that's a rather convenient and simplistic way of looking at the situation. Certainly, corruption plays a role in many of the safety lapses. Counterfeit inputs are substituted for real ones in an effort to shore up the bottom line. Or duplicate sets of books are used to dupe safety auditors. But often China's safety issues are not simply a matter of morality. Inferior technology, differing standards, undercapitalization, lack of organizational accountability, or just plain screwing up – all these factors conspire to add risk to the outputs. It's not always a case of good and evil. And China's supply chain is so complex and opaque that these errors usually pass through the system unnoticed, despite good intentions. Remember, Mattel's vendors had lead-detecting equipment and had been faithful suppliers to Mattel for years.

The "Made in China" safety lapses, then, are not so much a symbol of China's ethical collapse. Framing them in moral terms plays into the perception that the Chinese are somehow intentionally trying to poison us. This fuels the kind of hate and fearmongering that we heard so often from politicians in the last few election cycles, narratives that demonized China and cast America in the role of hapless victim.

Rather, the safety lapses are the result of a manufacturing and agricultural platform riddled with risk, in which errors and omissions are refracted and magnified through concentric circles of danger. The whole system is to blame for these ongoing safety failures, not a handful of evildoers.

Logistics

A good example of how the system, and not a discrete set of bad actors, can spoil a product can be seen in China's logistics industry. We often hear about how China's investments in roads and bridges have created a formidable competitor, how we're falling behind because of our aging infrastructure. Never mind that these roads and bridges keep collapsing. Or the glaring fact that the infrastructure China has built has yet to be integrated into a smoothly working system.

Like every other industry in China, its logistics sector is severely afflicted by fragmentation. Local protectionism and barriers to foreign firms' investment have created an unruly monster. It's estimated that China has more than 700,000 trucking companies, most of which have small fleets of just a few trucks. In comparison, the United States has about 7,000 trucking firms.[11] The rise of e-commerce in China has exacerbated this problem. Thousands of transportation companies have sprouted up to handle "last mile" order deliveries, many of which are merely a guy with a bicycle and a cell phone.

The delivery giants FedEx and UPS, so ubiquitous in the United States, have managed to carve out a tiny sliver of the Chinese market, with FedEx commanding just 1 percent of share. With local deliveries being handled by little trucking companies that win business by cutting their prices, the big firms are starting to abandon the local markets. DHL recently pulled out of a money-losing partnership with Chinese state-owned Sinotrans, quitting local deliveries to focus on the international market.

It's easy to understand why. The way goods flow in China is a lot like a late-night taxi ride I once took from Ningbo to Hangzhou. As we bumped through the night, each time we entered a new town, the taxi was flagged down and stopped, and I was hustled from one car into another. Goods are treated the same way as they pass from one municipality to the next – the local firm gets control. The goods are moved from one truck to another, documents and manifests are handed over, sometimes money must change hands, and the next mom-and-pop operation takes over. Goods are often transferred up to a dozen times in their journey from point to point, adding to their total delivered cost and, of course, the risk that they could become damaged or spoiled.

Imagine you're trying to expedite perishable products through this labyrinth. In the West, perishable goods travel along what is known as a "cold chain," and there is a high degree of technology and coordination involved. Products move from climate-controlled warehouses to climate-controlled trucks to climate-controlled ships and planes without a breach in the chain.

China's cold chain is often sketchy or non-existent. A typical example is ice cream which, in China, usually proceeds from a freezer at the ice-cream maker to a series of hot trucks and warehouses, where it melts. Then it's refrozen at the destination point. Most warehouses in China are old and lack refrigeration. But even logistics companies that do have cold facilities often leave the refrigeration off to save costs. Then they switch on the cooling when the goods arrive. So the cold products are going into hot rooms that gradually cool down: again, a case of hardware that may be comparable to the West, such as a modern cooler, but procedures and standards that are sub-par.

Ice cream that's melted and has been refrozen tastes gray and crystalline. But imagine if the product moving through

China's logistics is a medicine that needs to be kept cool. You see how fragmentation and different operating standards can lead to contamination and danger. It's not always a case of corruption or unethical behavior. The risk that comes with fragmentation in and of itself is often enough to poison your product.

Pharmaceuticals

But sometimes, when corruption is involved, fragmentation obscures the wrongdoing and makes it harder to identify the lapse. With the tragic case of heparin, a blood thinner manufactured by Baxter International, counterfeit inputs were at fault, but blame can't be placed only at China's door. Baxter could have been doing a much better job at policing its own upstream supply chain. And the US Food and Drug Administration was also asleep at the switch.

In 2008, tainted batches of heparin killed almost 150 Americans and injured hundreds more. This incident, which occurred in US hospitals, drove home how dangerous Chinese imports can be. This wasn't a case of babies dying in some faraway clinics halfway around the world. This was a case of Americans dying in American hospitals from tainted medicine.

Heparin, an anticoagulant, is made from the mucous tissues found in pig intestines. Given China's vast swine supply, the country is therefore a major producer of the raw materials for heparin.[12] The medicine's supply chain, then, begins at pig slaughterhouses, which in China are famously unsanitary. The intestines are trucked to small workshops that extract the mucous tissue. The trucking is a risk point in which heat could contaminate the goods, and the workshops, you can bet, are not what is known in the industry as "clean rooms." What comes from the pig intestine scraping is called "heparin crude," which often in China is sold to a consolidator (a middleman, which adds another opportunity for risk of contamination), to still other factories that refine the crude heparin into the "active pharmaceutical ingredient" (API) – at which point the API is combined, often at still another factory, with other inactive ingredients to form the finished product.[13]

The Centers for Disease Control and Prevention discovered patients were having adverse reactions to heparin in early 2008, yet the regulators and inspectors struggled to determine exactly where the bad batches came from, though the source has been confirmed as China.[14] In 2012, the FDA discovered fourteen Chinese suppliers of contaminated heparin, in addition to the original eight that the FDA had red-flagged in 2008.[15]

What is known is that the contaminated heparin batches were adulterated with a substance that mimics crude heparin but is about a hundred times cheaper to make and can go undetected in standard testing. Investigators believe that an outbreak of swine flu in 2007 caused a sharp tightening of the pig supply, driving up prices, and putting pressure on firms to wring profits out of faking the crude. But exactly where in the murky, long chain this happened investigators are still not sure. In trying to pinpoint the source of the bad batches, they found adulterated heparin in the active pharmaceutical ingredient made at Baxter's API producer, Scientific Protein Laboratories-Changzhou (SPL-CZ), and also in the crude heparin supplied by SPL-CZ's upstream consolidators.

That the bad batches of heparin wended their way into the US drug supply illustrates why Chinese fragmentation is so risky – and how far-reaching the problem goes. Really, the trouble starts with a gaping loophole in Chinese law. Chemical suppliers that are not qualified to make pharmaceutical-grade products often produce medicines anyway, but are not regulated by the China Food and Drug Administration (CFDA). SPL-CZ was registered as a chemical company and therefore fell outside the regulatory jurisdiction of the CFDA.[16]

Then Baxter, the company on the front lines, assumed a lax stance regarding its Chinese suppliers. Though it began to source product from SPL-CZ in 2004, it did not actually audit the factory until three years later. Baxter instead took the word of a different company which had done its own audit on SPL-CZ.[17] In what would be comic, save for the fact that so many lives were lost, the Food and Drug Administration also approved SPL-CZ sight unseen because they mistook SPL-CZ for another firm in the FDA database[18] (this from the agency that assures us it screens 100 percent of imports electronically). And to make matters worse, the US Government Accountability Office discovered the FDA's databases were in disarray, making it impossible to determine which plants had been approved for export and which hadn't.[19]

Once Baxter and the FDA started to investigate how bad batches were originating from China, it was discovered that there was significant manufacturing risk at the API supplier, SPL-CZ. Typical of Chinese firms, SPL-CZ was found to have lax quality control of its own manufacturing process and of the raw material inputs it would source from upstream suppliers to make its products.[20] SPL-CZ is a familiar sad case. Whether making pharmaceuticals or offshore drilling rigs or signal switches for high-speed rail, Chinese firms tend to lack effective quality control of their in-house process and of the components they source from other firms.

When Baxter and the FDA dispatched investigators to try to find the source of the adulterated heparin, upstream consolidators and workshops barred their doors.[21] All too often, Chinese firms and officials block US inspectors – whether they're from the FDA or the buyer. And at the government-to-government level, Chinese authorities have resisted American attempts to beef up the FDA's local staff of inspectors. Today, the FDA has a woefully small skeleton crew in China – just 27 people tasked with policing the vast amount of Chinese food and drug exports to the United States. The FDA sees this as a victory, having had to fight hard to increase its staff from just thirteen and, before that, from two.

It was the heparin incident that prompted the FDA to open an inspection office in China in the first place. Until then, the United States had no inspectors stationed in China at all. Yet pharmaceutical exports to the United States from China had been rising sharply year after year. From 2003 to 2013, that volume increased 192 percent. After the heparin-induced deaths and injuries in 2007 and 2008, Congress appropriated funds for the FDA to increase its local staff, but China pushed back. The new inspectors were not granted visas from the Chinese government until Vice President Joe Biden interceded in the fall of 2013.

Still, with 27 inspectors to police more than 4,000 Chinese exporters, the FDA is trying to hold back a tidal wave with a drinking cup. It is estimated that about 80 percent of the active ingredients and chemicals in American drugs are imported – and about half of the volume of those imports comes from China and India.[22] But about 90 percent of India's pharmaceutical raw materials are sourced in China. (And India has yet to set up an inspection office in China.)[23] So we can presume that it's really China that is the primary upstream source for about half of the imported APIs and pharmaceutical chemicals that are used to make the drugs we ingest.

In the face of ongoing Chinese resistance, the FDA still tries to obtain temporary visas for US inspectors to travel to China to conduct inspections. In 2010, the FDA did 46 drug inspections, and in 2011 that number nearly doubled to 84. But, at the current pace, it would take over a decade for the FDA to inspect all of China's drug exporters.[24] In testimony before the US–China Economic and Security Review Commission in March 2014, Christopher Hickey, who runs the FDA's China office, in noting that at the time of the hearing, the number of full-time drug inspectors stationed in China was still at a pathetic *two*, said, "We place primary responsibility on industry."

That's not very reassuring, as industry has demonstrated again and again that it shirks its responsibility. With the heparin case, Baxter, like so many other multinationals faced with safety issues in China, took a laid-back approach to policing its supply chain, choosing to not even inspect its primary API suppliers, much less *their* upstream suppliers. In any commercial interaction, the buyer wields great power. It's the power of the purse. Either you comply with my quality standards, or I take my business elsewhere. Unfortunately, Baxter chose to put patients at extreme risk by relying on audits from other companies, on the totally overwhelmed FDA, and on China's own authorities who often look the other way when a local favored company is in the crosshairs.

The scary reality, then, is that the drugs emerging from China are dangerous and largely unregulated, moving through a long, complex, and opaque supply chain that not only includes thousands of manufacturers with dubious quality control but also layer after layer of intermediaries – often six or more – each of which adds risk that the products will be contaminated, while the last line of defense is a US industry which the FDA is hoping will step up but typically doesn't. The sheer complexity of these supply chains contributed to why Baxter and 14 other US firms were caught flat-footed by the heparin contamination scandal.

The Pentagon

But Baxter is by no means alone. The US Department of Defense, with a yearly budget approaching half a trillion dollars, has been hamstrung by China's fragmented supply chain, too. In November 2011, the Senate's Committee on Armed Services held a hearing to review results from an investigation it had conducted to expose counterfeit electronic parts being incorporated into US defense systems. Over a two-year period, defense contractors and testing companies flagged more than 1,800 instances of counterfeit items across a total of one million individual parts. Of these cases, committee investigators selected a hundred, over 70 percent of which were traced back to China.

The trail is circuitous and sheds light on the complexity not just of China's supply chain, but of cross-border supply chains in the defense industry. According to the committee's findings, most counterfeit electronic parts begin as "e-waste" – discarded electronics, such as computers, circuit boards, and cell phones – exported from the United States and other countries to China as scrap, where the parts are dismantled and hand washed, often in rivers, dried in the sun on city sidewalks, then disguised to look new and sold to Chinese retailers, which export them back to the United States.

One example cited by the committee described how counterfeit parts found their way into the night vision and targeting capability of a particular model of navy helicopter. The US navy procured the system from Raytheon, the large defense contractor, which purchased the parts from Texas

Spectrum Electronics, a subcontractor. Texas Spectrum, in turn, bought the counterfeit transistors from an electronics recycler and distributor, Technology Conservation Group, which bought them from Thomson Broadcast of Massachusetts, a purveyor of "e-scrap." Since the parts appeared to be in their original packaging, Technology Conservation Group marketed these parts as unused. But the trail doesn't end there. Thomson Broadcast bought the parts from E-Warehouse in California, which bought them from a distributor in the United Kingdom, Pivotal Electronics, which purchased the parts from Huajie Electronics Limited in Shenzhen, China, which procured them from e-scrap recyclers.

Aside from the systemic failure of all these intermediaries to inspect the parts they procured from China, like Baxter, Mattel, and Aston Martin, the buyer in this case, the US government, also shares the blame. The buying criteria for the Department of Defense usually dictate that contracts must be awarded to the cheapest bidder, and so companies like Raytheon pursue low-cost inputs on the open market, exposing product integrity to risk. Additionally, government contracts often stipulate that a certain amount of the work must be carried out by small businesses, a requirement which also adds risk to the integrity of the supply chain, as a guy with a phone and a laptop adds no value or oversight to the process but often adds risk by making the chain more opaque.[25]

No matter how sophisticated your product – whether a blood thinner or an oil rig – it's as safe as its riskiest part. So an unknown number of US navy helicopter night vision systems are powered by scrap that was scrubbed in rivers and drip-dried on pavements. Interestingly enough, the recycling of e-scrap into counterfeit products is often not viewed by the Chinese as fraudulent. In his testimony before the

Senate Armed Services Committee, Thomas Sharpe, Vice President of SMT Corporation, which authenticates and sources parts for the defense industry, visited Shantou, a city where most of the counterfeiting seems to occur. "It is interesting to note that counterfeiting performed in Shantou," says Sharpe, "from speaking to the people there, was not regarded as IP theft or wrong in any way whatsoever. It was seen more as a positive green initiative for the repurposing and reuse of perfectly good used product."

That's quaint, until you hear about the many steps the counterfeiters take to evade detection. "These include a new surface recoating material that is immune to acetone surface-permanency tests that has a surface that looks just like the manufacturer's top coat," says Sharpe, "a process to remove manufacturer part markings without requiring surface recoatings...And a process to remove and recondition the top surfaces of ceramic components."

These counterfeit parts are then sold in large marketplaces, such as one in Shenzhen, known as the largest of its kind. Of all the parts sold there, 30–40 percent are thought to be counterfeit. Local buyers know they will receive as much as a 70 percent discount on these fake items versus the real McCoy, so it's a popular spot.[26]

Other cases were cited in the hearing, including informational display units deployed in US air force C-27J military aircraft. The display units let the pilot know about the status of the airplane, such as fuel usage, navigation, and any warning notices. After one of these units failed in the field, testing revealed that a memory chip was counterfeit and the investigation began.

The chips were supplied to the US air force by L-3 Display Systems, a division of L-3 Communications. Predictably, L-3 sits atop a long chain of suppliers wending back to China. L-3 purchased the goods from Alenia Aeronautica, a subcontractor to L-3. Alenia sourced the goods from sub-subcontractor Global IC Trading Group, a California-based electronics distributor, which bought the parts from sub-sub-subcontractor Hong Dark Electronic Trade in Shenzhen, China. According to Senator Carl Levin's opening statement, "In total the committee discovered that Hong Dark supplied more than 28,000 electronic parts to divisions within L-3 Communications, and at least 14,000 of those parts have already been identified as suspect counterfeit."

A third example was provided: a critical component used in the ice detection module for a navy P-8A aircraft used for anti-submarine and anti-surface warfare purposes. Counterfeiting was discovered when one of these modules failed mid-flight. The component in question broke loose from the module.

At that point, Boeing, the airplane's manufacturer, started to retrace the supply chain to figure out what happened. The supplier of the part was BAE Systems, which provided the ice detection module to Boeing. When BAE engineers warned Boeing that the part in question created a liability risk to the functioning of the aircraft, Boeing did not alert the navy and its other customers for more than a year – and only after it had been contacted by the Senate Committee.

It seems BAE bought the parts from Tandex Test Labs in California. Tandex had, in turn, bought them from Abacus Technologies of Florida. Abacus had bought them from A Access Electronics in Shenzhen – actually *an unnamed affiliate* of A Access Electronics, but the payment was wired to A Access's bank account in Shenzhen, China.

Interestingly enough, the chairman, Senator Levin, and ranking member, Senator John McCain, drew differing conclusions from this investigation. Levin stated emphatically, "let us be clear, though. The risk is not created by the contractors." True, but the risk is perpetrated by the contractors.

Ultimately, the contractors are the last line of defense. Sophisticated companies with deep, deep pockets, they certainly have the capability and the means to test these systems to insure that they work properly and that counterfeit parts haven't insinuated themselves into the mix. They also have the personnel to police their supply chain and should have been wary when the ultimate sources of their parts were based in China. That fact, in and of itself, should have thrown up red flags – given that these parts would be going into "mission critical" military aircraft.

Senator Levin recommended that "We must change our acquisition rules to ensure that the cost of replacing suspect counterfeit parts is paid by the contractor, not the taxpayer." Well, that's a good suggestion, but what about changing the procurement rules so that they stop incentivizing contractors to seek out lowest-bid, cheapest parts – which puts pressure on the supply chain to go counterfeit over genuine in the first place?

Senator John McCain, on the other hand, had this to say in summation: "The Chinese Government can stop it. And if the Chinese Government does not stop it, then it continues to pose a national security risk." But the Chinese government can't stop it, and they're trying. After the myriad safety scandals started to emerge in 2007, the central government deployed thousands of inspectors and police across the country in an attempt to shut down firms that were making harmful, fake products – especially in food and drugs, but also in electronics. The problem is that most of these offending firms are small and can disappear, reopening in some other incarnation in the future.

Senator McCain's formulation portrays an omnipotent Chinese autocracy that can simply flip a switch to get favored outcomes. If anything, the Chinese government has both hands tied behind its back. Its own policies, most notably its

closed financial system, have exacerbated this problem, pro-
hibiting the free flows of capital to integrate and rationalize
markets. But they're damned-if-they-do, damned-if-they-
don't once again. The system is kept closed to avoid the kind
of financial crisis that led to the collapse of Thailand's
economy in the 1990s. But in keeping their system closed,
they're hobbling their competitiveness and preventing the
modernization of their economy, not to mention threatening
the health and safety of their citizens and of every country
they export to. China's policy of federalism also hampers
their efforts to stop counterfeiting. If a local counterfeiting
firm makes big money, hires many workers, and is politically
well connected, local party bosses will fight to protect that
firm from any Beijing-mandated crackdown. So the authorities are left with having to rout out offending grains of sand
on a coastline.

Dairy

China's scandals in the dairy industry are another good
example of how fragmentation in the supply chain can sub-
stantially increase risk – and how blame is shared among
many stakeholders, not just corrupt counterfeiters. Though
several dairy companies were entangled in the melamine
controversy, the main antagonists were Sanlu, a Chinese
state-owned dairy company, and its partner Fonterra, the
giant New Zealand dairy firm, which owned 43 percent of
Sanlu at the time. Like Baxter and Mattel, Boeing and BAE,
Fonterra is an industry leader, with a top reputation for
quality. But Fonterra ran aground on China's fragmented
supply chain like the rest of them.
    The raw material input to baby formula is milk. So we
start our journey on the farm. China has millions of tiny
family farms, as many as 180 million or more. And it's

estimated that there are about 12 million dairy cows in China, most of which live on these small farms, milked by hand. Bad inputs lead to bad outputs. The farmers are poor, the land is unforgiving. Malnourished cows yield milk that's low in protein.

Dairy farmers go on to sell their milk to local consolidators, but if the milk comes from a sickly dairy cow, tests would reveal low protein levels. So the common practice has been for "protein boosting" powders to be added to liquid milk, either by farmers or by milk collection agents.

Put yourself in their sandals for a moment. Imagine you're a farmer barely eking by. You've got one pathetic cow. And a local businessman shows up at your door selling you something in a brown paper bag that he says will improve the quality of your milk. If it means the milk from your one cow will sell – and not potentially be rejected – allowing you and your family to stay alive longer, then you take the brown paper bag and mix the powder into your milk.

This practice has been going on for years, and dairy processors downstream got wise to the additives in "protein boosters" and adjusted their testing to screen them out. So melamine became a popular additive, as it's difficult to detect. A nitrogen-rich industrial chemical used in fertilizer and plastics, it looks like protein in dairy tests. This new, sneaky way to deceive dairy buyers caught on quickly. Additives companies would purchase scrap melamine from the local chemical factories to create their protein-booster. There are more than half a million additives companies in China, most of which are small, with ten or fewer employees. These little, local additive companies would then sell the melamine-spiked powder to farmers or milk collection agents, who would add it to their liquid milk supply, which would then go on to be sold to more middlemen and wholesalers (adding to the risk) and finally to large dairy processors.

As with heparin, pricing pressure was certainly a cause of the widespread adulteration of milk. The price of the inputs kept rising. Farmers complained that soy meal prices had increased 60 percent in the two years leading up to the scandal, while buyers like Sanlu kept lowering their offer prices for milk. As margins were squeezed, adding melamine allowed farmers and middlemen to scrape by. So Sanlu and Fonterra share blame for exacerbating the conditions that gave rise to the melamine scandal. Aside from being asleep at the switch, and failing to detect industrial fertilizer in their baby formula, they created top-down pressure when input costs were rising. A recipe for certain danger.

"The problem was and still is that anyone can become a dairy supplier," a professor at Renmin University, Xiang Zhikong, commented, "and anyone can own or invest in third-party dairy stations. There are no licensing requirements or any other sort of quality regulatory standards."[27] This makes for an impossible situation from a regulatory standpoint. As with trying to police the pesticides in crops or the antibiotics in meat and fish, whatever feeble screening mechanisms are in place at collections stations or local wholesale markets are totally overwhelmed.

And those that could have intervened were often on the take. A criminal prosecution found that 30 firms were involved in spiking the milk and bribing the local inspectors. But the melamine problem was much more far-reaching than just Sanlu-Fonterra products. Dairy from 20 companies around the world was tainted, including major multinationals like Cadbury, Unilever, Heinz, and Pizza Hut.

Sanlu broke the news of its safety lapse just days before the start of the Beijing Olympics. The central government had already made it clear. China would put its best foot forward to the world. There was to be *no bad news*. So the authorities hid the scandal from parents for many months.

Once word got out, several ministries in the central government tried to crack down on melamine adulteration in the dairy industry. Yet, despite beefing up enforcement and rewriting the laws governing the dairy industry, melamine-laced products continue to be exported from China.

As of 2014, pets were still being poisoned by melamine. An investigation into Nestlé Purina's Waggin' Train, the object of many pet owners' complaints, found misleading labeling in which the treats were labeled "Made in the USA," but several ingredients came from China. This, unfortunately, is a widespread problem caused by the vagaries of our antiquated labeling system. The FDA's website warns, "Packages that do not state on the label that they are made in another country may still contain ingredients sourced from China or other countries that export to the US."[28] And so consumers are left in the dark about what's safe and what's not.

Yet dairy is only the tip of the iceberg. A new investigation into food products by the Chinese magazine *Caixin* states ominously, "These publicized food safety scandals represent only a fraction of unsafe food production practices. Hundreds of chemical food additives are pumped into products that Chinese people consume every day."[29] And despite the best efforts of China's regulators, the problems won't be going away anytime soon. To Senator McCain's point that "the Chinese Government can fix it" – again, clearly, it can't. The whole system needs to be reformed to "fix it." "What we see in China is particular to a country that has a medieval farming system serving a product to a twenty-first century market," said David Mahon, managing director of Mahon China Investment Management, a Beijing research and investment advisory firm.[30]

In many ways, China's medieval agricultural sector resembles all of China's industries – primitive, undercapitalized, disorganized, and not ready for prime time. Yet the rush by multinational firms to globalize their supply chains has moved China's agriculture and manufacturing sectors to center stage, when China needed several decades – arguably a century – of development before being able to reliably perform its function as a supplier to the world.

And so, the threat from China's not-ready-for-prime-time fragmented supply chain is a dire threat to us. And to the Chinese. The latest scandal to emerge in China is rancid chicken feet being sold to Chinese restaurants – some of them with original date labels going back to 1967.[31] Beijing is working to address the continuing food safety crises. Inspectors have been dispatched across the country, laws and regulations are being rewritten, and ministries are being restructured. Yet the safety lapses continue. And they will continue for years to come, if not generations, until China can successfully implement the ground-up reforms needed to improve the system as a whole.

In the meantime, Chinese middle- and upper-class consumers see the outputs of China's broken safety system in the news, as ongoing scandals frequently make the headlines with tainted food and drugs, collapsing bridges and roads, and crumbling buildings. America looks like a utopia in comparison. Of course, we know America's system is far from perfect. Corruption, flawed regulatory oversight, and unsafe business practice afflict our system, too. But, in comparison to China, which has seen thousands of safety incidents over the past few years, it's ultimately a matter of perception. Chinese consumers believe American and European products are safer, and therefore overwhelmingly prefer them to local products.

Dairy is a good illustration. As of September of 2014, US milk futures were up 26 percent. There are a few factors that are driving this upswing. The first is dairy deregulation. As recently as ten years ago, US and EU dairy markets were essentially local, providing milk for domestic consumption. Governments stockpiled milk, which was released into the market in lean times. Dairy markets, therefore, were typically oversupplied and prices remained lower. Since then, dairy has become a global trade, and many governments have exited the industry. Pricing, therefore, is more responsive to the dips and spikes in supply and demand. The year 2013 was one of drought for New Zealand. Since many of New Zealand's cows graze in fields, which were hit hard by the lack of water, the country's dairy production sank about 30 percent, further driving up price.

But also China's demand for baby formula and dairy products keeps surging. Ongoing reports of melamine in milk products and a lack of trust in the ability of China's authorities to address the structural safety problems in China's food system are causing strong demand for imported dairy products. Usually, China accounts for about 15–20 percent of global dairy imports, but in just three months – from December of 2013 to February of 2014 – they shot up to 20–25 percent of all dairy imports.

"The demand for infant formula has gone sky high," dairy market analyst Matt Gould told the BBC. "There's a premium for foreign dairy products. People would rather have a product that says 'Made in New Zealand' or 'Made in the USA.' "[32] With hundreds of thousands of babies suffering from renal failure, you can see why.

That preference is driving up prices and supporting thousands of jobs in the US dairy industry, which is, as China's Academy of Science correctly noted, a century ahead of China's. Though the typical dairy supply chain in America involves small- to medium-sized dairy farms that sell into collectives that, in turn, sell to big processors, this system is much safer than China's for many reasons. Modern sanitary and testing practices are employed at the dairy farms, which are overseen by a functioning regulatory system and anchored by rule of law. The supply chain that connects farms to collectives to processors is much more integrated than China's. And it's not glutted with small middlemen and traders, which often use their position in the chain to wring more profits from transactions by adulterating the goods.

The pernicious problem of systemic risk in China's fragmented supply chain, then, gives rise to both the threat of unsafe Chinese imports but also to the opportunity for job creation. Milk isn't the only category. Agricultural exports to China are booming in general. And as China struggles to safely manufacture higher-value goods, American exports to China grow in aerospace, aviation, automotive, medical devices and equipment, construction machinery, nuclear power equipment, and many other products – as do Chinese investments in complementary US firms.

But fragmentation is not the last concentric circle of danger that magnifies risk in China's system. If you think the firms and farms were risky, wait till you see the regulators.

6

When Regs are Dregs

Often, we hear politicians refer to China as "Red China." They mean Communist China. Authoritarian China. Dictatorship China.

The idea of autocracy conjures up certain associations: that because China is run by an authoritarian system, somehow this makes the Chinese a more lethal competitive threat; that officials in Beijing can pull a lever and produce an outcome. This notion feeds the whole China-is-taking-over-the-world shtick. Surely, an autocratic government can "get the job done" more efficiently in maneuvering an economy. Surely, the marriage of a market economy with an authoritarian government is an unbeatable combination, making "the rise of China and the decline of America" inevitable.

When Senator John McCain says, "The Chinese Government can stop it," he's tapping into this conventional wisdom. So is former Secretary of Transportation Ray LaHood, who remarked in July 2011 that "The Chinese are more successful because in their country only three people make the decision. In our country three thousand people do."[1]

But these notions couldn't be farther from the truth. Three people don't rule China. A byzantine, infighting, opaque, and sprawling bureaucracy does. The opposite of what McCain and LaHood contend is true. China's government and regulatory structures hinder competitiveness, add risk to its economic outputs, and actually *prevent* China from fully asserting power in the world. Zooming out from chains of companies to the regulatory regimes that must govern them, one encounters another concentric circle of danger. Just as severe fragmentation afflicts China's industries, introducing further risk into the system, fragmentation also afflicts China's regulators. So, as a product moves through China's supply chain, it encounters increasing exposure to risk that it will be unsafe. From the contaminated ground, to poorly run firms, to long, opaque supply chains, and finally to a regulatory regime so fractured, infighting, and often corrupt, that what should be the last line of defense is another ring of risk.

Regulatory Fragmentation

There are two types of fragmentation in China that obstruct effective oversight. There's horizontal fragmentation, in which the regulation of a portfolio, such as food safety or environmental protection, is divided among several competing bureaucracies. And there's vertical fragmentation, in which power is then divided among central and local authorities. China's regulatory regimes are fractured in both directions. This makes regulatory enforcement especially difficult.

Of course, it's not a new problem. Fragmentation in China's modern governmental bureaucracies dates back to Mao. The central government was divided into ministries and departments according to function. This arrangement is known in bureaucrat-speak as "silo-ing" – creating a stovepipe effect in an organization, so that the management of a portfolio is divided among several groups. As usually happens in such an organizational design, bureaucracies fight with each for budget and power to the detriment of the larger goal of effective regulation of the portfolio.

With the decentralization of power under Deng, the fracturing of the system got worse. Now you had horizontal fragmentation, in that regulatory portfolios were apportioned among several departments, and vertical fragmentation, in that these departments were further splintered into central, provincial, and municipal levels. What has emerged is a sprawling bureaucracy at war with itself.

Since the early 2000s, in an effort to improve oversight, Beijing has tried to recentralize control over certain portfolios, such as product safety and environmental protection. But the federalist system already in place, in which so much power has been vested to the localities, makes enforcement of centrally dictated regulations difficult, especially if these regulations will cost local favored companies money or restrict their ability to do business. There's an old saying in China, which is especially apt today: "The mountains are high, and the emperor is far away."

Environmental Protection

As with the business practice of a typical Chinese firm, in which the signing of a contract is the beginning of negotiations, not the end of them, the enforcement of laws often entails a protracted negotiation with the provinces.[2] You can see this play out with environmental protection regulations. Despite Beijing's aggressive efforts to crack down on the pollution of water and air, for example, many local factories still dump untreated chemicals into China's rivers and fail to curb their emissions. That's because local governmental authorities give them cover from Beijing's edicts.

When China's Ministry of Environmental Protection (MEP) tried to reduce carbon-intensive emissions in the steel industry, for instance, the enforcement of its regulations was blocked in Jiangxi and Hunan provinces, which rely on steel production as a major driver of economic growth. The Jiangxi and Hunan metal industry commissions, agencies of local government, successfully overrode the MEP's regulations in favor of local steel producers. So even when the central government's MEP tries to promulgate well-publicized and popular policies, it struggles to get these policies enforced locally.

The Green Credit Policy is another example, which seeks to tie bank lending for carbon-intensive industries to environmental assessments and the implementation of carbon-reducing standards. Yet a powerful alliance of industry, local government officials, and banks demonstrates how these sorts of central regulations are often evaded.

The Xianglu Corporation, a large Taiwanese petrochemical manufacturing company, sought to build a paraxylene (PX) plant in Changzhou, a city in Jiangsu province. PX is a chemical used in the production of PTA and PET, inputs for textiles, plastic bottles, and tires. This new factory would be a big deal for Changzhou – boosting GDP and employing many workers. Yet the PX plant would have had difficulty complying with the MEP's environmental regulations, making funding difficult. So billions of renminbi in loans were secured from Agricultural Bank of China, China Merchants Bank, and Everbright Bank. Then, Xianglu Corporation, with the support of the Changzhou government, made the case to the MEP that these loans had been secured before the Green Credit Policy was enacted (when they hadn't), and the project went forward.

As is shown in the diagram of China's environmental protection regulatory regime (Figure 6.1), the local governments sit smack in the middle of the chain of command. And when their local interests conflict with the

When Regs are Dregs

6.1   Bad air: The regulatory structure for environmental protection

Source: Christopher Marquis, Jianjun Zhang, and Yanhua Zhou, 2011, "Regulatory Uncertainty and Corporate Responses to Environmental Protection in China," *California Management Review* 54(1): 39–63

interests of central government, they will usually disregard or try to evade the dictates of Beijing. Local governments often oversee several developmental agencies, such as the Bureaus of Commerce, Transportation, and Industry and Information Technology, as well as regulatory agencies, such as local branches of the MEP. Predictably, local officials will often side with the economic development agency over the regulator if it helps grow the local economy.

Beijing is trying mightily to overcome lax law enforcement at the local level. After the heparin and dairy scandals hit, a major piece of reform was enacted to great fanfare, the 2009 Food Safety Law, which was intended to regulate the tens of thousands of tiny firms making additives for food. But Chinese shoppers on the streets of Beijing gave voice to how the system really works in a *USA Today* piece that ran in March 2009. A husband said he hoped the new law would force food producers to be safer. His wife laughed and said, "There are so many people and factories in China. At the local level they don't obey the laws of the central government. Why should this law be any different?"[3]

Quite right. Because since the law was passed in 2009, food safety scandals have not abated: if anything, they've got worse, especially in the dairy supply chain, which the new law was specifically meant to address. Tons and tons of melamine-tainted milk continue to be discovered and seized by authorities since the law was enacted.[4] Exploding watermelons, glow-in-the-dark pork, tainted meat, recycled gutter oil, fake eggs – these scandals, and more, have all broken since the Food Safety Law was enacted.

Nuclear Power

Civilian nuclear power is another example of how regulators magnify risk. Historically, the regulation of civilian nuclear power got off on the wrong foot from the very beginning. Other nuclear-powered countries enacted atomic energy laws in the early stages of their nuclear development in order to establish a legal framework for research and development, regulation, and emergency management. Great Britain enacted its atomic energy law in 1946; the United States, also in 1946; Japan in 1955; Korea in 1958.

And China? Not yet. China's central government has struggled unsuccessfully for the past three decades to produce a unifying legal foundation to govern atomic energy. A set of piecemeal laws and regulations has been promulgated instead. And many of these laws are out of date, unsuitable for the next generation of nuclear power plants that are currently being planned and built.

One important reason why China has failed to enact a basic atomic energy law is the difficulty in uniting the fractured and warring nuclear bureaucracy. As a basis for comparison, the United States has a comparatively streamlined regulatory structure for its nuclear industry. The Nuclear Regulatory Commission has jurisdiction to oversee the management of civilian nuclear reactors, their materials, and their waste – one agency to regulate the entire portfolio.

China's nuclear regulatory regime, on the other hand, is extremely complex and vague, with overlapping functions and unclear lines of authority. Typical of Beijing's piecemeal and incrementalist approach, the central government has tried to reform its fragmented regulatory structure in 1998, 2003, and 2008. But these changes have done no more than move boxes around on an organizational chart and have not succeeded in integrating and rationalizing the basic structure.

Figures 6.2 and 6.3 illustrate the regulatory structure before and after the 2008 reforms. Compared with the United States and the United Kingdom, both of which have a single civilian nuclear power regulator, notice in Figure 6.2 how many separate ministries and departments have oversight in China. Then compare this with after the reorganization as shown in Figure 6.3.

Um, how did this help? There's still a highly complex and fractured system in place. Different ministries and departments have been given authority, but the underlying complexity has not been alleviated. To get a sense of how these departments and ministries interact within the Chinese government, take a look at Figure 6.4.

It's like three-dimensional chess. And the latest reorganization hasn't helped matters much. It has placed a key

6.2 Before the government organization change in March 2008

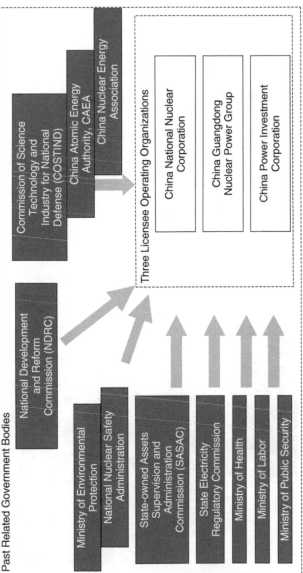

Source: NRDC (Natural Resource Defense Council), 2013, "Recommendation for the Reform of China's Nuclear Safety Regulatory System", www.nrdc.cn

6.3 Government organization change after March 2008

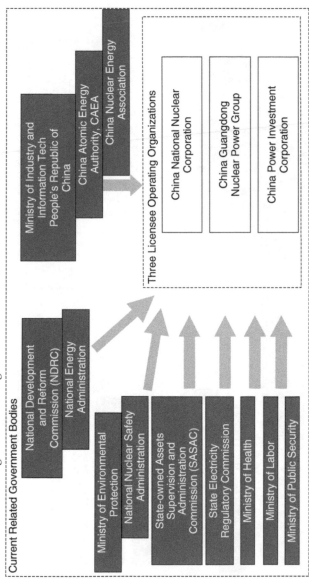

Source: NRDC (Natural Resource Defense Council), 2013, "Recommendation for the Reform of China's Nuclear Safety Regulatory System", http://www.nrdc.cn

6.4 China's nuclear regulatory structure

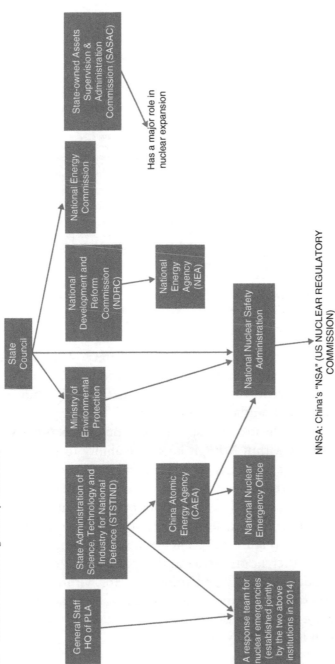

State Council

National Energy Commission

State-owned Assets Supervision & Administration Commission (SASAC)

Has a major role in nuclear expansion

National Development and Reform Commission (NDRC)

National Energy Agency (NEA)

Ministry of Environmental Protection

National Nuclear Safety Administration

NNSA: China's "NSA" (US NUCLEAR REGULATORY COMMISSION)

State Administration of Science, Technology and Industry for National Defence (STSTIND)

China Atomic Energy Agency (CAEA)

National Nuclear Emergency Office

General Staff HQ of PLA

A response team for nuclear emergencies (established jointly by the two above institutions in 2014)

Source: World Nuclear Association

6.5   Too many cooks in the kitchen

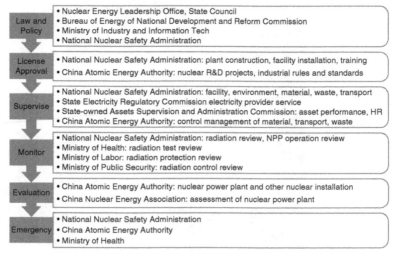

Law and Policy
- Nuclear Energy Leadership Office, State Council
- Bureau of Energy of National Development and Reform Commission
- Ministry of Industry and Information Tech
- National Nuclear Safety Administration

License Approval
- National Nuclear Safety Administration: plant construction, facility installation, training
- China Atomic Energy Authority: nuclear R&D projects, industrial rules and standards

Supervise
- National Nuclear Safety Administration: facility, environment, material, waste, transport
- State Electricity Regulatory Commission electricity provider service
- State-owned Assets Supervision and Administration Commission: asset performance, HR
- China Atomic Energy Authority: control management of material, transport, waste

Monitor
- National Nuclear Safety Administration: radiation review, NPP operation review
- Ministry of Health: radiation test review
- Ministry of Labor: radiation protection review
- Ministry of Public Security: radiation control review

Evaluation
- China Atomic Energy Authority: nuclear power plant and other nuclear installation
- China Nuclear Energy Association: assessment of nuclear power plant

Emergency
- National Nuclear Safety Administration
- China Atomic Energy Authority
- Ministry of Health

Source: NRDC (Natural Resource Defense Council), 2013, "Recommendation for the Reform of China's Nuclear Safety Regulatory System", www.nrdc.cn

regulator – the National Nuclear Safety Administration (NNSA) – under the jurisdiction of the MEP. The NNSA has a direct reporting line to the State Council, China's top administrative authority, which is led by the premier and includes the heads of each agency. But since NNSA is a department within MEP, it lacks the ability to plan its own budget or the authority to select regulatory personnel.

When you consider how these various agencies and departments are supposed to collaborate in regulating discrete aspects of civilian nuclear power, you see how tangled everything gets (Figure 6.5). Each regulatory function is split between different ministries and departments – each with its own budget, agenda, and priorities. So, within each function, there are overlapping duties, unclear lines of authority, and therefore a lack of ultimate accountability for the effective regulation of any function.

The maze-like organizational structure of China's nuclear regulatory regime undermines the broader policy objective: to develop and manage safe, modern, and efficient civilian nuclear power. The regulatory regime that should be mitigating risk is actually exacerbating it.

Bearing that in mind, think about China's nuclear construction bonanza. Experts like Bo Kong believe China has already outstripped its ability to regulate this industry safely. And as next-generation reactors come online, the risk of an accident will increase, as regulators scramble to keep up.

Food and Drugs

But the equivalent of a Chernobyl has already happened in the area of food and drug safety. After the mother-of-all-food-safety scandals hit China in 2008 with melamine-contaminated milk poisoning over 300,000 Chinese babies and killing six, authorities rushed to overhaul China's food safety regulatory regime. Ecce: the 2009 Food Safety Law, which was a reform of the old Food Hygiene Act.

Although the law was meant to tighten food safety regulation, it failed – as have subsequent amendments – to deal with the broader structural problem of multiple agencies policing overlapping areas with unclear lines of authority, fractured both horizontally and vertically. As with the nuclear power industry, in which the regulation of discrete aspects of the production and distribution of nuclear power is vested in several competing government authorities, food safety follows a similar scheme. Each stage of the food supply chain is divided up among several bureaucracies. Seed, cultivation, fertilizer, transportation, processing, wholesale, retail – each phase is regulated by various competing authorities, each with its own budget, culture, and mission, which they vie to maintain and expand. As with nuclear safety, this dynamic puts food safety squarely in the middle of a bureaucratic turf war.

Beijing knows fragmented regulators are risky. A fairly recent amendment to the 2009 Food Safety Law in the spring of 2013 attempts to centralize regulation by subsuming some departments into the China Food and Drug Administration (CFDA). The CFDA, which was demoted from ministerial level in 2007 when its director was convicted of corruption and executed, has been promoted back to ministerial status, and a number of departments that were in other agencies have now been swallowed by this new ministry (Figure 6.6).

Still, too many cooks are in the kitchen: the newly established ministerial-level CFDA (a rebranding of the old State Food and Drug Administration), plus the Ministry of Health, the Ministry of Agriculture, the State General Administration of Quality Supervision, Inspection and Quarantine (AQSIQ), and the Ministry of Commerce all oversee discrete and overlapping parts of the food chain. The AQSIQ maintains control over regulating all imports and exports of food. So two powerful government agencies, the CFDA and the AQSIQ, remain entangled in each other's bureaucratic knitting.

It's not like Beijing didn't *try* to wrangle everyone into a single superagency. The original plan was to have the CFDA be the master regulator, having oversight over everything from farm to table. But rival bureaucracies, with powerful protectors in the State Council and state-owned industries, resisted diminution. The Ministry of Health (MOH), for example, was granted the power in the Food Hygiene Law to regulate food safety and levy fines against offenders – a major source of revenue. So the MOH fought hard to prevent the new CFDA from re-obtaining ministerial status, lobbying instead for it to be placed under the MOH's control. And though the CFDA was granted ministerial status anyway, it

6.6 Reform of the Chinese Food and Drug 1Administration

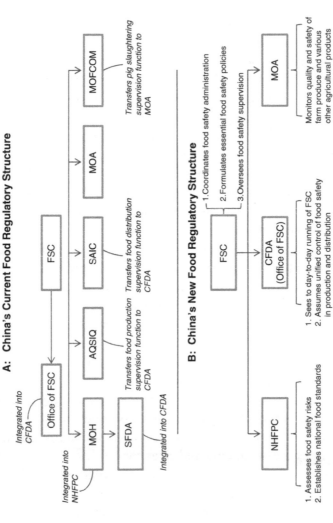

A: China's Current Food Regulatory Structure

Integrated into NHFPC

Integrated into CFDA

Office of FSC

FSC

MOH

AQSIQ

SAIC

MOA

MOFCOM

SFDA

Integrated into CFDA

Transfers food production supervision function to CFDA

Transfers food distribution supervision function to CFDA

Transfers pig slaughtering supervision function to MOA

B: China's New Food Regulatory Structure

1.Coordinates food safety administration
2.Formulates essential food safety policies
3.Oversees food safety supervision

FSC

NHFPC

CFDA (Office of FSC)

MOA

1. Assesses food safety risks
2. Establishes national food standards

1. Sees to day-to-day running of FSC
2. Assumes unified control of food safety in production and distribution

Monitors quality and safety of farm produce and various other agricultural products

Source: Reproduced with permission of David J. Ettinger and Mark Thompson, Keller and Heckman LLP, The Bund Center, Suite 3604, 222 Yan'an Dong Lu, Shanghai, China

has encountered fierce resistance from other agencies that refuse to cooperate with its directives.[5]

So the chief result of the 2013 streamlining reforms is still more overlap and conflict. The regulation of food contact materials, such as packaging and processing equipment, remains with the AQSIQ. The Ministry of Agriculture is in charge of regulating food before it's processed and enters the market. It also regulates pig slaughterhouses. And, finally, the National Health and Family Planning Commission is in charge of establishing industry standards. The CFDA regulates everything else – the processing, distribution, and consumption of food.

These four rival agencies will probably not join hands and sing "Kumbaya" anytime soon. If past is prologue, they'll keep fighting bitterly over budget, resources, and authority. This kind of fragmented regulatory structure also leads to jurisdictional blind spots. Where there are loopholes in the law, agencies tend not to want to extend themselves beyond their prescribed authority. For example, the CFDA is trying to patch up a gaping loophole in the regulations governing food, pharmaceuticals, and the chemicals industry. The CFDA has jurisdiction to regulate food and pharmaceutical companies – not chemical companies. But many chemical companies are producing additives for food, such as sweeteners, as well as active pharmaceutical ingredients (APIs) for medicines, yet evade oversight by refusing to register with the CFDA, maintaining their classification as chemical companies.[6] "We have never investigated a chemical company," said Yan Jiangying, deputy director of policy and regulation at the State Food and Drug Administration (now, the CFDA). "We don't have jurisdiction."[7]

Regulators in China have been aware of this loophole for at least 20 years. Between 1995 and 1996, nearly a hundred children in Haiti suffered acute renal failure from ingesting

acetaminophen laced with counterfeit glycerin – an industrial solvent, diethylene glycol, used in brake fluid and glue.
Almost half the children were under the age of two. Invited
by the Haitian government, the USFDA conducted an investigation to determine the source of the poison pills.

The glycerin that was provided to the pill manufacturer
was tracked to Chemical Trading and Consulting, a German
middleman, which had purchased it from Vos B.V., a Dutch
middleman. Vos says it bought the counterfeit glycerin from
another German trading company Matall-Chemie, which
claims it bought the syrup from Sinochem International
Chemicals Company, a marketer of Chinese-made APIs. In
1996, the US Embassy in Beijing asked Sinochem to provide
a list of its glycerin suppliers; after many months, it complied
with the request. The maker of the counterfeit glycerin was
identified as Tianhong Fine Chemicals Factory in Dalien, a
prosperous industrial city in northeast China. A year and a
half after it began its investigation, the FDA deployed an
inspector to Tianhong Fine Chemicals, but the plant had
already been closed.

This is yet another case that shows how China's concentric
rings of danger can all conspire to infuse a product with
deadly risk. An unscrupulous chemical factory sells its
product into a long, opaque chain of middlemen; it slips
through a gaping regulatory loophole in China and kills a
bunch of unsuspecting kids. Apparently, the Dutch company
Vos B.V. had even tested the glycerin and discovered it
was tainted but went on to sell it anyway. So blame must
be shared among many stakeholders here, not just the
counterfeiter.

But since that tragic event, Chinese regulators and legisla-
tors have been unable to plug the loophole and stop chemical
companies from supplying dangerous ingredients to the food
and drug industries. Diethylene glycol has been the cause of

multiple deaths in at least eight cases around the world since Haiti. Researchers of this issue estimate that literally thousands have died from the poisonings.[8] Most of these incidents have been traced back to China.

In 2006, a government dispensary in Panama, which failed to test its ingredients, prepared 260,000 bottles of cough medicine with the fake glycerin. As of 2007, there have been 365 reported deaths, with 138 confirmed. The tainted ingredients were traced through a Panamanian buyer, Social Security Laboratories, by way of a Panamanian trading company, Grupo Comercial Medicom, which in turn purchased the goods from Rasfer Internacional, a Barcelona-based trading company. The trail leads from Rasfer to CNSC Fortune Way, a Chinese trading company, which purchased the tainted goods from Taixing Glycerine Factory. Tellingly, the US Embassy in Beijing requested the CFDA to investigate these firms, but the regulator determined that, as companies officially classified as chemical suppliers, they fall outside of the CFDA's jurisdiction.[9]

The supplier that made the active pharmaceutical ingredient for Baxter's heparin slipped right through this loophole, too. And as of this writing, the underlying regulatory gap has not been addressed. It's estimated that China has 80,000 chemical companies.[10] Neither the CFDA nor the USFDA has a clue about how many of these are selling chemicals to the pharmaceutical industries. Independent auditors have discovered hundreds of fraudulent chemical companies producing APIs made from unregulated chemicals that are not safe for human consumption.

Yet the loophole for chemical and drug manufacturers isn't the only weakness in the regulations. The exporting of unsafe food and drugs is not expressly prohibited in the 2009 Food Safety Law, despite the fact that China is one of the world's largest food and drug exporters.

Importing regulations are much more explicit. There are six provisions governing the obligations of China's food importers in the "Import and Export of Food" section of the law, but only one provision governing China's exporting obligations – namely that "sample inspectors and food exporters go through the record-filing formalities of entry/exit inspection."[11]

As such, getting food into China is a highly regulated affair. Chinese customs and AQSIQ are all over your business. If one word is wrong on a food label, for example, your goods will be seized indefinitely. Jumping through bureaucratic hoops often takes years before you can get your product into market. Yet, on the export side, it's anything goes. When the heparin scandal hit, and the FDA and Baxter tried to figure out what happened, the CFDA and the AQSIQ grudgingly cooperated, but clearly placed the blame for what occurred at a *Chinese API manufacturer* squarely on the shoulders of the buyer, making the following chilling statement: "Safeguarding the legality, safety, and quality of raw materials imported for use in pharmaceuticals is the responsibility of the importing country."[12]

That's very reassuring to know, given that the FDA has only 27 people deployed in China, who must police thousands of firms that vehemently resist inspection and are abetted by the local authorities.

When China's government has tried to address food safety regulation in a piecemeal fashion, other problems emerge. For example, the ongoing melamine crisis is an unintended consequence of the attempt to integrate small, primitive farmers into a modern agricultural supply chain. Beijing recognized that China's sprawling agriculture sector must be rationalized. Small farmers were therefore allowed access to the supply chains of large dairy companies, a move that was supposed to have helped them evolve. But without an effective local and central regulatory framework in place, or the ability to police inputs throughout the long, opaque supply chain, large dairy processors, and ultimately consumers, were exposed to great risk.

Clearly, then, the worthy goal of rationalization needs to be attacked from many different angles – law, policy, and governmental structure. A gradualist approach, the strategy most often embraced by China's leaders, has not solved this multi-dimensional problem. So while the latest move toward more bureaucratic consolidation of China's food and drug regulation seems like the right idea, it doesn't go far enough in addressing the root problems.

Ultimately, China's leaders will have to figure out a way to create a system that is centrally controlled, with a unified foundation in law, but with accountable authority vested locally to respond to the complexities on the ground. Right now, centrally mandated regulations don't effectively trickle down to actual local implementation. China's gradualist approach is failing to create the kind of comprehensive regulatory system that is needed, says Dr John Yasuda, a post-doctoral fellow at the University of Pennsylvania, who specializes in China's food safety regulatory regime. Even with the latest moves to centralize control under the CFDA, "regulators at different levels of government don't understand how they are to function as part of a system…New food safety bodies that are created at the central level have no real impact at the county level."[13]

But it's not just a matter of poor information flow. Yasuda concedes that corruption plays a role in undermining regulatory oversight. Since counterfeiting firms make money, hire people, and flow tax revenues to local coffers (and bribes to local billfolds), officials can advance in the Party and make money by abetting criminal activities. But Yasuda says that it would be an "oversimplification" to blame China's regulatory failures solely on unethical bureaucrats. The whole agricultural system in China is to blame, posing such a complex problem that even well-meaning officials at all levels of government are failing to remedy the situation, causing more problems as they try to fix them.[14]

Consumer Products

Food, drugs, and civilian nuclear power are not isolated cases. Indeed, every regulatory regime in China is organized along similar lines: with competing and overlapping bureaucracies, horizontal and vertical fragmentation, arbitrary and inconsistent enforcement, and, ultimately, ineffective oversight. The regulation of consumer products is another example. Predictably, as with nuclear power and food and drugs, China does not have a unified consumer product safety law. It's more like a patchwork quilt of many laws and regulations. These include the General Principles of the Civil Law, the Law on Protection of the Rights and Interests of Consumers, the Criminal Law, and the Administration of Pharmaceuticals on Product Quality.[15] Heaped on top of these laws, there are myriad industry-specific regulations.

So the legal framework is weak. And the regulators are fragmented and overlapping in their duties to police product safety and quality. The AQSIQ – splintered among central and local offices – is tasked with oversight of product quality and safety – but so is the State Administration for Industry and Commerce – also splintered among central and local offices. Other agencies overlap according to their particular industry, such as the Ministry of Agriculture, the Ministry of Health, and the CFDA.

From food and drugs, to energy, to consumer products, China's regulatory regime, which should serve to mitigate risk, exacerbates it, feeding a vicious cycle of risk in China's economy. Local factories are protected from Beijing over-sight, so they're free to dump chemicals and untreated sewage in China's waterways and to belch pollution into the air, to counterfeit medicines and foodstuffs. The vicious cycle goes around and around – with ever-diminishing quality of China's soil, water, air, food, medicines, and manufactured goods.

This is not to say that America's regulatory structure is by any means close to perfect. We have horizontal fragmen-tation too. For example, both the USDA and the FDA oversee overlapping parts of the food chain. The USDA regulates meat and poultry, while the FDA regulates nearly the entire food chain.

National security in America is another regulatory struc-ture that is fragmented. The Department of Homeland Secu-rity (DHS), like China's Food and Drug Administration, was created by grafting departments from many agencies into one giant superagency. The morale in the bureaucracy is famously bad, as top managers depart at a rate four times faster than the federal government as a whole.[16] And the oversight of this agency is highly convoluted. Congress's 9/11 Commission recommended that the governance of DHS be streamlined in order to mitigate risk of another attack, but that has yet to occur.

It's not easy to rationalize a fragmented regulatory struc-ture. A bureaucracy is a tribe. It has its own language and its own culture. Just look at the US Secret Service, the group tasked with protecting the president. A series of scandals has revealed a culture more akin to a raucous fraternity house than a professional law enforcement agency. Putting a new person in charge of the agency has done nothing to change the bureaucratic culture of the Secret Service, and the scandals continue. It's hard to change the mores of a group. And moving departments from one bureaucracy to another, as with the US Department of Homeland Security and China's Food and Drug Administration, often breeds culture clash, resentment, and conflict.

Americans are divided in their views on regulations. Many believe that we have too much regulation and that government should get off the backs of business and let the market work its magic. Others believe that we have too little regulation, and that agencies like the USDA, the FDA, the Securities and Exchange Commission, and other regulators, should receive more funding, more staffing, and more of a legal mandate to do their jobs.

But wherever you fall on this ideological spectrum, America by comparison is arguably *centuries* ahead of China in terms of its regulatory system. For one thing, there's a functioning system of laws and enforcement. Of course, our system is not without corruption – high and low. Critics point out how many regulators, such as the FDA and Nuclear Regulatory Commission, are far too cozy with industry. Others lament the corrosive influence of big money in our political system. However, on the whole, there is a bedrock rule of law in America, a system to redress cases of fraud, abuse, and liability, and a civil society, which has the freedom to speak out against abuses.

Not so in China. Parents who have complained about the melamine poisoning of their kids have been put in prison for disrupting social harmony.[17] Also, though we are certainly not free from our own lapses in safety in manufacturing and agriculture, the proof of our system's superiority is in the pudding. We have lapses, but we don't have thousands of them over the course of a few years – spanning the breadth of basic manufacturing and agricultural industries, from food and drugs to infrastructure and consumer goods. And, truth be told, often the safety lapses in American products can be traced to Chinese imports.

General Motors (GM), for example, has recently determined that its defective ignition switches, which caused a recall of over three million cars, were made ... guess where? In a filing with the US National Highway Traffic Safety Administration, the automotive safety regulator, GM stated that the faulty switch used in the Cadillac DeVille and DTS, Buick LaCrosse and Lucerne, and Chevrolet Monte Carlo and Impala was manufactured by the Chinese firm, Dalian Alps Electronics Co. Ltd.[18] In 2012, almost half of all the product recalls from the Consumer Product Safety Commission were Chinese imports. And from 2011 to 2014, of the FDA's 1,861 import alerts, 131 alerts were for Chinese imports, as compared to 45 for Taiwan, 41 to Japan, and 39 for South Korea.

Though our regulatory system is far from perfect and struggles with fragmentation and corruption, it's much more highly evolved than China's. And the Chinese know it. They trust American-made products, not just because they believe US companies are safer in their outputs but because they regard their very system as safer.

Chinese watch their local news and see high-placed party officials abscond with billions of renminbi, as their children career through the streets in Ferraris, plowing through pedestrians and acting with wanton disregard for the law. They see America, in comparison, as a society in which laws are generally enforced, and where goods produced are generally safe because firms are generally better at making things and regulators are generally better at doing their jobs.

Which is why middle- and upper-class Chinese consumers don't just seek out American and European luxury brands for status. They flock to buy western staples, like food and drugs. Distrusting the safety of their own food supply – and disbelieving the strenuous protestations by government and corporate officials that Chinese-produced food is safe – they do anything they can to buy imported food.

When imported food is restricted, such as with baby formula, Chinese consumers will engage in very creative ways to purchase it. They'll have their kids attending college overseas send back baby formula via FedEx. Or they'll even smuggle the goods into China from Hong Kong, Taiwan, and other Asian nations where western-made baby formula can be purchased.

A *New York Times* article of July 25, 2013 describes how the Chinese are buying baby formula anywhere they can lay their hands on it around the world, causing shortages in at least six countries. The large retailers Boots and Sainsbury's in the United Kingdom have instituted a new limit on baby formula to two cans per customer. And Hong Kong customs is enforcing the two-can limit as well for anyone trying to spirit baby formula through Hong Kong into China. A recent sting by Hong Kong customs officials targeted three baby formula smuggling syndicates, with the arrest of ten people and the confiscation of nearly 220 pounds of contraband.[19]

Chinese don't even trust the imported milk powder being sold on Chinese retail shelves. Since the melamine scandal of 2008, there have been media reports of imported formula being mixed with Chinese-made formula. So consumers insist on buying formula outside China.

Health Care

Affluent Chinese are increasingly leaving China for medical care, too. Upstream products in China like food, drugs, and energy are weakly regulated, as are downstream industries like health care, a recipient and client of China's pharmaceutical industry. Drugs wend their way through a long, byzantine, opaque, and, inevitably, risky supply chain before they arrive at hospitals and medical clinics.

It is estimated that China has more than 13,000 distributors of pharmaceuticals, each of which feeds into one or two hospitals (see Figure 6.7). Japan has 147 pharmaceutical distributors. The United States has 75.[20] China's three largest distributors (China Resources, Shanghai Pharmaceuticals, and Sinopharm) command about 20 percent market share, as opposed to the top three distributors in the United States (AmerisourceBergen, Cardinal Health, and McKesson), which command more than 95 percent of a market that's nearly triple the size of China's. China's distribution of pharmaceuticals, then, is glutted with layer after layer of small middlemen. Medications must move through national distributors to multiple local distributors – from province to city to town – before they arrive in hospitals and clinics. The drugs, risky to begin with because of the way they've been made, accumulate additional risk with each middleman that handles them along the way – the risk they'll be tampered with, the risk they'll spoil.

And once they arrive at hospitals and clinics, they are absorbed into a healthcare system that is weakly regulated. Predictably, as with food, drugs, environment, nuclear energy, and consumer products, China's healthcare industry is fragmented both vertically and horizontally. At the national level, the system is divided by healthcare function, such as prevention, medical service, rehabilitation, education, and research.[21] But other governmental departments are also thrown in for good measure. Private medical facilities are regulated by the Ministry of Civil Affairs. State-owned enterprises that operate their own medical services for employees are regulated by the Ministry of Commerce.

The regulatory structure is then fractured vertically. Each province, city, and town has its own regulators that mirror

6.7   Overview of China's pharmaceuticals distribution chain

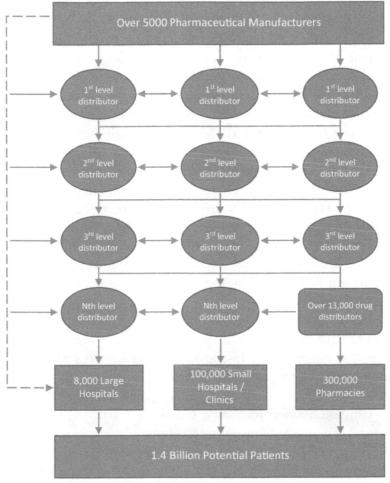

Source: Edward Tse, Kevin Ma, Paul Pan, and Simon Sun 2012, "Changing Landscape of China's Pharmaceutical Distribution Industry," Booz & Company Inc., www.strategyand.pwc.com/media/file/Changing_Landscape_of_China's _Pharmaceutical_Distribution_EN.pdf

the pattern at the national level. And, not to be outdone, regional administration also includes regulators that oversee traditional Chinese medicine (see Figure 6.8).

Of course, the outcome of this jumble is patchy and inconsistent health care. Patients complain of long wait times at hospitals, an inability to choose their own surgeon, a lack of advanced medical treatments and devices, as well as poor quality of care. An example is how cancer is treated in a typical Chinese hospital. Medical specialties are divided across independent departments. You have to go back and forth from department to department, wait in long lines for the chance to talk to a doctor for a few minutes, and try to piece together the advice from the different specialists. By contrast, American hospitals like the Mayo Clinic provide patients with a cross-disciplined team of doctors that provides a holistic diagnosis and treatment approach. And that treatment is delivered by the most up-to-date medical techniques and devices.

Consequently, affluent Chinese are increasingly seeking health care in Europe and the United States, where Chinese medical tourism is a fast-growing industry. It's estimated that approximately 60,000 Chinese go abroad each year for health care.[22]

Chinese medical tourists are driving a growing industry, a market which McKinsey and Company estimates is expanding at a rate of 20 percent per year and valued at approximately US$100 billion in 2013. That means jobs and revenue for hospitals and their localities. Chinese medical tourists at the Mayo Clinic, for instance, doubled in 2012–13 and continued to increase significantly in 2014.[23] And, according to *Medical Tourism* magazine, eighteen of England's National Health Trust hospitals report that 7 percent of their patients are medical tourists, who pay full price and account for nearly one-quarter of all the hospitals' private income. From

6.8 China's healthcare regulatory system

Health administration agencies in China

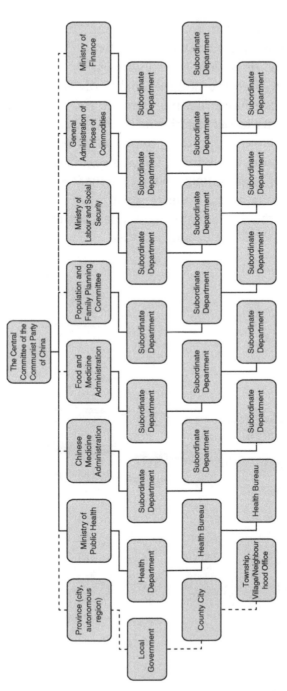

Note: dotted lines in the chart refer to subordinated relations and unbroken lines refer to the relevant professional guidance and management relations.

Source: Li Zhen, Wang Baozhen, and Zhou Yun, 2007, "The Current Situation and Analysis of Medical and Health Service Regulation in China," www.oecd.org

2010 to 2011, that comprised about US$71.9 million in hospital revenues with about US$350 million going to hotels, restaurants, retail, and transportation.[24]

And so, from the tangled thicket of China's regulators, which imbue more risk into already risky products, come grave threats to our health and safety. Our own regulators are totally overwhelmed by the flood of imported Chinese products, and, terrifyingly, China's regulators, the last line of defense, aren't doing their jobs either. But that risk also supports jobs in this country, as affluent Chinese citizens, who see their regulators as ineffective too, clamor for American-made goods and services.

7

What to Do

America is not a hapless victim. It is not about to be overrun by China. Yes, China poses a threat to our health and safety but also an opportunity to create lots of new jobs. And we have the ability to mitigate the threat and maximize the opportunity.

But we first need to focus on the *right* threat. Our myopia causes us to see threats where none exist. We rail against China's currency. It's a non-issue. There's no correlation between US employment rates and China's currency value. And the prescribed cure, jacking up tariffs, would kill jobs. We rail against outsourcing. It's highly overblown. Millions of jobs are created and destroyed in our economy every year. To blame China for a symptom of capitalism is dishonest and distracts us from creating policies that can speed the re-employment of those out of work. We rail against intellectual property theft. Yet many of the leading multinationals doing business in China don't take the basic steps to protect their ideas and their technologies, failing even to apply the most rudimentary oversight of their subcontractors. And in the case of advanced technologies, such as high-speed rail, China's risky system hinders reverse-engineering and safe deployment.

The true threat from China arises from this risky system, and it's a problem that isn't going to go away anytime soon.

The Chinese government *can't* stop it. And the reforms needed to mitigate risk will require a ground-up transformation of China's political economy. In the meantime, we're exposed to a significant threat to our health and safety. Our floodgates are wide open to unsafe products that are not policed by China's regulators, our regulators, or, for the most part, US corporations.

Unfortunately, we can't just stop buying Chinese imports, as Peter Navarro recommends in *Death by China*. After all, many ingredients in the food, drugs, and products we use may originate from China, but there's no way of telling that from the label. Your fish sticks may say they're made in the United States, but they were probably deboned and breaded in China. Your headache remedy may say it was "Made in the USA," but the active pharmaceutical ingredient probably came from China. The apple juice your kid is drinking may say it's American, but the apples are probably Chinese. So simply stopping your purchase of "Made in China" products is impossible.

And even if you could just stop buying Chinese-made goods, you'd harm a broad swath of the American economy, as many Chinese imports contain US-made inputs: the cotton in clothes, the pulp in cardboard, the recycled steel in faucets, the chips in iPhones, the PV polysilicon in solar panels, and so on. Then there are all the jobs associated with bringing these imported products to market. Boycotting Chinese-made goods would ultimately kill a lot of US jobs.

But the same systemic risk that gives rise to the threat also gives rise to a windfall opportunity. China supports millions of jobs in our economy through trade and investment. As China struggles to make things safely and reliably, it must import them. And although US exports to China are booming – in just about every congressional district across the country – our export intensity to China remains low. There's still much more we could be selling China. America's share of China's imports lags behind the EU, Taiwan, South Korea, and Japan. There are many steps we could take to boost exports further still, while encouraging more job-creating investment.

All of us can work together to mitigate the threat and maximize the opportunity – consumers, corporations, and policy makers alike.

What You Can Do

Despite the vagaries of the US product labeling system, there are proactive things you can do to guard yourself from unsafe Chinese imports. Go to your pantry and take out a box of any processed food. Look at the list of ingredients. That litany of chemicals has an anonymous source. Food manufacturers are not required to state where the xanthum gum was made or the soy lecithin, the Yellow Dye Number 6, the garlic powder, or the nonfat milk solids.

Consider the recall of Super Veggie Tings Crunchy Corn Sticks, brought to you by Robert's American Gourmet, the company that makes Pirate's Booty. These types of snacks are marketed as healthy alternatives and are sold in stores like Whole Foods. Yet, in the summer of 2007, kids were getting really sick from eating the Super Veggie Tings: high fever, diarrhea, hospitalization. Responding to pressure from the FDA, Robert Ehrlich, the CEO of Robert's American Gourmet, directed 50 distributors to pull the product from supermarket shelves and manufacturing was stopped. An investigation started. It was discovered that the kids were getting sick from salmonella poisoning. Testing traced the salmonella to a spray-on vegetable additive imported from China. Ehrlich insists he thought the ingredients for his product were sourced in the United States and fired the supplier, Atlantic Quality Spice & Seasonings of Edison, NJ. But Atlantic countered that Ehrlich knew most of its additives were imported and had a letter from Ehrlich to prove it. The two companies went to court to battle it out.[1]

The moral of the story here is that even "healthy" processed snacks can expose you to dangerous Chinese ingredients. So if you really want to minimize your exposure to unsafe Chinese imported foodstuffs, stop buying processed foods. Anything in a box, jar, bag, bottle, or can is suspect.

Even if it's labeled organic. Because China still does not grant the United States permission to inspect its farms. So any additives coming from China that go into an organic product need only be stamped "organic" by two independent Chinese authorities. Unfortunately, document forgery is practically its own industry in China. You can actually buy fake receipts on the street to provide your boss for expense reimbursement. And these shenanigans go on in the inspection industry all the time. China's law that pork imports must be free of a hormone called ractopamine has spurned a whole cottage industry in which fake ractopamine-free certificates are mocked up after the ractopamine-full pork is imported.

So independent certificates attesting that certain Chinese ingredients are organic cannot be trusted. The organic crystallized ginger that goes into that bottle of chai tea may easily have come from a farm that doused the ginger in harmful chemicals and paid off a local inspector to look the other way.

Should you buy something in a container, read the list of ingredients. If there's a long list of unrecognizable chemicals, you're at risk of being exposed to an unsafe import from China. Really, the only way you can be sure that your food is not coming from China is to buy fresh fruit, vegetables, meat, poultry, and fish from local sources, like farmers' markets.

Our deceptive food labeling system forces families to become students of the global supply chain. The best defense against unsafe Chinese imports is knowledge. The more you know, the more defensive action you can take. A good website that helps you track where your food is being imported from is provided by the advocacy group, Food and Water Watch: http://www.foodandwaterwatch.org/food/global-grocer.

As for medication, this is a real problem. Given that about 80 percent of the active pharmaceutical ingredients and chemicals in the medicines we take are imported, and half of them come from China and India (and that India sources 90 percent of its pharmaceutical raw materials from China), you're basically accepting this risk when you take a pill. So, not to be too simplistic about it, the best medicine is prevention. Eat a balanced, healthy diet, and exercise regularly. Recent studies show that even a modicum of exercise is exponentially better than no exercise at all. Researchers determined that, compared with total inactivity, those who engaged in low-volume activity – just 15 minutes a day – "had a 14% reduced risk of all-cause mortality...and had a 3 year longer life expectancy."[2]

In other words, eat well and get off your duff so you don't have to take pills that could contain unsafe Chinese ingredients. And try to avoid dietary supplements, which are not regulated by the US FDA at all. In 1994, President Bill Clinton deregulated the supplements industry, now a US$32 billion industry, exempting them from FDA oversight. This means the FDA is not permitted to study and screen supplements before they come to market – it may take action only after they're on the shelves, after complaints of adverse effects are made by consumers and doctors, and *only if* the

FDA can prove "significant or unreasonable risk of illness or injury."

That's not good. Studies are revealing an industry that has run amok. In November 2013, the *New York Times* ran a story about how Canadian researchers conducted DNA tests on the ingredients contained in 44 different herbal products from 12 leading supplements companies. They discovered that one-third of the products had zero trace of the herb advertised on the bottle. And that 59 percent contained additives that were not listed in the ingredients, such as rice, soybean, and wheat used as fillers. "Only 2 out of 12 companies had products without any substitution, contamination or fillers."[3] Sometimes the fillers were the only ingredients found in the supplement – a hazard for people with allergies or who are gluten-intolerant. Echinacea supplements, a popular American remedy for colds, for example, "contained ground up bitter weed, Parthenium hysterophorus, an invasive plant found in India and Australia that has been linked to rashes, nausea, and flatulence."[4]

Lovely. Try to stop your cold, and you get gas. But it gets worse. New data have revealed that dietary supplements caused almost 20 percent of the drug-related liver injuries diagnosed in US hospitals – a sharp increase from 7 percent ten years ago. This research was conducted nationally by a group of liver specialists who considered only the most severe cases. In other words, the actual number of cases was undercounted.[5]

Of course, many of the ingredients that go into supplements come from China, a cheap and ready source. I once gave a talk at a conference held by the Council for Responsible Nutrition, a major trade group for the supplements industry. My remarks focused on the risk that Chinese ingredients pose to the health of American consumers of supplements. There was stunned silence. I was not invited back.

Trust me, if you want to avoid unsafe Chinese imports, avoid dietary and herbal supplements. Get your vitamins from fruit and vegetables. And if you must take supplements, you've got to do diligent research on the efficacy of the companies in question and their quality control methods.[6]

As for protecting ourselves from unsafe consumer products, this is even trickier – as unsafe Chinese-made ingredients can find their way into just about anything. From an Aston Martin accelerator pedal to a night vision system in a navy helicopter to a Dora the Explorer toy to the deck panels on the San Francisco Bay Bridge. One thing you can do is stay up to date on product recalls from the Consumer Product Safety Commission (CPSC) which offers the following website: www.cpsc.gov/en/Recalls. You can also check out www.saferproducts.gov, where you can report an unsafe products and keep up to date on the latest recalls. The CPSC regulates about 15,000 different consumer products – mostly everything that falls outside of automobiles (regulated by the National Highway Traffic Safety Administration), alcohol, tobacco, and firearms (regulated by the Bureau of Alcohol, Tobacco, Firearms, and Explosives), airplanes (regulated by the Federal Aviation Administration), and food and drugs (regulated by the Food and Drug Administration).

Educate yourself, and be your own advocate. Companies respond to consumer feedback. Reach out to them. Contact companies whose products you buy and the retailers you buy them through. Find out where products are coming from and express your preference for increased safety checks. If you want to buy a dietary supplement, contact the company and ask if they perform DNA barcoding on their ingredients. If they say they don't, ask them why not.

If you're buying toys for your kids, you can ask where they're being made and under what quality control parameters. When the Mattel recalls happened, I went to our local toy stores and asked the owners about what brands to avoid. I got very frank advice about which companies had good safety track records and which didn't. If enough people demand that companies establish better and tighter quality controls on their imports from China, that will help. Be vocal. Vote with your pocketbook.

Same with your politics. No matter your political persuasion, you can be an informed and vocal voter. If politicians are blaming China for our own policy mistakes, call them on it. If they give you the China-is-stealing-our-jobs canard, ask them where they're getting their information. If they tell you it's that fictional EPI study, you know better, and you can tell them so. Politicians bash China because it's politically expedient. The pollsters tell them it wins votes. It plays on our fears and anger. And it distracts our attention away from the real issues in domestic policy that need to be addressed.

You can also take advantage of the opportunity that China brings this economy in jobs. If you're in the job market or are an entrepreneur, the first thing to do is not buy into the false narrative of American defeatism. If you believe that China is the world's leading superpower that is rapaciously stealing our jobs, it'll be hard to see all the areas in our economy where China is supporting jobs – and where we're successfully competing.

When politicians like Jennifer Granholm, Sherrod Brown, Lindsey Graham, Chuck Schumer, and Mitt Romney tell us all our jobs are going to China, it contributes to a larger failure of entrepreneurial imagination. Think of all the new businesses that could be started in Detroit to supply and service the largest, fastest-growing car market in the world, had the governor of Michigan used her bully pulpit to show us all the job-creating trade and investment flowing from China. When politicians like Mitt Romney tell us to "Believe in America," yet at the same time focus their talking points on how China is strong enough to steal our jobs right out from under us, it's hard to believe in America.

We actually should believe in America. Yes, there's so much about our system that we could improve, but there's still so much about the American experiment that we're getting right. Across the street from me lives a family where the dad is a Greek Cypriot and the mom is Japanese. Both are bright and accomplished – the one a successful economist at an international fund, the other a veterinarian. Both speak passionately about why they came to America to study and build a family. They each said that, had they stayed in the countries of their birth, neither would have been as success-ful or happy.

As Americans, we tend to overlook some basic things about our country that are fundamentally good. We've got the best higher education in the world, and the freedom to say and think and be what we wish. Émigrés will be the first to tell you why they came to America and why they stay.

And if imitation is the sincerest form of flattery, we should be flattered, not threatened, by all the Chinese who are moving to the United States to study, work, and build lives. From 2011 to 2012, the United States hosted 764,495 international students. The highest number of that group was from China: 194,029, or just over 25 percent of the total.[7]

Critics of America's educational system often point to China as proof that America has lost its mojo and that China is where it's at. "US students, who once led the world," according to *Newsweek*, "currently rank 21st in the world in science and 25th in math."[8] This kind of talk gets louder around the time when the results are posted from the big global evaluations on education, such as the Programme for International Student Assessment (PISA) and the Third International Mathematics and Science Study (TIMSS).

But let's consider a few facts. Tom Loveless, a senior fellow at the Brown Center on Education Policy at the Brookings Institution, who is an expert on PISA and TIMSS, reminds us that we need to put these test results in perspective. First, China is a very large, poor, rural country that cannot possibly administer this kind of assessment nationwide, so only discrete parts of China participate. Shanghai participates. Beijing participates. Yes, Shanghai scored first place on the PISA, but that tells us nothing about how China as a whole would do. That's like having Manhattan compete on the PISA and claim the results represent America as a whole. Loveless writes that "Shanghai's municipal website reports that 83.8% of high school graduates enter college. The national figure is 24%. The American figure is about 66%."[9]

Second, the notion that America is in free fall from a perch as number one in the world for math and science is also a myth. "The United States never led the world," says Tom Loveless. "It was never number one and has never been close to number one on international math tests. Or on science tests, for that matter. It is more accurate to say that the United States has always trailed the world on math tests." If you look at assessments on math and science going back to 1964, in fact, America always scored a Gentleman's C. Mediocre: not the world leader.

And yet, even with middling test grades on math and science, the United States has been a world leader in science and innovation. Why? University of Oregon professor Yong Zhao goes beyond the PISA scoring to assess China's education in his book, *Who's Afraid of the Big Bad Dragon?* Zhao is highly critical of the authoritarian culture of Chinese schooling, which teaches rote memorization, linear thinking, and obedience to teachers.

"This is an excellent and convenient way," writes Zhao, "for the authorities to deny any responsibility for social equity and justice and to avoid accommodating differently talented people."[10] Chinese students in Shanghai and Beijing may score well on math and science tests, but they tend to lack the creativity and non-linear thinking that is the mother of invention and innovation.

China may even mint more engineers than the United States. In 2011, China reports over one million engineers graduated.[11] But China's definition of an engineer is much broader than ours; it includes auto mechanics and factory workers. Our best and brightest engineers are studying the very latest thinking in tomorrow's technologies. The engineers that China churns out tend to learn more basic science and are not taught how to think creatively or work in teams. There's a reason that China has yet to produce a Nobel laureate in science, and why China's top students vie to study in the United States. It's not just China. Talk to a tiger mom from any Asian country and she'll tell you how many spots are open at Harvard and Stanford in a given year, and what she's doing to prepare her four-year-old to get in.

Yes, US advanced engineering and science education is still the envy of countries like China, but there's something more. It's the soft skills taught in the United States that sow the seeds of innovation. To build the next Google or GE or invent a cure for cancer, you need good math and science fundamentals, but you also need much more. The ability to think creatively, the ability to buck authority – not kowtow to it – and the ability to inspire others in helping to implement your vision. These are traits vital to an innovation economy that are not reflected on the PISA test but, arguably, are more important than whether kids ace their math and science scores.

So rather than stress out about getting your kid into next year's Mandarin class, remember: the Chinese are teaching English in their Shanghai and Beijing schools, and chances are, most of those kids will want to come here to help grow our pie anyway.

What Companies Can Do

There's a lot more our corporations could be doing to mitigate the threat of unsafe Chinese imports. When the head of the FDA's office in Beijing said that it is incumbent on US firms to police their own supply chains, he wasn't kidding. The FDA is totally overwhelmed in terms of its oversight. And while the FDA and the CPSC work hard to maintain good relations with the relevant Chinese authorities and even to train their inspectors in American standards, there are many thousands of firms in question that need to be monitored, so no amount of money would be sufficient to ramp up the inspections and training to the level needed to inspect every export firm and its outputs.

We can't rely on the regulators to safeguard us. US firms are on the front lines. They're our first line of defense. True, China is one of the toughest places to do business in the world. It's highly complex. And fraught with risk. Attempts to mitigate that risk are usually met with stiff resistance. Authorities prevent you from proper inspections. Business owners bar their doors.

But remember: in any commercial interaction, the buyer holds tremendous leverage. With costs coming closer and closer to parity between China and the United States – plus the added risk of unsafe business practice that comes with

China sourcing – the case for making something in America is strong. So companies have a choice.

Be prepared to push hard in insisting that you forward-deploy your resources up the entire length of China's supply chain. You need to inspect your contractors, your subcontractors, and your sub-sub-subs. To truly mitigate risks, you actually need to rationalize your own supply chain, eradicating middlemen that add risk but little value. Like Mattel, even if you own factories in China but still employ outside vendors, you're at risk.

If your Chinese interlocutors refuse to open their doors to you, then be prepared to take your marbles and go home. Look at Google. China's internet users number twice the total US population. The temptation is strong to do anything to market to them. Yet Google had had enough of Chinese government interference and hacking, so moved its service to Hong Kong. There is a point in your business trajectory where you may feel you need to back off on China. And that's fine. I would imagine that Baxter, Mattel, Aston Martin, Boeing, and the many other companies burned by China's systemic risk all wish they could have pushed back harder on China's intransigence.

And although policing China's supply chain is highly complex, comprehensive testing of your imported products is not. It's just expensive. But consumers, increasingly aware of the danger from Chinese imports, would welcome knowing that your company is on the front lines inspecting everything before it reaches our supermarkets and drug stores. As a dad, I certainly would pay more for an imported product I was confident was tested for safety. And I mean *directly* tested for safety, not randomly batch-tested, which is not a fine enough net to stop dangerous goods from slipping through.

As for the opportunities, companies can also do more to create jobs through tapping into Chinese trade and investment. Though there are thousands of firms of every size across the country that have been bold and persistent enough to support jobs here at home through doing business with China, there are many many more that have chosen to shutter the shop in the face of hard economic times. It's tough to blame them when our politicians and media tell us China is the leading superpower and America is going down the tubes.

But look at all the companies that have turned to China in the most unlikely of product exports and are thriving. Toys. Wallpaper. Chopsticks! And there are so many products and services that China desperately needs that America can provide: environmental remediation; water treatment technology; dairy farm management; healthcare products and services; safe agricultural products, especially perishable items; energy services. The list goes on and on. If you want to start a business or grow your current one, just look at the trends where China is expanding. You don't need to source products in China to do business there. Sell them something. To be sure, some Chinese industries are closed or highly restricted to foreign investment and exports. Don't plan on opening up your own bank or oil field anytime soon. But most industries are open for business. All that is required is your persistence and creativity.

What the US Government Can Do

As for policy, we've got a long way to go. Our politicians need to understand that currency is a red herring, a distraction from the real threat posed by China: unsafe Chinese imports. With China as the largest exporter to both the US and the EU, the volume of Chinese imports has overwhelmed our regulators.

The United States must take defensive measures to support what companies need to do on the front lines. First, the US inspection and screening capabilities in China must be vastly expanded. And our executive branch must make product and food safety a top priority.

There are two official bilateral exchanges that occur between China and the United States: the Strategic and Economic Dialogue, led by the State Department and the Treasury Department, and the Joint Commission on Commerce and Trade, led by the Commerce Department. In the most recent meetings, food and drug safety was relegated to a pretty low rung on the "to do" lists. Safety needs to be made a much higher priority. And it needs to be a topic that the US president advocates for directly to China's president. Given China's institutional resistance to America's beefing up its inspection regime, political support must be won at the top levels in China first.

Then, the budgets for the FDA, the USDA's Foreign Agricultural Service, and the CPSC must be commensurately expanded to fund a radical overhaul of our inspection system. It's not just a matter of increasing our inspectors in the field. We need to adopt a more comprehensive system. Japan, which imports a lot more food from China than the United States, is a model we can emulate. After detecting high concentrations of pesticides in frozen spinach in 2002, Japan enacting an aggressive quality control inspection system coupled with a strict supplier certification process. Japan operates two giant inspection clearinghouses where they randomly test batches from 10 percent of all the food imported from China. Yet Japan's health ministry reported that, in 2006, China was still the largest food safety violator, accounting for one-third of all non-compliant food products that Japan imports.[12] So Japan still has a way to go in protecting itself too.

I would argue that this screening system is a step in the right direction. And a 10 percent inspection rate is a heck of a lot better than how we're doing, which is about 2 percent. But random batch testing is hardly an effective shield against unsafe imports. So much danger can slip through undetected.

So America should open national inspection centers like Japan, but we should test a lot more than 10 percent of what comes in. And not just food; drugs and consumer products as well. Industries and congressional appropriators may balk at the costs, but we're talking about protecting lives here, saving babies from renal failure, hospital patients from blood poisoning.

We should also emulate Japan's supplier certification program. Japan dictates the standards by which Chinese suppliers must grow food, and licenses are awarded to the suppliers that comply. But the licenses are issued by Chinese authorities, and that's a problem. Authorities can be bribed and don't always follow the standards to the letter. Really, the FDA, USDA, and CPSC should have supplier-certification inspectors in-country as well to screen firms before granting export licenses. At this time, the United States uses something closer to an honor system, in which suppliers self-certify that they are compliant. It's called a "supplier cert," and it's about as flimsy as the paper it's printed on.

Finally, there needs to be a change in the mindset of our regulators stationed in China. At a food expo in Shanghai in 2012, Michael Taylor, the deputy commissioner for food at the FDA, said, "Most consumers understand that food is not risk-free. They are not asking for the impossible. But they do expect that everyone involved in producing, processing, transporting, and marketing food is doing what they reasonably can to prevent problems and make food safe."[13]

That's pathetic and scary. As someone with a family, who spends a lot of time and hard-earned money to put nutritious food on the table, I actually do expect it to be safe and that it won't poison my wife and children. Most consumers in the United States don't give a fig about all the players in the upstream food supply chain doing what they "reasonably can" because, too often, "reasonably can" means putting poison in our shopping baskets. We've seen what course of action is taken when companies "reasonably" do what they "can" to keep our food and drugs safe.

They look the other way.

Baxter, which is considered an industry leader in safety, didn't even bother to inspect the Chinese facility that it was sourcing active pharmaceutical ingredients from. Robert's American Gourmet, the maker of Pirate's Booty, let poison additives be sprayed on products without inspecting them before they were marketed to children. Fonterra of New Zealand, a global dairy giant, was caught flat-footed when the melamine safety lapses occurred.

American consumers actually do demand that their food is safe and that, when they buy food, they're not going to be putting poison on the dinner table. The FDA must do a much better job to protect American families, and so must the top leaders of our federal government and Congress. We have no business sourcing anything in such a dangerous market as China if we can't do a much, much better job of making sure that what we import is safe.

US lawmakers can help. They can bring the dietary supplements industry back under the regulatory framework of the FDA. They can expand the budget and authority of the FDA, the USDA, and the CPSC. And they can increase fines and liability exposure to companies that take a lax attitude toward policing their own imports. We can't legislate our

7.1   Top five PRC import sources, 2013 (US$ billion)

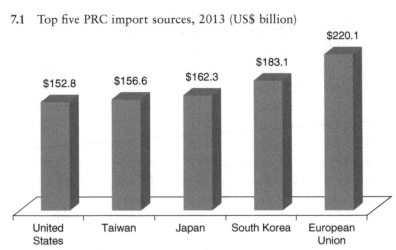

Source: The US–China Business Council

way out of this safety crisis, but smart policy can help a great deal.

In the meantime, policy makers can help the push to create more jobs through China trade and investment. It's true exports from nearly every congressional district are on the rise – and often rising steeply. And inbound investment is hitting record numbers. Yet our exports to China comprised about 8 percent of the total market of China's imports – down from 10 percent in 2000. We lag behind Europe, South Korea, Taiwan, and Japan (Figure 7.1).

So, in many ways, our economic competition in the coming century is not with China at all, as the conventional wisdom holds, but with Europe. China's lower-value, assembly-driven operations largely complement American advanced manu-facturing. Europe's exports of food, high tech, and services are much more directly in competition with America than with China.

Ramping up exports still further and encouraging more inbound direct investment in strategic sectors would create many jobs across our economy. From a policy perspective, there's a lot that could be done to make this happen. First, funding needs to be increased to US government agencies that help grow our exports. There's the Foreign Commercial Service (FCS) – part of the US Commerce Department – which is a powerful advocate for American exporters. The FCS helps US companies large and small identify and capitalize on export opportunities. The FCS has staff stationed in several cities in China that provide real business leads and local hands-on help to exporters, as well as local offices in every state that can help you export your products. Then, there's the US Trade Representative, which works to remove market barriers to American exports, as well as to enforce trade rules. And, finally, there's the Export-Import Bank, which provides financing to foreign importers of American goods. It also extends financing for exporters large and small. The Ex-Im Bank is a resource many companies cite as keeping them operating onshore. It helps to combat competitive advantages afforded to other countries through governmental subsidies without engaging in the same beggar-thy-neighbor policies.

All three of these agencies deserve stepped-up funding to support their important activities in growing US exports, not just to China but to the world. Funding must also be increased for our federal economic statistical agencies, such as the Bureau of Labor Statistics, the Bureau of Economic Analysis, and the Census Bureau. These agencies produce the numbers that guide our policy decisions, and these days, they're understaffed, underfunded, and woefully behind the times, in terms of accurately measuring America's trade flows and economic activity. What results is a myopic view of China's size in the global economy and its relationship to the United States. Bad statistics support bad conclusions about "rising China and declining America."

Most broadly, data collection and reporting must be reformed in order to reflect more accurately the realities of global trade. The World Trade Organization is developing methods to improve the way it collects and analyzes data. So is Japan. The basis of their efforts lies in tracking and measuring value captured at each point in the global supply chain. With more accurate data, many of the alarmist claims about China would dissipate.

And rather than the binary trade numbers we see each quarter, in which the trade imbalance is depicted in the crudest terms, severely distorted, we'd see the more nuanced picture of how products are actually made. That many "Made in China" products are usually just assembled there and contain inputs from all over the world, including from the United States. With better measurement of the service industries, we'd also be able to discern all the value added to products from US service industries – how imported products from China are transported, warehoused, marketed, and retailed, and how those services support jobs.

Improving the accuracy of our data would probably go a long way toward improving public perception of America's role in the global economy, too. After all, it's misleading statistics that are the basis for so much political and journalistic rhetoric – how the moderator in a presidential debate can say that Apple products are manufactured in China, when they're only put together there; how broadcast news reports can claim that millions of jobs are being lost to China because of a greatly exaggerated and misleading trade imbalance; how institutions like the IMF can claim China will overtake the United States economically in just a few years. These claims are all based on bad data. Improving the data will help arm journalists, economists, politicians, and pundits with a more accurate understanding of American competitiveness.

We also need more accurate labeling. Products that are only assembled in China should say so. Ingredients that are sourced in China should no longer be anonymous. Consumers should be able to tell where the various inputs to their purchases are coming from. It would help us make more informed and safe decisions, and it would give us a clearer picture of China's true position in global trade.

We need improvements in education and outreach as well. Certainly, within the business community there's a concerted effort to get the word out about exports. For example, the US Chamber of Commerce sponsors workshops and symposia around the country that provide information about tapping into export markets. These events attract many local businesses and usually feature experienced China-trade hands, such as representatives of the US commercial service from China, export specialists, and sometimes members of China's ambassadorial corps.

But in many ways, US exports to China are a well-kept secret. If select members of the business community know about booming exports to China, the public at large certainly does not. Schools could help. In the 1950s and 1960s, many elementary and high schools taught "home ec" and "shop" in an effort to impart what was considered then as practical life skills. A course that studies how products are made in today's globalized economy would go a long way to dissipate myths about China's economic preeminence. Too often, as consumers, we just buy things without knowing how they're made or where they come from. Such a course would help provide context to America's role in the global economy.

Politicians could do a much better job in this area as well. Too often, they prefer to hide behind the rhetoric of fear and defeatism. After all, fear sells. But a message of abiding strength and competitiveness would also sell. To ask

Americans to believe in America – and then to list all the reasons why we *should*: how we're competing and winning, how we're innovating and creating jobs, how we're exporting our goods and services to a country we once thought was wiping the floor with us. Instead, we are told to believe in America, then are told all the reasons why we're going down the tubes.

That kind of talk contributes to an overall head-in-the-sand mentality and a larger failure of entrepreneurial imagination. If kids aren't growing up understanding the opportunities out there – if all they hear is that "Rising China is Eating Our Lunch" – then it becomes especially difficult to imagine participating in the global workforce or starting a company that would capitalize on China's markets.

Finally, smarter policies at the federal and local levels regarding China trade would help accelerate job creation. The US Congress needs to stop its Quixotic missions of fear by attacking China's currency policies. These bills invariably fail to pass both chambers, yet they attract more and more sponsors each time they move through the legislature because lawmakers can be seen to be "tough on China" without the consequences of the bill actually becoming law.

Similarly, efforts to penalize China's imports by slapping duties and tariffs on certain products is a blunt cudgel that actually harms US industry and kills jobs. We should stop using tariffs as a means to retaliate against unfair trade practices.

For one thing, we could turn to international bodies that we helped create, like the World Trade Organization. China's subsidies are usually against WTO rules, and we can use that forum to push back on them. But, at the end of the day, as the old garmentos on Manhattan's Lower East Side used to say, "The best revenge on a lousy customer is to sell him more goods." We should bear in mind that, despite China's undervalued currency and market-distorting subsidies, America is still exporting so much to China – and we could be exporting a whole lot more.

To that end, holistic policies encouraging more Chinese trade and investment need to be enacted at the federal and local levels. A shining example is a policy promulgated in British Columbia, Canada, called the BC Jobs Plan, and it stands in stark contrast to Missouri's chuckleheaded China Hub as an example of a comprehensive, effective policy to create jobs and economic growth.

British Columbia pursued a three-pronged strategy: aggressively funding training; boosting investment in small business and infrastructure; and expanding markets, especially in China, through increased transportation routes and lowering trade barriers. While the Missouri legislature has been wrangling over whether to fund a mission of economic silliness since 2008 – hoping freight forwarders will act against their own interests by routing cargo away from a hub in Chicago to St Louis, which has none of the necessary infrastructure – British Columbia has created over 50,000 jobs since 2011. The United States would do well to adopt a similar policy, embracing a coordinated strategy of job training, infrastructure investment, and increased access to China's markets. As it stands, our strategy is piecemeal and disconnected, spanning several federal government agencies and statehouses with little coherent vision.

Finally, America needs to take a page out of China's playbook. The Chinese take a long view on history when looking into the future. We tend to remember as far back as the last media cycle as we lurch from tweet to tweet. It's worth remembering that a deep undercurrent of fear and self-doubt runs through the American psyche. We saw this in the 1980s when Japan's economy was expanding. Americans believed

Japan would rule the world economically. And many serious academics agreed. Before that, in the 1970s, America feared rising Middle East Gulf States like Saudi Arabia, which were investing their oil riches in US assets. And, before that, there was the fear of a rising Soviet empire, encapsulated in the Sputnik moment.

We can look back even further. Charles Dickens documented this peculiarly American fear in 1844. In *The Life and Adventures of Martin Chuzzlewit*, the protagonist, arriving in New York from England, is told that America is in "a season of great commercial depression," "an alarming crisis," and "a period of unprecedented stagnation." To this, the narrator responds: "Martin knew nothing about America, or he would have known perfectly well that if its individual citizens, to a man, are to be believed, it always is depressed, and always is stagnated, and always is at an alarming crisis, and never was otherwise."[14]

But these fears seem to have taken on a greater intensity lately amidst the trends of globalization and technology. Since the prevailing view of Chinese economic might is predicated on a belief in the supremacy of its manufacturing base, understanding systemic risk in China's supply chain from the ground up necessitates a rethinking of China's economic rise. That includes discarding simplistic theories, like the "flat world" paradigm. Information technologies, the flattening agents in this scheme, do not place China on a competitive footing with the West, since they do nothing to mitigate China's systemic supply chain risk. If anything, they magnify it, linking your desktop computer straight to the Chinese labyrinth.

Technology can't extricate China from its unique challenges either. They've got a long road to hoe, and a web browser won't help much. The acculturation of rule of law, a more balanced economy, a sustainable growth model – these will be very hard to achieve and are necessary before systemic risk can be mitigated.

It's easy to assume that because Japan moved up from low value to advanced manufacturing, China can too. But Japan and China are radically different. Japan in the 1960s was a society ruled by law, with a business culture that painstakingly mastered technology and organizational excellence from the bottom up. Its companies, like Sony, staunchly refused to make products under other brand names. China, on the other hand, flailing in a system with no rule of law and still healing from the national trauma of Mao's mass murder, aims to get rich quick by trying to leapfrog development through any means necessary – counterfeiting, making products for western brands, reverse-engineering. But the fact remains that to build something reliably, you need transparent, well-run companies with trained workers in a context of enforceable laws and effective regulators. Merely having the spec for a stealth bomber or bullet train doesn't mean you can build and operate it safely.

In many ways, the ongoing experiment of China's modernity is America's experiment, too. Our two economies are locked in an ardent embrace. China's export sector is dominated by American-owned firms. Its factories belch pollution-making products for our consumption. And simply packing up and going home – even if it were possible – would not create a desired outcome. China's risks would grow more acute and the rewards would wither on the vine. Rather, a smarter engagement is required. We must recalibrate our perspective, focusing on where the danger actually lies – not so much in lethal economic competition but in lethal products; and where the opportunities lie – in creating jobs and prosperity through tapping into China's dire need for safe goods and for services that can ameliorate the risks in China's economic system.

The only way to minimize the threat and maximize the opportunity is through cooperation. Trying to hurt China only hurts ourselves. The Chinese need a lot of help, and it's in our best interests to roll up our sleeves and give it to them.

Notes

Preface

1 PewResearch Global Attitudes Project 2012, "Global Opinion of Obama Slips, International Policies Faulted," www.pewglobal.org/2012/06/13/global-opinion-of-obama-slips-international-policies-faulted/
2 Brooks Jackson and Kathleen Hall Jamieson (2007), *UnSpun: Finding Facts in a World of Disinformation*, Random House Trade Paperbacks.
3 Cecilia Malmström, "China-EU Trade: Mutual Support for Growth and Jobs," 2015. http://trade.ec.europa.eu/doclib/docs/2015/january/tradoc_153066.pdf

1 Three Myths

1 Charles Kenny, 2014, "America is No. 2 and That's Great News," *The Washington Post*, www.washingtonpost.com/opinions/america-is-no-2-and-thats-great-news/2014/01/17/09c10f50-7c97-11e3-9556-4a4bf7bcbd84_story.html
2 Jamil Anderlini, 2014, "China has 'Wasted' $6.8tn in Investment, Warn Beijing Researchers," www.ft.com/intl/cms/s/0/002a1978-7629-11e4-9761-00144feabdc0.html#axzz3LKEirTl3
3 Reuters, 2010, "China's GDP is 'Man-made,' Unreliable: Top Leader," www.reuters.com/article/2010/12/06/us-china-economy-wikileaks-idUSTRE6B527D20101206

4 Yueran Zhang, 2013, "A Baffling Trend in China's GDP Statistics," TeaLeafNation, www.tealeafnation.com/2013/04/a-baffling-trend-in-chinas-gdp-statistics/

5 Tom Orlik, 2011, "Chinese GDP Data: How Reliable?," *The Wall Street Journal*, http://blogs.wsj.com/chinarealtime/2011/06/10/chinese-gdp-data-how-reliable/

6 Yueran Zhang, 2013, "A Baffling Trend in China's GDP Statistics," TeaLeafNation, www.tealeafnation.com/2013/04/a-baffling-trend-in-chinas-gdp-statistics/

7 Robert J. Samuelson, 2014, "Robert Samuelson: Economic Power Shifting in China's Favor," *The Washington Post*, www.washingtonpost.com/opinions/robert-samuelson-economic-power-shifting-in-chinas-favor/2014/05/14/bee0d608-daf3-11e3-b745-87d39690c5c0_story.html

8 Joe McDonald, 2014, "China Rejects Sign It May Soon Be No. 1 Economy," Associated Press, http://bigstory.ap.org/article/china-rejects-sign-it-may-soon-be-no-1-economy

9 China Daily, 2010, "Beijing's Middle Class Expands to 5.4 Million," http://china.org.cn/china/2010-07/19/content_20524810.htm

10 Jacob Poushter, 2013, "Inflation, Corruption, Inequality Top List of Chinese Public's Concerns," Pew Research Center, www.pewresearch.org/fact-tank/2013/11/08/inflation-corruption-inequality-top-list-of-chinese-publics-concerns/

11 China Quarterly Update, 2008, "Special Focus – New PPPs and China's Economy," World Bank, http://siteresources.worldbank.org/INTCHINA/Resources/318862-1121421293578/cqu_jan_08_en.pdf

12 Derek Scissors, 2011, "The United States vs. China – Which Economy is Bigger, Which is Better," The Heritage Foundation, www.heritage.org/research/reports/2011/04/the-united-states-vs-china-which-economy-is-bigger-which-is-better

13 Credit Suisse, 2013, "Global Wealth Databook 2013," www.international-adviser.com/ia/media/Media/Credit-Suisse-Global-Wealth-Databook-2013.pdf

14 Bloomberg News, 2013, "China's Local Debt Swells to 17.9 Trillion Yuan in Audit," www.bloomberg.com/news/2013-12

-30/china-s-local-debt-swells-to-17-9-trillion-yuan-in-audit
.html

15 Xinhua, 2013, "Fortune 500 List Reveals Need for Structural
Reform," http://english.peopledaily.com.cn/90778/8324216
.html

16 Ibid.

17 Nicholas R. Lardy, 2012, "Sustaining China's Economic
Growth after the Global Financial Crisis," Peterson Institute
for International Economics, Washington, DC.

18 David Shambaugh, 2012, "Don't Expect Reform from China's
New Leaders," *The Washington Post*, www.washingtonpost
.com/opinions/dont-expect-reform-from-chinas-new
-leaders/2012/11/15/82cd4402-2f47-11e2-9f50-0308e1e75445
_story.html

19 Mark J. Perry, 2014, "Despite China's Impressive Growth, on
a Per Capita Basis, The US Economy is Still a Century Ahead
of China, AEIdeas," www.aei-ideas.org/2014/04/on-a-per
-capita-basis-the-us-is-still-a-century-ahead-of-china/

20 Derek Scissors, 2011, "The United States vs. China – Which
Economy is Bigger, Which is Better," The Heritage Foundation, www.heritage.org/research/reports/2011/04/the-united
-states-vs-china-which-economy-is-bigger-which-is-better

21 Derek Scissors, Charlotte Espinoza, and Ambassador Terry
Miller 2012, "Trade Freedom: How Imports Support U.S.
Jobs," The Heritage Foundation, www.heritage.org/research/
reports/2012/09/trade-freedom-how-imports-support-us-jobs

22 Yuqing Xing and Neal Detert, 2010, "How the iPhone Widens
the United State Trade Deficit with the People's Republic of
China", ADBI Working Paper Series, www.adbi.org/files/2010
.12.14.wp257.iphone.widens.us.trade.deficit.prc.pdf

23 *The Economist*, 2012, "iPadded: The Trade Gap between
America and China is Much Exaggerated," www.economist
.com/node/21543174

24 Ibid.

25 *The Wall Street Journal*, 2010, "Flawed Math Seen in Unemployment Tied to China," http://online.wsj.com/articles/
SB10001424052702303284604575582293236501172

26 Ibid.
27 Galina Hale and Bart Hobijn, 2011, "The US Content of 'Made in China,'" Federal Reserve Bank of San Francisco, www.frbsf.org/economic-research/publications/economic -letter/
28 Derek Scissors, Charlotte Espinoza, and Ambassador Terry Miller, 2012, "Trade Freedom: How Imports Support US Jobs," The Heritage Foundation, www.heritage.org/research/ reports/2012/09/trade-freedom-how-imports-support-us -jobs
29 Ibid.
30 Laurence Caramel and Harold Thibault, 2012, "China at The Centre of 'Illegal Timber' Trade," *The Guardian*, www .theguardian.com/environment/2012/dec/11/china-illegal -logging-deforestation
31 Allen T. Cheng, 2007, "Cardboard Queen Zhang Recycles to Become China's Richest Person," Bloomberg, www.bloomberg .com/apps/news?pid=newsarchive&sid=aX2DENqYvouU
32 Thomas Danjczek and Alan Price, 2010, "Scrap Supply in the Global Steel Industry: A Better Path," OECD Steel Committee, www.oecd.org/industry/ind/46584778.pdf
33 *The New Yorker*, 2008, *American Scrap*, www.newyorker.com/ magazine/2008/01/14/american-scrap
34 The US–China Business Council, 2013, "China and the US Economy: Advancing a Winning Trade Agenda," www.uschina .org/sites/default/files/USCBC-Trade-Agenda-Report.pdf
35 Outdoor Industry Association, 2013, "Should 'Made in USA' Rules Be Updated to Reflect the Global Value Chain?" http:// outdoorindustry.org/education/library.php?newsId=17732&n ewsSubType=Manufacturing&action=display
36 Brent Balinski, 2013, "China's Manufacturing Advantage over the USA Disappearing," *Manufacturer's Monthly*, www .manmonthly.com.au/news/china-s-manufacturing-advantage -over-the-usa-disap
37 Lori Montgomery, 2012, "Siemens Plant in Charlotte Offers Lessons as Obama, Romney Talk Job Creation,"

The Washington Post, www.washingtonpost.com/business/economy/siemens-plant-in-charlotte-offers-lessons-as-obama-romney-talk-job-creation/2012/09/04/f52304fa-f30c-11e1-adc6-87dfa8eff430_story.html

38 Charles Fishman, 2012, "The Insourcing Boom," *The Atlantic*, www.theatlantic.com/magazine/archive/2012/12/the-insourcing-boom/309166/
39 Ibid.
40 GTM Research Study, 2011, "US Solar Energy Trade Assessment 2011," www.seia.org/sites/default/files/resources/GTM-SEIA%20U%20S%20%20Solar%20Energy%20Trade%20Balance%202011.pdf
41 Ibid.
42 Gary Clyde Hufbauer and Sean Lowr, 2012, "US Tire Tariffs: Saving Few Jobs at High Cost," Peterson Institute for International Economics, www.iie.com/publications/pb/pb12-9.pdf
43 Daniel J. Ikenson, 2011, "Made in America: Increasing Jobs through Exports and Trade," CATO Institute, www.cato.org/publications/congressional-testimony/made-america-increasing-jobs-through-exports-trade
44 Face the Facts USA, 2012, "Factories Bounce Back, Hirings Hangs Back," www.facethefactsusa.org/facts/factories-bounce-back-hiring-hangs-back
45 Linda Levine, 2012, "Offshoring (or Offshore Outsourcing) and Job Loss among US Workers," Congressional Research Service, http://fas.org/sgp/crs/misc/RL32292.pdf
46 Generation Opportunity, 2012, "Poll: Michigan Young Adults Worry about Losing Jobs to China, Support Lowering Taxes to Encourage Hiring," http://generationopportunity.org/press/poll-michigan-young-adults-worry-about-losing-jobs-to-china-support-lowering-taxes-to-encourage-hiring/
47 Tom Gantert, 2013, "Despite Rhetoric, United State Outsourced Less than 3,000 Jobs in 2012," Michigan Center for Public Policy, www.michigancapitolconfidential.com/18373

2   Jobs and Jeopardy

1 US Food and Drug Administration, "Number of Import Alerts by Country/Area," www.accessdata.fda.gov/cms_ia/countrylist .html

2 Stephanie Strom, 2013, "China's Food Deal Extends Its Reach, Already Mighty," *The New York Times*, www.nytimes .com/2013/05/30/business/wariness-over-a-deal-intended-to -deliver-more-pork-to-china.html?pagewanted=all&_r=1&

3 Penny Pritzker, Kathryn Sullivan, and Samuel D. Rauch, III, 2013, "Fisheries of the United States 2012," National Marine Fisheries Service office of Science and Technology, www .st.nmfs.noaa.gov/Assets/commercial/fus/fus12/FUS2012 .pdf

4 Fish Watch, 2012, "The Surprising Sources of Your Favorite Seafoods," www.fishwatch.gov/features/top10seafoods_and _sources_10_10_12.html

5 Nicole Gilbert, 2011, "Tainted Seafood Reaching US, Food Safety Experts Say," *News 21*, http://foodsafety.news21.com/ 2011/imports/seafood/

6 Nancy Huehnergarth and Bettina Siegel, 2014, "Chicken from China? Your Seafood is Already Being Processed There," *Food Safety News*, www.foodsafetynews.com/2014/03/chicken -from-china-your-seafood-is-already-being-processed-there/ #.VCTS97KJuTV

7 Ibid.

8 Ching-Fu Lin, 2013, "Taking China's Food Safety Problem Seriously (I)," Harvard Law Petrie-Flow Center, http://blogs .law.harvard.edu/billofhealth/2013/10/10/taking-chinas-food -safety-problem-seriously-i/

9 US Food and Drug Administration, 2013, "Ensuring the Safety of Imported Products: Q&A with David Elder," www.fda.gov/ ForConsumers/ConsumerUpdates/ucm048631.htm

10 Gardiner Harris, 2011, "FDA Confronts Challenge of Moni-toring Imports," *The New York Times*, www.nytimes.com/ 2011/06/21/health/policy/21food.html

11 Sharon LaFraniere, 2011, "In China, Fear of Fake Eggs and 'Recycled' Buns," *The New York Times*, www.nytimes.com/2011/05/08/world/asia/08food.html?pagewanted=all

12 Sharon LaFraniere, 2011, "Despite Government Efforts, Tainted Food Widespread in China," *The Seattle Times*, http://seattletimes.com/html/foodwine/2014994537_chinafood08.html

13 Edward Wong, 2013, "Chinese Search for Infant Formula Goes Global," *The New York Times*, www.nytimes.com/2013/07/26/world/asia/chinas-search-for-infant-formula-goes-global.html?pagewanted=all&_r=0

14 Ibid.

15 M. Melinda Meador and Wu Bugang, 2012, "China Agricultural Trade Report," USDA Foreign Agricultural Service, http://gain.fas.usda.gov/Recent%20GAIN%20Publications/China%20Agricultural%20Trade%20Report%20in%202012_Beijing_China%20-%20Peoples%20Republic%20of_2-25-2013.pdf

16 Fred Gale, 2013, "US Exports Surge as China Supports Agricultural Prices," United States Department of Agriculture, www.ers.usda.gov/amber-waves/2013-october/us-exports-surge-as-china-supports-agricultural-prices.aspx#.VCTWQrKJuTV

17 Mark Perry, 2010, "Food Exports and Food Trade Surplus with China Set Record High in 2009: Are They Beholden?" Get.com, https://get.com/economy/2010/05/16/food-exports-and-food-trade-surplus-with-china-sets-record-highs-in-2009-are-they-beholden/

18 The US–China Business Council, "US Exports to China," www.uschina.org/reports/us-exports/national-2013

19 International Trade Administration, 2014, "US Export Fact Sheet," http://trade.gov/press/press-releases/2014/export-factsheet-february2014-020614.pdf

20 Ibid.

21 Emilia Istrate and Nicholas Marchio, 2012, "Export Nation 2012: How US Metropolitan Areas are Driving National Growth," Brookings, www.brookings.edu/~/

media/Research/Files/Reports/2012/3/08exports/0308
_exports.pdf

22 Office of the United States Trade Representative, "US–China
Trade Facts," www.ustr.gov/countries-regions/china-mongolia-
taiwan/peoples-republic-china

23 Pamela Prah, 2013, "States Use Connections to Boost China
Exports," The Pew Charitable Trusts, www.pewtrusts.org/en/
research-and-analysis/blogs/stateline/2013/06/07/states-use
-connections-to-boost-china-exports

24 International Trade Administration, 2013, "Trends in US
Vehicle Exports," US Department of Commerce Office of
Transportation   and   Machinery,   www.trade.gov/mas/
manufacturing/oaai/build/groups/public/@tg_oaai/documents/
webcontent/tg_oaai_004086.pdf

25 NEI Summary, 2012, "Growth Trends in US Vehicle
Exports,"   www.trade.gov/mas/manufacturing/oaai/build/
groups/public/@tg_oaai/documents/webcontent/tg_oaai
_003833.pdf

26 Norihiko Shirouzu and Alex P. Kellogg, 2008, "Chrysler and
Chery End Small-Car Project," *The Wall Street Journal*, http://
online.wsj.com/articles/SB122884793853691953

27 Andrew Osborn, 2007, "Crash Course in Quality for Chinese
Car," *The Wall Street Journal*, http://online.wsj.com/articles/
SB118651314364590719

28 United States of America Department of Commerce, *China
Business Handbook 2013*, www.export.gov/china/build/
groups/public/@eg_cn/documents/webcontent/eg_cn_055956
.pdf

29 Jean Murphy, 2012, "W. S. Darley & Co. Recognized for
Growth, Longevity," *Daily Herald*, http://dhbusinessledger
.com/Content/Suburban-Trends-and-Issues/Suburban–Trends
-and-Issues/Article/W-S–Darley—Co–recognized-for-growth
–longevity/87/172/5214

30 CNN, 2014, "Made in America. Sold in China," http://
money.cnn.com/gallery/smallbusiness/2014/01/08/made-in
-america-china/2.html

31 Ibid.
32 Jim Dwyer, 2012, "In Manufacturing Shift, Made in US but Sold in China," *The New York Times*, www.nytimes.com/2012/09/21/nyregion/a-manufacturing-about-face-made-in-america-but-sold-in-china.html
33 Rick Nicholas, 2013, "Bassetts Scooping up the Market in China," *The Inquirer*, http://articles.philly.com/2013-03-22/food/37906582_1_ice-cream-china-trade-china-market
34 CNN, 2011, "Georgia's Hottest Export: Chopsticks!," http://money.cnn.com/video/smallbusiness/2011/12/05/smb_sbt_chopsticks.cnnmoney/index.html
35 CNN, 2014, "Made in America. Sold in China," http://money.cnn.com/gallery/smallbusiness/2014/01/08/made-in-america-china/2.html
36 John Grossmann, 2013, "New Path for Trade: Selling in China," *The New York Times*, www.nytimes.com/2013/01/24/business/smallbusiness/tips-for-companies-that-want-to-sell-in-china.html?pagewanted=all&_r=1&
37 NPR, 2012, "Transcript: Mitt Romney's Acceptance Speech," www.npr.org/2012/08/30/160357612/transcript-mitt-romneys-acceptance-speech
38 Glenn Kessler, 2013, "Sarah Palin's Claim about China, US Debt and the 'Foreign Master,'" *The Washington Post*, www.washingtonpost.com/blogs/fact-checker/wp/2013/11/12/sarah-palins-claim-about-china-u-s-debt-and-the-foreign-master/?hpid=z3
39 www.realclearpolitics.com/video/2013/03/13/flashback_obama_talks_unpatriotic_debt_in_2008.html
40 Comedy Central, 2012, *The Daily Show*, http://thedailyshow.cc.com/videos/2o7ucm/herman-cain–an-american-presidency—chinese-debt-crisis
41 Tony Capaccio and Daniel Kruger, 2012, "China's US Debt Holdings Aren't Threat, Pentagon Says," *Bloomberg News*, www.bloomberg.com/news/2012-09-11/china-s-u-s-debt-holdings-aren-t-threat-pentagon-says.html

42 Ibid.
43 Ibid.
44 Ibid.
45 Thilo Hanemann, 2012, "Chinese FDI in the United States: Q3 2012 Update," Rhodium Group, http://rhg.com/notes/chinese-fdi-in-the-united-states-q3-2012-update
46 Thilo Hanemann, 2012, "The Employment Impacts of Chinese Investments in the United States," Rhodium Group, http://rhg.com/articles/the-employment-impacts-of-chinese-investment-in-the-united-states
47 Timothy Williams, 2013, "In Blue-Collar Toledo, Ohio, A Windfall of Chinese Investments," *The New York Times*, www.nytimes.com/2013/12/27/us/in-blue-collar-ohio-a-windfall-of-chinese-investments.html?pagewanted=all&_r=0
48 sherrodbrown.com, 2012, "Protecting Ohio Jobs," www.sherrodbrown.com/video/tv-ad-protecting-ohio-jobs/
49 Bob Davis, 2012, "Bill for China Ads in US Election: $54.3 Million," *The Wall Street Journal*, http://blogs.wsj.com/chinarealtime/2012/11/14/bill-for-china-ads-in-u-s-election-54-3-million/
50 Jeremy W. Peters, 2012, "In Dueling Ads, Candidates Seek to Politicize Issues of China and Manufacturing," *The New York Times*, www.nytimes.com/2012/09/16/us/politics/in-dueling-ads-candidates-seek-to-politicize-issues-of-china-and-manufacturing.html
51 Bob Davis, 2012, "Bill for China Ads in US Election: $54.3 Million," *The Wall Street Journal*, http://blogs.wsj.com/chinarealtime/2012/11/14/bill-for-china-ads-in-u-s-election-54-3-million/
52 David W. Chen, 2010, "China Emerges as a Scapegoat in Campaign Ads," *The New York Times*, www.nytimes.com/2010/10/10/us/politics/10outsource.html
53 South Carolina Department of Commerce, 2013, "Foreign Investment in South Carolina: Highlighting China," http://sccommerce.com/sites/default/files/document_directory/foreign_china_may_2014.pdf

3 The Bad Earth

1 Elizabeth C. Economy, 2007, "The Great Leap Backward?," *Foreign Affairs*, September/October 2007, p. 41.
2 Ibid.
3 Christina Larson, 2013, "Losing Arable Land, China Faces Stark Choice: Adapt Or Go Hungry," Sciencemag.org, http://english.igsnrr.cas.cn/ue/ne/201302/P020130217334597774774.pdf
4 Elizabeth C. Economy, 2007, "The Great Leap Backward?," *Foreign Affairs*, September/October 2007, p. 42.
5 Ibid.
6 Ibid.
7 Elizabeth C. Economy, 2007, *The Great Leap Backward?*, Foreign Affairs, September/October 2007, p. 43.
8 BBC News, 2013, "China Acknowledges 'Cancer Villages,'" www.bbc.com/news/world-asia-china-21545868
9 Elizabeth C. Economy, 2007, "The Great Leap Backward?," *Foreign Affairs*, September/October 2007, p. 42.
10 Barbara Demick, 2014, "China Looks Abroad for Greener Pastures," *Los Angeles Times*, www.latimes.com/world/asia/la-fg-china-foreign-farmland-20140329-story.html#page=1
11 J. Shi, L. Li, and G. Pan, 2009, "Variation of Grain Cd and Zn Concentrations of 110 Hybrid Rice Cultivars Grown in a Low-Cd Paddy Soil," *Journal of Environmental Sciences* 21(2): 168–72; J. Fu, Q. Zhou, J. Liu et al., 2008, "High Levels of Heavy Metals in Rice (Oryza Sativa L.) from a Typical E-Waste Recycling Area in Southeast China and its Potential Risk to Human Health," *Chemosphere* 71(7): 1260–75; Q. Chi, G. Zhu, and A. Langdon, 2007, "Bioaccumulation of Heavy Metals in Fishes from Taihu Lake, China," *Journal of Environmental Sciences-China* 19(12): 1500–4; K. Cheung, H. Leung, and M. Wong, 2008, "Metal Concentrations of Common Freshwater and Marine Fish from the Pearl River Delta, South China," *Archives of Environmental Contamination and Toxicology* 54(4): 705–15.

12 China Council for International Collaboration on Environment and Development, 2010, "CCICED Special Policy Study Report: Developing Policies for Soil Environmental Protection in China," www.cciced.net/encciced/policyresearch/report/201205/P020120529358298439639.pdf; N. Chen, 2013, "Heavy Metal Pollution in China: Implications for Food Safety". Report prepared for the Social Science Research Council. Working Paper.

13 Louisa Lim, 2007, "Air Pollution Grows in Tandem with China's Economy," NPR, www.npr.org/templates/story/story.php?storyId=10221268

14 Eric Larson, 2014, "China's Growing Coal Use is World's Growing Problem," Climate Central, www.climatecentral.org/blogs/chinas-growing-coal-use-is-worlds-growing-problem-16999

15 Elizabeth C. Economy, 2007, "The Great Leap Backward?," *Foreign Affairs*, September/October 2007, p. 40.

16 Bloomberg News, 2012, "China Overtakes US as Largest Crop Importer, WTO Data Show," www.bloomberg.com/news/2012-09-20/china-overtakes-u-s-as-largest-crop-importer-wto-data-show.html

17 United States Department of Agriculture, "China," www.fas.usda.gov/regions/east-asia-and-pacific/china

18 European Commission, Directorate-General for Trade, "European Union Trade in Goods with China" 2014. http://trade.ec.europa.eu/doclib/docs/2006/september/tradoc_113366.pdf

19 Arian Campo-Flores, 2013, "Catchy Idea: To Battle Asian Carp, Send Them to Asia," *The Wall Street Journal*, http://online.wsj.com/news/articles/SB10001424052702304027204579332674266477290

20 The US–China Business Council, 2013, "US Exports to China," www.uschina.org/sites/default/files/2013%20US%20Exports%20to%20China%20by%20State.pdf

21 Dan Stone, 2013, "Why China Wants (and Needs) Foreign Farm Land," *National Geographic*, http://newswatch

.nationalgeographic.com/2013/09/25/countries-like-china
-want-foreign-farm-land/
22 Heather Timmons, 2013, "China's Growing Food Demands
Stoke Fears of a Global Factory Farming Boom," *Quartz*,
http://qz.com/225182/chinas-growing-food-demands-stoke
-fears-of-a-global-factory-farming-boom/
23 Associated Press, 2014, "Jar of French Mountain Air Sells for
£512 in Polluted Beijing," *The Guardian*, www.theguardian
.com/environment/2014/apr/10/jar-french-mountain-air
-polluted-beijing
24 Peter Calthorpe, 2012, "Weapons of Mass Urban Destruction," *Foreign Affairs*, www.foreignpolicy.com/articles/2012/
08/13/weapons_of_mass_urban_destruction
25 Jennifer Baumert Powell, 2013, "Environmental and Related
Services," US International Trade Commission, www.usitc.gov/
publications/332/pub4389.pdf

4 Risky Business

1 HSBC, 2012, "100 Years Behind: New Eye-Opening
Report on Chinese Farming," *Week in China*, 20 July,
p. 15.
2 BBC News, 2012, "China's Yantai City in 'Toxic Apple'
Check," www.bbc.com/news/world-asia-china-18406012
3 Ge Ruijiang and Jiang Gang, 2011, "Tainted Greens: From
Field to Market, China Dialogue," https://www.chinadialogue
.net/article/4520-Tainted-greens-from-field-to-market
4 Michael Stumo, 2011, "CPA White Paper: How China's
VAT Massively Subsidizes Exports," Trade Reform, www
.tradereform.org/2011/07/cpa-white-paper-how-chinas
-vat-massively-subsidizes-exports/
5 Ibid.
6 Lydia Guo, 2013, "China Exports: Doing the Rounds,"
Financial Times, http://blogs.ft.com/beyond-brics/2013/05/10/
china-exports-doing-the-rounds/?Authorised=false

7 ISO Survey, 2013, International Organization for Standardization, www.iso.org/iso/home/standards/certification/iso-survey.htm

8 Leo Lewis, 2011, "China Troubled by Steel-Thinning Scam in Building Foundations," *The Times*, www.theaustralian.com.au/archive/business/china-troubled-by-steel-thinning-scam-in-building-foundations/story-e6frg90o-1226136555319?nk=4621bbab429baf4d90d069b2ec77850a

9 Jim Ostroff, 2007, "New Threat from China: Shoddy Steel Imports," Kiplinger, http://marcchamot.blogspot.com/2008/05/china-earthquake-reveals-new-threat.html

10 Ibid.

11 David Barboza, 2011, "Bridge Comes to San Francisco with a Made-in-China Label," *The New York Times*, www.nytimes.com/2011/06/26/business/global/26bridge.html?pagewanted=all

12 Philip Matier and Andrew Ross, 2009, "Questions over Welds Delay Bay Bridge Project," SFGate, www.sfgate.com/bayarea/article/Questions-over-welds-delay-Bay-Bridge-project-3175088.php

13 Ibid.

14 Ibid.

15 Ibid.

16 World Nuclear Association, 2014, "Nuclear Power in China," www.world-nuclear.org/info/Country-Profiles/Countries-A-F/China–Nuclear-Power/

17 Liu Werui, 2010, "Cultivating the Culture of Nuclear Safety, Achieving Sustainable Nuclear Power Development," http://sns.sinap.cas.cn/kjlt/201310/P020131105704782212711.pdf

18 Yang Yuze, 2014, "The Lack of Supervision is More Dangerous than the Missing of Radioactive Material," *China Youth Daily*, http://zqb.cyol.com/html/2014-05/14/nw.D110000zgqnb_20140514_2-02.htm

19 Katie Thomas, 2013, "Drug Research in China Falls under a Cloud," *The New York Times*, www.nytimes.com/2013/07/23/business/global/drug-research-in-china-falls-under-a-cloud.html?pagewanted=all&_r=0

20 Ibid.
21 Matthew L. Wald, 2011, "Nuclear Industry Thrives in the US, but for Export," *The New York Times*, www.nytimes.com/2011/03/31/business/energy-environment/31NUKE.html?pagewanted=all&_r=0
22 Ibid.
23 Barack Obama, 2011, "State of the Union Address," www.whitehouse.gov/the-press-office/2011/01/25/remarks-president-state-union-address
24 Tom Yam, 2013, "China's High-Speed-Rail Programme a Case of Too Far, Too Fast," *Southern China Morning Post*, www.scmp.com/lifestyle/technology/article/1299188/chinas-high-speed-rail-programme-case-too-far-too-fast
25 Evan Osnos, 2012, "Boss Rail: The Disaster that Exposed the Underside of the Boom," *The New Yorker*, www.newyorker.com/magazine/2012/10/22/boss-rail
26 Keith B. Richburg, 2011, "Are China's High-Speed Trains Heading Off the Rails?," *The Washington Post*, www.washingtonpost.com/world/are-chinas-high-speed-trains-heading-off-the-rails/2011/04/22/AFHzaNWE_story.html
27 Evan Osnos, 2012, "Boss Rail."
28 Ibid.
29 Tom Yam, 2013, "China's High-Speed-Rail Programme a Case of Too Far, Too Fast," *Southern China Morning Post*, www.scmp.com/lifestyle/technology/article/1299188/chinas-high-speed-rail-programme-case-too-far-too-fast
30 Evan Osnos, 2012, "Boss Rail."
31 Trefor Moss, 2012, "$100 Billion for China's Railroads," *The Diplomat*, http://thediplomat.com/2012/10/if-railways-are-this-corrupt-what-about-pla/
32 John Garnaut, 2012, "Rotting from Within: Investigating the Massive Corruption of the Chinese Military," *Foreign Policy*, www.foreignpolicy.com/articles/2012/04/16/rotting_from_within?page=0,0&wp_login_redirect=0
33 Evan Osnos, 2012, "Boss Rail."

5   Chain of Fools

1 Zhong Weijun, 2011, "The Logic of 'Causing No Trouble' in the Social Management of Local Governments: An Analysis Framework," *Zhejiang Social Sciences* 9, www.chinareform .org.cn/society/manage/Forward/201112/ P020111208329806967114.pdf

2 Bin Jiang and Edmund Prater, 2002, "Distribution and Logistics Development in China: The Revolution has Begun," http:// wweb.uta.edu/insyopma/prater/IJPDLM%20logistics%20 in%20China.pdf

3 David Barboza and Louise Story, 2007, "Toymaking in China, Mattel's Way," *The New York Times*, www.nytimes.com/2007/ 07/26/business/26toy.html?pagewanted=all&_r=1&

4 Ibid.

5 Ben Klayman, 2014, "Aston Martin Recalls 17,590 Due To Counterfeit Material," Reuters, http://uk.reuters.com/ article/2014/02/05/uk-autos-astonmartin-recall -idUKBREA141T420140205

6 John Gapper, 2014, "Aston Martins Recall Is an Embarrassment for China," *Financial Times*, http://blogs.ft .com/businessblog/2014/02/aston-martins-recall-is-an -embarrassment-for-china/?Authorised=false

7 Steve Toloken, 2014, "Molder Claims to Be Victim in Aston Martin Recall," Plastic News, www.plasticsnews.com/ article/20140221/NEWS/140229982/molder-claims-to -be-victim-in-aston-martin-recall#

8 Ibid.

9 Jane Spencer, 2007, "Toy Recalls Shows Challenge China Poses to Partners," *The Wall Street Journal*, http://online .wsj.com/articles/SB118607762324386327

10 Huang Yanzhong, 2012, "China's Corrupt Food China," *The New York Times*, www.nytimes.com/2012/08/18/opinion/ chinas-corrupt-food-chain.html?pagewanted=all

11 *The Economist*, 2014, "The Flow of Things," www.economist .com/news/china/21606899-export-superpower-china-suffers -surprisingly-inefficient-logistics-flow-things

12 Drug Safety Project, 2012, "Heparin: A Wake-Up Call on Risk to the US Drug Supply," The Pew Charitable Trusts, www.pewtrusts.org/en/research-and-analysis/issue-briefs/2012/05/16/heparin-a-wakeup-call-on-risks-to-the-us-drug-supply

13 David G. Strunce, 2008, "Statement of David G. Strunce President and Chief Executive Officer Scientific Protein Laboratories LLC, Subcommittee on Oversight and Investigations Committee on Energy and Commerce, United States House of Representatives," www.baxter.com/downloads/information/safety_information/heparin/SPL_testimony.pdf

14 Steve Usdin, 2009, "The Heparin Story," *The International Journal of Risk and Safety in Medicine* 21(1–2): 93–103, http://iospress.metapress.com/content/w047418983941g21/

15 Jennifer Corbett Dooren, 2012, "Suppliers Linked to Impure Heparin," *The Wall Street Journal*, http://online.wsj.com/news/articles/SB10001424052970203960804577239624228625522

16 Jia Hepeng, 2008, "Regulators Scramble to Tighten Loopholes after Heparin Debacle," *Nature Biotechnology* 26: 477–8, www.nature.com/nbt/journal/v26/n5/full/nbt0508-477.html

17 Robert L. Parkinson, 2008, "Testimony before Subcommittee on Oversight and Investigations Committee on Energy and Commerce, US House of Representatives," www.baxter.com/downloads/information/safety_information/heparin/RLP_testimony.pdf

18 Janet Woodcock, 2008, "Heparin Testimony before Committee on Energy and Commerce Subcommittee on Oversight and Investigations, US House of Representatives," US Department of Health and Human Services, http://wayback.archive-it.org/4150/20131202180042/http://www.hhs.gov/asl/testify/2008/05/t20080429a.html

19 Gardiner Harris, 2008, "Chinese Factory Linked to Drug under Inquiry in US," *The New York Times*, www.nytimes.com/2008/02/14/business/worldbusiness/14heparin.html?_r=0

20 Department of Health and Human Services, 2008, "Warning Letter WF: 320-08-01," www.fda.gov/downloads/Drugs/ GuidanceComplianceRegulatoryInformation/Enforcement ActivitiesbyFDA/WarningLettersandNoticeofViolation LetterstoPharmaceuticalCompanies/ucm054109.pdf
21 United States Government Accountability Office, 2010, "Food and Drug Administration: Response to Heparin Contamination Helped Protect Public Health; Controls That Were Needed for Working with External Entities Were Recently Added," www.gao.gov/assets/320/311879.pdf
22 Reuters, 2014, "US FDA Ups China Drug Inspections and Global Supply-China Concerns," www.reuters.com/article/ 2014/04/03/us-fda-china-idUSBREA322CO20140403
23 Zachary Brennan, 2013, "US FDA Looks to Speed Placement of More Inspectors in China," in-Pharma Technologies.com, www.in-pharmatechnologist.com/Regulatory-Safety/US- FDA-looks-to-speed-placement-of-more-inspectors-in -China
24 Gardiner Harris, 2008, "Chinese Factory Linked to Drug under Inquiry in US," *The New York Times*, www.nytimes.com/ 2008/02/14/business/worldbusiness/14heparin.html?_r=0
25 The Committee on Armed Services, 2011, "The Committee's Investigation into Counterfeit Electronic Parts in the Department of Defense Supply China," www.gpo.gov/fdsys/pkg/ CHRG-112shrg72702/pdf/CHRG-112shrg72702.pdf
26 Ibid.
27 David Barboza, 2008, "China's Dairy Farmers Say they are Victims," *The New York Times*, www.nytimes.com/ 2008/10/04/world/asia/04milk.html?pagewanted=all& _r=0%20NYT
28 Sarah Matheson, 2014, "Dog Treats Made in China Linked to Kidney Failure, Death," *Epoch Times*, www.theepochtimes .com/n3/726160-dog-treats-made-in-china-linked-to-kidney -failure-death/
29 Mark McDonald, 2012, "From Milk to Peas, a Chinese Food- Safety Mess," *The Rendezvous*, http://rendezvous.blogs.nytimes

.com/2012/06/21/from-milk-to-peas-a-chinese-food-safety
-mess/

30 Alexa Olesen, 2012, "No Quick-Fix for China's Troubled
Dairy Industry," Associated Press, http://bigstory.ap.org/
article/no-quick-fix-chinas-troubled-dairy-industry

31 Reuters, 2014, "China Police Seize 30,000 Tonnes of Tainted
Chicken Feet," *Chicago Tribute*, www.chicagotribune.com/
news/sns-rt-us-china-foodsafety-20140824-story.html

32 Debbie Seigelbaum, 2014, "How Chinese Babies and Mid-East
Pizza Tip US Markets," BBC News, www.bbc.com/news/
world-us-canada-29133022

6   When Regs are Dregs

1 Evan Osnos, 2012, "Boss Rail: The Disaster that Exposed the
Underside of the Boom," *The New Yorker*, www.newyorker
.com/magazine/2012/10/22/boss-rail

2 Zheng Yongnian, 2009, "Power to Dominate, Not to Change:
How China's Central-Local Relations Constrain Its Reform,"
EAI Working Paper No. 153, www.eai.nus.edu.sg/EWP153.pdf

3 Calum Macleod, 2009, "Some Skeptical of China's New Food
Safety Law," *USA Today*, http://usatoday30.usatoday.com/
money/industries/food/2009-03-01-chinafood01_N.htm

4 Ching-Fu Lin, 2013, "Taking China's Food Safety Problem
Seriously (II)," Harvard Petrie-Flow Center, http://blogs.law
.harvard.edu/billofhealth/2013/10/11/taking-chinas-food
-safety-problem-seriously-ii/

5 Waikeung Tam and Dali Yang, 2005, "Food Safety and the
Development of Regulatory Institutions in China," *Asian Perspective* 29(5): 5–36, http://china.praguesummerschools.org/
files/china/14china2012.pdf

6 Melaine Lee and Ben Hirschler, 2012, "Special Report: China's
'Wild East' Drug Store," Reuters, www.reuters.com/
article/2012/08/28/us-china-pharmaceuticals
-idUSBRE87R0OD20120828

7 Walt Bogdanich, 2007, "Chinese Chemicals Flow Unchecked onto World Drug Market," *The New York Times*, www .nytimes.com/2007/10/31/world/asia/31chemical .html?pagewanted=all&_r=0

8 Walt Bogdanic, 2007, "From China to Panama, A Trail of Poisoned Medicine," *The New York Times*, www.nytimes.com/ 2007/05/06/world/06poison.html?pagewanted=all

9 Ibid.

10 Walt Bogdanich, 2007, "Chinese Chemicals Flow Unchecked onto World Drug Market," *The New York Times*, www.nytimes.com/2007/10/31/world/asia/31chemical. html?pagewanted=all&_r=0

11 Ching-Fu Lin, 2013, "Taking China's Food Safety Problem Seriously (II)," Harvard Petrie-Flow Center, http://blogs.law .harvard.edu/billofhealth/2013/10/11/taking-chinas-food -safety-problem-seriously-ii/

12 Elaine Kurtenbach, 2008, "China SFDA: Buyers Must Vet Drug Safety," *USA Today*, http://usatoday30.usatoday.com/ news/world/2008-02-27-1916541804_x.htm

13 Tom Levitt, 2013, "China's Top-Down Food Safety System Is Failing," *China Dialogue*, www.chinadialogue.net/article/ show/single/en/6369-China-s-top-down-food-safety-system -is-failing

14 Ibid.

15 Barbara Li, 2010, "Overview of China's Product Safety Regime," *China Business Review*, www.chinabusinessreview .com/overview-of-chinas-product-safety-regime/

16 Alice Crites, Ellen Nakashima, and Jerry Markon, 2014, "Top-Level Turnover Makes It Harder for DHS to Stay on Top of Evolving Threats," *The Washington Post*, www .washingtonpost.com/politics/top-level-turnover-makes-it -harder-for-dhs-to-stay-on-top-of-evolving-threats/2014/09/ 21/ca7919a6-39d7-11e4-9c9f-ebb47272e40e_story.html

17 Andrew Jacobs, 2010, "China Sentences Activist in Milk Scandal to Prison," *The New York Times*, www.nytimes.com/ 2010/11/11/world/asia/11beijing.html

18 Reuters, 2014, "GM Says Other Defective Ignition Switch Made in China," www.reuters.com/article/2014/06/25/us-gm-recall-china-idUSKBN0F01BF20140625

19 Edward Wong, 2013, "Chinese Search for Infant Formula Goes Global," *The New York Times*, www.nytimes.com/2013/07/26/world/asia/chinas-search-for-infant-formula-goes-global.html?pagewanted=all&_r=0

20 Edward Tse, Kevin Ma, Paul Pan, and Simon Sun, 2012, "Changing Landscape of China's Pharmaceutical Distribution Industry," Booz & Company Inc., www.strategyand.pwc.com/media/file/Changing_Landscape_of_China's_Pharmaceutical_Distribution_EN.pdf

21 Li Zhen, 2007, "The Current Situation and Analysis of Medical and Health Service Regulation in China: Background Discussion Paper to Inform the Regulatory Reform Review of China," www.oecd.org/gov/regulatory-policy/39218123.pdf

22 China Daily, 2012, "Medical Tourism Becomes Popular with Affluent Chinese," eTN Global Travel Industry News, www.eturbonews.com/31317/medical-tourism-becomes-popular-affluent-chinese

23 Li Yan, 2014, "Getting a Healthy Interest in Medical Tourism," Caxin Online, http://english.caixin.com/2014-07-18/100706007.html

24 Wang Chao, 2014, "Chinese Tourists Spark Growth of Global Medical Tourism Market," Skift Travel IQ, http://skift.com/2014/07/21/chinese-tourists-spark-growth-of-global-medical-tourism-market/

7 What to Do

1 Helen Coster, 2008, "Tainted Booty," Forbes, www.forbes.com/forbes/2008/0421/084.html

2 Chi Pang Wen et al., 2011, "Minimum Amount of Physical Activity for Reduced Mortality and Extended Life Expect-

ancy: A Prospective Cohort Study," *The Lancet*, www
.thelancet.com/journals/lancet/article/PIIS0140
-6736(11)60749-6/abstract

3 Steven G. Newmaster et al., 2013, "DNA Barcoding Detects
   Contamination and Substitution in North American Herbal
   Products, MBC Medicine, www.biomedcentral.com/1741
   -7015/11/222/abstract

4 Anahad O'Connor, 2013, "Herbal Supplements are Often Not
   What They Seem," *The New York Times*, www.nytimes
   .com/2013/11/05/science/herbal-supplements-are-often-not
   -what-they-seem.html?pagewanted=all&_r=1&&gwh=616CB
   B19C8E4A724008602CBBBB34615&gwt=pay

5 Anahad O'Connor, 2013, "Spike in Harm to Liver is Tied to
   Dietary Aids," *The New York Times*, www.nytimes.com/2013/
   12/22/us/spike-in-harm-to-liver-is-tied-to-dietary-aids
   .html?pagewanted=all

6 Ibid.

7 Project Atlas, "International Students in the United States,"
   www.iie.org/Services/Project-Atlas/United-States/
   International-Students-In-US

8 Jay Mathews, 2011, "The Myth of Declining US Schools:
   They've Long Been Mediocre," *The Washington Post*, http://
   voices.washingtonpost.com/class-struggle/2011/02/myth_of
   _declining_us_schools.html

9 Ibid.

10 Jay Mathews, 2014, "Why Admiring Chinese Test Scores
   Might Hurt US Schools," *The Washington Post*, www
   .washingtonpost.com/local/education/envy-of-chinese-kids-is
   -bad-for-us-and-china/2014/09/14/39dc6910-3951-11e4
   -8601-97ba88884ffd_story.htmlv

11 Vivek Wadhwa, 2011, "President Obama, There Is No Engineer Shortage," *The Washington Post*, www.washingtonpost
   .com/pb/national/on-innovations/president-obama-there
   -is-no-engineer-shortage/2011/09/01/gIQADpmpuJ_story
   .html

12 Martin Fackler, 2007, "Safe Food for Japan," *The New York
   Times*, www.nytimes.com/2007/10/11/business/worldbusiness/

11safety.html?gwh=66DF73F918A3FE882DB47A13D07ADF1D&gwt=pay

13 Ted Agres, 2013, "Despite Regulatory Reform, China's Food Safety Remains Problematic," *Food Quality and Safety Magazine*, www.foodquality.com/details/article/4366181/Despite_Regulatory_Reform_Chinas_Food_Safety_Remains_Problematic.html?tzcheck=1

14 Michael Taylor, 2012, "China Spin and Economic and Military Confusion," Georgetown University course, "China, The Media, and Politics."

Index